HORSE POWER AND MAGIC

# Horse Power and Magic

by

## GEORGE EWART EVANS

*faber and faber*

This edition first published in 2008
by Faber and Faber Ltd
3 Queen Square, London WC1N 3AU

Printed by CPI Antony Rowe, Eastbourne

A CIP record for this book is available from the British Library

ISBN 978–0–571–24664–9

Cyflwynir y llyfr hwn

i

Iorwerth a Nansi Peate

*Think when we talk of horses, that you see them*
*Printing their proud hoofs i' th'receiving earth.*

Shakespeare: Prologue to
*Henry the Fifth*

# Contents

# Illustrations

# Abbreviations

# Acknowledgements

In writing this book I have become a debtor to many people, most of all to those who entered wholeheartedly into the project, contributing their own experiences and views and allowing me to record them here. They are chiefly responsible for whatever vitality this book has; and I greatly appreciate the help they gave me.

Many whose names are not mentioned in the text of the book also gave me information or made useful suggestions. They are: Mr Aston Gaze, Mr W. D. Akester, Mr C. R. Hannis, Dr J. D. A. Widdowson, Mr Sanders Watney, Mr David Y. Evans: I here acknowledge their kind help. I am particularly grateful to Mrs Sharon Cregier of the University of Prince Edward Island, Canada for the numerous pieces of information she has given me about British and American horse trainers; also to Mr A. F. H. Arnold, former Governor of H.M. Borstal and Detention Centre at Hollesley, Suffolk.

I wish to thank Lord Clark and his publishers, John Murray, for permission to quote from one of his books; also Sir Emrys Jones who allowed me to use a passage from one of his lectures. Faber and Faber and the Oxford University Press gave me permission to use the Edwin Muir poem; and Bernard Dixon and Maurice Temple Smith to use the quotation on page 89. The following kindly gave permission to use photographs: Mr Arthur Brown for Plates 1, 6, 14, 15 and 16; Mr Charles Saunders and Miss Jennie Caldwell for 2, 3 and 11; Mr C. R. Hannis for 4 and 5; Mr K. J. Neale and the Home Office for 7 and 8; Mr John Osborne for 9; *The Farmers Weekly* and Mr Keith Huggett for 12 and 13; The Royal Photographic Society for 10 and 21; Mr Sanders Watney for 17; Mrs Jane Bixby for 18, one of her late husband's prints. I am greatly indebted to Mrs Valerie Dzija and Mr Tony Mitchell of New Jersey for reproducing 19 from the original coloured lithograph; also to Mrs Ida Sadler for 20; and Mrs Susan Gentleman for 22. My thanks are due to Faber and Faber for allowing me to use the line drawings of Percherons from Lowes D. Luard's book, *The Horse*; to Aston

Gaze for his sketches on which Peter Branfield's drawings of the timber appliances are based; and to Mr Stanley Miller for the broadsheet.

Mr Peter du Sautoy, Mr Michael Wright and Mrs Elizabeth Renwick made the final stages of compiling the book much easier and I am very grateful to them.

# Part One

---

## HORSE POWER

# *I*

# A Place for the Heavy Horse?

This book is essentially a plea for conserving and increasing the stock of working horses as a reserve against a possible disastrous decline in energy resources; and for recording the traditional lore connected with the heavy horse, empirical lore that has accrued over many centuries and which has therefore historical and anthropological as well as severely practical value.

Twenty years ago horses were going off the land in great numbers, and it was then that I began to collect in East Anglia material for a book[1] where I attempted to record the type of farming that was powered almost solely by the horse, and—in addition—to describe the social scene where the heavy horse was the proud centre. At the beginning of this century, in spite of the earlier advent of steam-power and the marginal use of the new invention, the internal combustion engine, the horse was still the main source of power both on the land and the road; and although his dominance was gradually eroded he did not completely yield place to the self-propelled machines until this period in the late 'Fifties and early 'Sixties. It seemed clear then— at least in Britain—that the last working horses were soon going from the land; and in fact during the next few years British farming became the most highly mechanized in the world.

But the process that displaced the horse was a slow one, and it was so for two reasons. First, during long periods in the first half of this century British farming was depressed and neglected. The small farmer, who by virtue of his numbers was still the typical farmer in Britain, kept his horses because he did not have the capital to invest in new and expensive machinery: this applied to nearly all those farmers who did not have access to capital taken from outside farm- ing itself. Secondly, the low wages of the farm workers, at the be- ginning of this century and during the inter-war years, relieved the farmer of any urgent pressure to mechanize. After the repeal of the

---

[1] *The Horse in the Furrow*, Faber and Faber, 1960.

Corn Production Act and the abolition of the Agricultural Wages
Board in 1921, many farm workers were by 1923 receiving wages that
were well below the recommended minimum of twenty-five shillings
a week. Indeed, the wages they were getting were in real value below
the 1914 level; and even as late as 1935 the average wage of the farm
worker in the east of England was only thirty shillings and eight-
pence.[2] While the wages were at this level it did not pay the farmers
of the small or middle-sized holdings to mechanize: to substitute
tractors and their allied machinery for horses. It made more sense
for them to keep them.

According to official statistics, however, horses continued to decline
right throughout the 'Thirties, and even during the last war;[3] but the
horses that were working on the farms after 1939 were valued as
highly as the tractors which were necessarily in short supply. Moreover, the tractor's fuel owing to the intensive U-boat campaign was
like liquid gold.[4] But as soon as industry readjusted to a peace-time
working the machines came on to the farm in a spate; and by the
early 'Sixties it was not easy in most districts of East Anglia to find
a farm that still had a complement of working horses. It is true that
many farmers still kept a horse or two, as I found out when I went
about collecting information from farmers and horsemen. But these
horses were chiefly old stalwarts that had spent their lives working
on the land and were kept out of sentiment or affection. They played
little part in the economy of the farm, and at most did an odd job
or two between the shafts of a tumbril or an occasional bout of
drilling. As one farmer told me about the last of his horses: 'I shan't
let him go. I like to see him around the farm. It wouldn't be the
same without him. He has been a good servant, and he can end his
days quietly here.' Or another: 'I dussn't let the knackers have owd
Boxer. The missus and the family would be after me right quick!'
But there was also a handful of traditionalists who stood out reso-
lutely against the tide and still worked their farms with horses; but

[2] Lord Ernle, *English Farming Past and Present*, Frank Cass (sixth
edition), 1961, p. 527.
[3] Sir George Stapledon, *Farming and Mechanized Agriculture*, London,
1946, p. 409.
[4] Adrian Bell recalls a directive from the War Agricultural Committee in
1943: 'Do not employ a tractor for a load that a horse can pull.' And there
was a 'sticker' gummed to the tank of every tractor delivered to the farmers.
It read: *Oil costs lives. We won't waste it, Sailor.*

by 1960 they were very rare indeed; and as time went on—although fashion and status-seeking or plain emulation, looking over a neighbour's hedge at his tractor or combine, played some part in mechanization—it was the economics of their position that compelled all but the most ardent traditionalists to change over to the self-propelled machine.

In the following years the almost complete disappearance of the horse from the farms of East Anglia was taken for granted. In spite of the tentative opinion of a few people, who could stand a little to one side from the rush to mechanize, that there was still a place for the horse on the land—as a working beast and not merely as an adornment or a concession to the days that we have seen—the general opinion was that the heavy horse was finished. One ploughman at that time went so far as to say: 'Horses are dying off on the farms, and they are not being replaced. Before long, if you want to see a farm horse you'll have to visit the zoo; and in about twenty years' time you'll see me a-settin' in there [pointing to his cottage] and doin' my ploughing by radio-control.' The twenty years have passed and both these predictions have proved wrong; but I remember that I myself was inclined to underwrite the ploughman's belief that we were seeing the last of the working horses on all but a few of the arable farms in Britain. In fact I had included, as an epigraph to the book, a quotation that seemed to justify its compilation at that particular time: 'the certainty that the plough teams would come to an end in the near future'.[5]

As time went on this general pessimism began to be shared by the men who were most directly concerned with the heavy horse—those who were responsible for promoting his breeding. In the early 'Sixties the Suffolk Horse Society met to consider its future. It seemed limited, but in the opinion of the President of the Society, Colonel Sir Robert E. S. Gooch, they could last another twelve years if they managed things economically. Wilfred J. Woods, Secretary of the Society, told me recently:

'From 1961 to 1965 was our worst period. But, as you see, the twelve years have gone; and during the last five years the Society has gained in strength. This year we've had sixty new members; and about two-thirds of these have horses that will be put to work in some form or other (the other members have joined to give a general support to

[5] H.I.F., p. 281.

5

the heavy horse). It is an encouraging sign. The oil crisis has greatly helped the return of the horse, and people are wanting Suffolks. Not so long ago a ten-months-old Suffolk foal sold for 1,000 guineas. (As you see, we still deal in guineas; but we haven't yet passed the record price paid for a Suffolk horse—Sudbourne Foch, an entire sold in 1919 for 2,200 guineas.)

'A number of our members are increasing their stock of brood mares: A. J. Wright of Bruisyard, near Saxmundham, is going to maintain a stud of ten to twelve mares; Peter Moorhouse of Ardleigh, Essex, is building a small select stud; and Richard Creek of Long Drove, Cottenham in Cambridgeshire has recently increased the number of his Suffolk mares. We have a scheme at present, aimed at the breeding of as many pedigree Suffolk mares as possible to meet the current demand. Stallion owners are also invited to make their horses available for service; and the Society offers grants for retaining the service of good horses for each season. We are also building up our export trade. We've recently been sending horses to Pakistan where they are breeding Suffolks pure and also crossing them to get mules for artillery work. But our trouble sending animals abroad is the high cost of freightage. I know some Australian buyers came over here to attend a Suffolk horse sale; and I am now certain that they would have bought much more stock were it not for the high cost of sending horses to Australia. That's one of the things the Government should do: assist breeders in their export drive by arranging some kind of concession for them when they are trying to sell horses to go abroad.

'But things look more hopeful now than they did fifteen years ago. The Suffolk horse is here to stay and I'm sure that horses will come back—though not to their former position on the farms—but to a degree. After all, the Suffolk was specially bred for use on the farm, and he has an unsurpassed reputation as a horse for the land. It's not generally known that for the first twenty-three years of the Royal Agricultural Society's existence a prize was offered for "the best horse for agricultural purposes": all the various breeds of heavy horse took their chances during that period (1838–60). Of these twenty-three First Prizes fourteen went to Suffolk horses—a convincing percentage. And if the oil dries up or is priced out of reach, it's on the farm that the Suffolk will find his true place again.'

It is fitting that Wilfred Woods should find the Suffolk Horse Society in such good heart again, a hundred years after its founding, and that his own fifty-nine years of service to the Society (forty-nine as assistant secretary and ten as full secretary) should be recognized at the Centenary Dinner recently held at Melton, Woodbridge.

There has been the same resurgence in the other heavy horse societies: Shire, Percheron and Clydesdale all report an increase in membership and in the number of horses registered. At the agricultural shows in the last few years there has been a noticeable increase in the number of heavy horse entries and of the interest of the lay-public in the heavy horse classes. Roy Bird, the secretary of the Shire Horse Society, recently estimated that, whereas in the early 'Sixties the number of Shire horses was down to about 5,000 (when the breed was in real danger of dying out), today there are 15,000 horses active in one form or other: 'The horse', he said, 'has become an economic proposition again.' In saying this he was not using a vague, almost meaningless phrase: he meant it literally. For the heavy horse has already become more efficient—that is, cheaper than a tractor—for a stockman to use on a farm; and brewers, coal merchants, and furniture removers are saving money by using a horse for short journeys up to two or three miles. The heavy horse sales reflect the new demand in the number of dealers present and demonstrate the general interest by the crowds that attend them.

The public interest in the heavy horse is also shown in the increasing number of rural museums that are keeping heavy horses to give their displays of rural exhibits a 'living quality'. This will be discussed in Chapter 6. Another sign of the times is that the Horse Race Betting Levy Board that administers a premium scheme for heavy horse stallions has recently sought to assist breeding still further by increasing its grant for a stallion at stud from £250 to £350. Again, the Agricultural Training Board has been for some time running a course near Dorchester where farmers and young people who wish to learn to handle heavy horses are given a chance to have practical training on a Dorset farm. That there is a need for this is to be seen from the kind of advertisement now appearing in the farming and horse press: 'Miss Y (of Lancashire) is interested in working with heavy horses—preferably with a show team.' 'Mr A would like to find employment on a farm where heavy horses are used. Has experience in general farm work.' 'Mr W is interested in working with horses, preferably in the timber hauling business.' How far this new and rather diffuse interest in the heavy horse will contribute towards practical results in enabling the horse to be used on the land and on the road again—even to a limited extent—will be our present task to explore. But we can say at this stage that the signs appear to show the basis for a moderate degree of confidence that, if at some time in the future the heavy horse is called upon to make a real contribution towards the country's depleted energy resources, he could do so with a minimum of delay.

This book, as already stated, has another purpose which is developed in its second half: to extend and amplify my previous study of the rich context of society when the heavy horse was an integral part of both rural and urban communities. In the countryside, the horse was the focus of a way of life that had lasted for centuries. The change, therefore, from horses to tractors was very much more than a technical change that only affected farming: it caused a revolution in the farming work but, more spectacularly, it helped to bring about a revolution in rural society. The shape of this revolution can be sketched by one bare example: a 250-acre farm in Suffolk under the old farming system carried ten to twelve horses (the traditional rating was a plough-team of two horses to every fifty acres) and eight or nine men in addition to the farmer. When the horses went so did most of the men. Many of them had passed retiring age but had kept on working because of the shortage of labour caused by the war and its aftermath. This applied especially to experienced horsemen. These left the farm in great numbers during the 'Fifties and early 'Sixties and retired to their cottages in the villages where they tended their gardens and looked over the fence, slowly shaking their heads at the increasing array of machines that was coming on to the land. By today, under full mechanization, it is likely that an active farmer will work that 250-acre farm himself with the help of only one man—depending whether or not it is completely arable—and with only occasional extra help at peak periods of the farming year.

The effect on the village in East Anglia, a predominantly arable area, has been momentous. Already by the 'Sixties this change was reaching its final stage, and the village ceased to be as it had been for centuries a community organized for the particular work of farming. At first it became a kind of gentle pasture where the old generation of farm workers were put out to grass like the occasional horse they had so lately tended. Even before the 'Seventies most of this generation had gone; and their cottages had been bought and furbished up either by retired people from outside, or by young executives from the nearby town who opted for a restored cottage as being either more comfortable or more likely to give them status than a house in the suburbs. The result is that the present-day rural village has tended to take on the character of a dormitory for the nearby town, alongside a well-kept geriatric compound. Many of the young people native to the village have to leave simply because they cannot find a place to live in, as most of the cottages are bought by people who have much better-lined pockets than they have. Without attempting a closer analysis of the changes or making explicit value judgements, I believe that this tendency alone is sufficient to show the extent of social change that has happened in the countryside; and that the change in farming technique that (along with the increased mobility) is made possible by the motor-vehicle, was its most potent cause.

While I was collecting material twenty years ago for the previous book on the farm horse, at a time when the above changes were rapidly reaching their climax, I assumed a more or less complete break with the farming of the past. For it looked then that I was recording the last men who would regularly work farm horses in this region. But during the last two or three years I have come to believe that the break was not as final as I had supposed. The horse is returning to the land, even if, as yet, in only negligible numbers. But even more important for my present purpose, I now believe that I underestimated the stamina of the tradition that the older horseman carried. Within the last couple of years I have found that a remarkable amount of the lore has been transmitted to a few of the younger generation by the men who had been involved in the full horse regime. This comes out in the account given later by Mervyn Cater, a horseman's son. From the age of three his father had carefully trained him to be a horseman; had schooled him in the discipline of his craft and had passed on to him most, if not all, of his craft secrets. But by the time the lad reached his majority, the horse had gone from the farm; his father had retired and he was left with the skills he had laboriously acquired but no longer a means of practising them. Roger Clark and his wife, Cheryl, who are even younger than Mervyn Cater, have the main body of the old lore as will be seen later; and it was through my meeting young people like these that I was induced to go back to gather this aftermath of lore I hardly expected to be still available. I have done this

9

both to supplement and confirm the work I had already done, and to suggest that some of this material will have its uses apart from its being a historical record: if the farm horse is used increasingly in the future some of the information recorded here will have direct practical value.

# 2

# Chickering Hall and Oakley Park: Suffolks

Charles Saunders has been breeding horses for well over fifty years; and since the last war he and his groom, Jennie Caldwell[1], have become known in heavy horse circles all over Britain. He has been king of the ring in numerous shows down the years. On one occasion at Euston Park, the Duke of Grafton's home, he had four champions in the ring at the same time. This year (1977) as President of the classic Suffolk event at Woodbridge, the first of the season, he saw his Suffolk gelding, Joker, take the top award. He has been coming regularly to this show for Suffolk horses for sixty-four years. His first interest, however, was in Shires; but since his change-over to Suffolks, stock from his Chickering and later his Oakley Park studs have found their way all over the country and to many parts of the world:

'I was born on a farm in 1898, and I am now at Hoxne [Suffolk] a mile from where I was born. Farming has been my life, all my life—and a good life! I've bought stock, light horse, heavy horse—all types of horses. I had a few light horses for a bit of a hobby. I ran horses in good company—racing, but I didn't take any harm. But none of my horses which I bought cost me too much money. I could always sell my horses at more or less a profit. These horses—light horses I'm talking about now—they earned their keep in prize money. About 1921–2 I had a small stable of horses: I stood ninth in the trainers' list. But things began to get worse, with stable lads and with girls, and I packed in the training job. I then went back and started to breed horses again from one mare. Well, I've been breeding Suffolks since 1932. We put a Suffolk over a Shire mare and her offspring came clean-legged, some chestnuts, some bays. We used to sell a lot of horses to Moyse the coal people of Colchester. They would take eight to ten horses every year; and a fellow by the name of Seago—F. B. Seago (his son is known better than the father; he was a great painter)—

[1] See Chapter 7.

11

once he came to look at these horses. He said: "What a lovely stock of horses you've got here." There was a horse just broken (I think he was just three) and he said: "Don't sell him, Mr Saunders, I shall want him next year: I'll have him a year younger than I should do." After that we had several coming along. They were by a well-known Suffolk horse, Freston Lord Kitchener. He belonged to a man called William Breese of Occold. We had a lot of mares after that; and when I was in business on my own I bought a Suffolk mare, and I also had one or two good chestnut mares by the Suffolk horse out of the Shire mare. Those mares carried more bone than a pedigree Suffolk. Crossing them again I got my fillies into the [stud] book. And that is where I got my weight and size of my animals, or Suffolk horses—whichever way you'd like to put it. There was a time when they were looking (as they are now) for taking horses into the book, for mares into the book, mares on inspection. And in that day these mares were inspected by a committee.'

Introduction of new blood, either openly or surreptitiously, into a recognized breed was not an uncommon practice and it is confirmed by another breeder on a later page.[2] The result of such experiments as Charles Saunders describes has been to make the Suffolk a bigger, more powerful looking horse, and the impact on the breed since the last war has been considerable. The Suffolk has tended to lose his stocky 'punchy' look, and this has been remarked upon by people not directly connected with breeding. For instance, Kenneth Clark (Lord Clark) records the difference between the Suffolk of a half-century ago and the Suffolk of today in his autobiography: [3]

'In the other part of the park [Sudbourne, Suffolk, where he was brought up] were two circles of beech trees which enclosed the stables of our Suffolk Punches. . . . They were solid and heavy, but as perfect in proportion as the horses of the Sforzas or Gonzagas. For ten years the Sudbourne stud was the most famous in the world and won prizes at every show. We all loved them, and visited their stables several times in a week; but the great moment was on Sunday mornings when they would have coloured ribbons put in their manes and be trotted round to stand for our admiration on the lawn in front of the house. My father would give them minute peppermints of a brand known as *Curiously Strong* which made them sneeze but seemed to give them

[2] p. 25.
[3] *Another Part of the Wood*, John Murray, 1974, pp. 10–11.

pleasure. After the ceremony they would trot home to their stables in the beech trees as complacent as Morris dancers. I have often thought that the memory of these dear animals, which I recapture every time I open a "conker", is the basis of my sense of form.'

In a note to the above passage Lord Clark writes: 'They [the Punches] are now bred for work, are 17½ hands instead of 15 and have lost the perfect proportion that so much delighted me.'

A number of old horsemen share Lord Clark's preference for the former conformation of the Suffolk. An old stager strongly disagreed with the verdict of the judges after they had given the prize at a recent show to a seventeen hands plus, entire 'chestnut'; and as the stallion came out of the ring he held forth: 'That's not a Suffolk! With a real Suffolk you should just be able to stand a walking stick under his belly and drive a wheelbarrow through his front legs!'

Purity of breed appears to be influenced by individual or subjective preference as much as does an appreciation of beauty. But Charles Saunders defends his experiments by pointing to what has gone on elsewhere:

'I don't think there is as much of this [crossing] as with our neighbours across the border: the *Clyde* [Clydesdale] and the Shire. But in my opinion it's the best thing that ever happened, putting the Clyde stallion over the Shire mare. At one time, the Shire—you know what they were like. It was a job sometimes to get a farrier to shoe some of these horses: full of grease! As soon as they put the Clyde over it, it cut all that out. It was a year or two ago. I can remember one buyer—one gentleman's farm: well, perhaps it was twenty or thirty years ago, down in the West Midlands district. Well, there were Shire mares on the meadow there, itching and stamping. They'd got a bush hedge; and that hedge was all dead where they'd rubbed it and rubbed it with their legs and feet. Por old devils! That's what started me breeding Suffolk.

'There was a gentleman called C. A. West about two or three miles from me, farming a lot of land, a lot of cows, and I should think he had thirty Shire horses on his farm. Talking to me he said:

"I don't know: these horses come home every night sweating. They are never dry—wet when they go out next morning. Well, I bought two Suffolks; and I worked them for twelve months; they come home as cool as they go out. I'm going to clear out the others!"

'And he did. C. A. West: he had some wonderful Suffolk horses.

13

When they had the sales at Ipswich he was nearly always the top twig of the tree. C. A.'s grandson now farms the land. He's got one horse. He's got a cowman who won't have a tractor. I sold him a wonderful horse, old Jock; and they had that horse for seven years, and then I found him another to take Jock's place. I used to put a lot of horses on to the farm where there was poultry: they ran the horse and cart with feed down to the hoppers. But now they got these big "upset" hoppers. That killed that. But that's the only thing I could see where the horse could save a man some money. But now they got these big hoppers: you see so many of them round these poultry and pig places. They pull the chute down, turn the crank and away she goes. The Fens? Well, I used to drive up that way, and I'd see twenty horses in carts: I drive up now and I don't see one. It looks as if they're not using so many. It used to be, just before the strawberry crop came on —maybe in March—they'd be looking for what we called "a strawberry walker". They didn't mind a pigeon-toed horse because that would bend over and keep right in the middle of the rows away from the crop. They didn't want a big one, something about sixteen hands. They walk up the middle and don't stamp on the plant. Pigeon-toed, and of course their foot was small compared with the Shire's.

'You talk about soil compaction, and I'll give you an instance of where a horse could still be useful in this connection. You drive about the country now—it was noticeable when we had that wet spring— no corn on the headlands at all. This year [1976] we had a very dry time. Everything in Suffolk has gone very well. But field after field I've been about recently the headlands are covered with water where the tractor has been turning round. Trampled it all down. . . . Yes, now in my opinion that's where the horse could come in. No, we've made a bit of a mess-up of that with the tractor. The way to do it is to pull your headlands up and drill them last not first. Put your cultivators in or whatever you've got, and break that pan, and that will let the water through. Cultivating that would be a job for the horse. But I cannot see the horse coming back in any numbers. He could be wanted for yard work, as I said before, or something like that. I think the horse in the farm yard is a very good thing.'

# 3

# Hasholme Carr (Humberside): Shires

Geoffrey Morton, owing to the showing of a successful television film[1] featuring his farm, is probably the most widely known of that small band of British farmers who cultivate their land entirely with horses. He farms at Holme-on-Spalding Moor in Humberside, and when I visited him in the late autumn of 1976 he was helped by his two sons, Andrew and Mark, and by a younger man, Tony Ashford, who was learning to use farm horses. Geoffrey Morton was born in Whitby in 1928 and he left school in 1942. He went to sea in the Merchant Service, and came back to farm in 1951. He worked a small-holding at Spalding Moor where his wife's family originated. In those days it was a good small-holding district: it is fairly light land and it was possible for a man to make a living off fifteen to twenty acres growing cash roots: potatoes, sugar-beet, red beet and so on.

'I started off on a small place about twelve acres and got up to where we are now—138 acres. I was always interested in horses and never wanted to change to tractors. We have twenty-five horses on the farm now: a dozen of those are broken to work at present, all mares; another five are waiting to be broken in this winter; three of those are fillies. We use an entire horse from the Yorkshire Hiring Society (this is one of the eight or nine hiring societies still functioning in the country). We have eighty to ninety acres of arable land most years, sixty acres of corn and grain, some potatoes, mangels, fodder roots of different kinds, one year leys for the hay. Very little is bought for horse-fodder, a bit of bran occasionally. If we were doing nothing but farming, I suppose six work horses would be ample for all we have to do here. But we are building up a stock of breeding mares partly because we think there's a demand for horses arising, and partly for any other work that comes to hand: advertising, carnivals, steam-engine rallies, various demonstrations, television work—anything like that that turns up and needs heavy horses. They are not important to

[1] *Command Performance*, Thames Television, 10.8.76.

15

the farm but quite an important source of income. Advertising usually means a film on commercial television. A few weeks back we supplied horses for a funeral, a wagon and a pair of black mares to the churchyard.

'Two or three years ago we did a film for the Central Office of Information: a ten- to fifteen-minutes' film, showing ploughing and harrowing and other jobs round the farm. It was made for showing in Africa, for the native population out there: I suppose you'd call it propaganda against mechanization. It was to counter the feeling the Africans have that tractors and so on must be right for them because that's what the white man is doing all the time. It was really designed to show them that there were some white men doing it with draught animals, suggesting in a nice sort of way that they would be better off doing that instead of getting something—the tractor—that their system can't support. This has some bearing on the position as it was here. Because there's no question about it that a lot of small farmers have gone out of existence because they had to mechanize and found that it didn't pay them to mechanize, especially as machinery developed to the sophisticated level we have today. There were plenty of farms working three or four horses that wouldn't stand for the cost of a Ferguson tractor plough. That's how it all started; but as things became more expensive and more complicated a lot of these farms disappeared because they couldn't stand the cost of bigger modern machinery.'

Geoffrey Morton is speaking from his own experience, and undoubtedly he must have felt the pressure about twenty-five years ago to mechanize. The majority of farmers were buying machines, and there was a sense of 'keeping up' if you bought a tractor; it did not have to be fed when it was not working; your wages bill was less; and, most inviting of all, you were a progressive farmer, you were 'in the swim'. But there was also a subsidiary reason at that time, compelling small farmers to mechanize: it was a time of meat shortage and I recall that small farmers were then complaining that when they went to horse-sales prices were sent up beyond their reach by the horse-slaughterers' men, agents who were shipping horses to the continent, chiefly to France, where horse-flesh was in great demand. But it was the beginning of the end for the small farmer, because even when he had bought a small tractor, his 'mechanization' couldn't stop there: for one thing—as will be discussed later in connection with soil compaction—he found that his small tractor became less capable of doing the work he had intended it to do, and in spite of oil being cheap he soon found that he was acquiring more machinery than his holding could economically carry. In connection with the price of oil Geoffrey Morton had this to say:

'Part of the trouble then, as it is even now, oil was too cheap. Oil as a source of energy is set at far too low a level. I know I grumble like mad when I get my petrol bill at the end of the month, but even so we are still not paying what we might be paying for it. Because it means that we are using that oil up for things that could be done in other ways. It's a highly expendable resource. There just won't be any more left when that's gone. We should husband those kind of resources and not use them as we are doing now. We use oil because it's so cheap for transporting stuff all over the place that doesn't need transporting at all. Bread, for instance: most of the bread in the East Riding gets baked in Hull now, and gets taken about by diesel or petrol engine instead of being made where it is eaten. The same applies to beer and bacon, and lots of other things for that matter. A lot of this is totally unnecessary. Besides, the quality is less good—that's another side of it and a big one, I agree.

'I was talking to a farmer who is farming in a big way. He had recently bought a pair of Percheron mares. He knows nothing about horses. I met him because I was concerned with the Agricultural Training Board course on working with farm horses: he'd come along on this. He said the reason he'd bought horses was that though he was farming on a large scale the farm really didn't belong to him! It had got so big. He'd got some cows but they really didn't belong to him: they belonged to the cowman. Although he signs the cheques and pays the bills and draws the Milk Marketing cheque, they're not really his cows. So he thought he'd get a pair of horses that would be something that were his. Well, he was getting them—well, he said that eventually he hoped he might do a little work round the farm. But he was saying that it was *totally impossible* to go back to farming with horses. And he was saying: "How can you justify it?" Well, let's start with ploughing. We were using two fourteen-inch furrow ploughs and we'd put a five- or six-horse team in. Now a man can plough six acres a day with that, which is acceptable from an economic point of view. He said: "That's all right; but ploughing is easy. What about potato picking?" (because it happened to be coming up to potato time) and

17

I said: "Well, a potato harvest is one of the occasions where horses are extremely useful. They stand up very well to the carting and so on". Well, he went on and he said that he'd got two potato harvesters and he was doing very well with them; and I told him that I'd be interested to see whether you have done 'em with those machines since it has been so wet. "But we can't do it by hand," he said; "we can't get the pickers."

'Now that sort of argument seems to me like putting the horses into a box and saying the choice is really whether we change back to horses as opposed to tractors but leave everything else exactly as it is. But I don't think that is the choice that lies before us. I think that the factor that will make us have to go back to animal-draught is the tremendous cost and the future scarcity of oil as energy source. I want to go back to horses! perhaps this is one of the minor effects at that level on our whole way of life (I'm referring now to the whole nation and not just the farmers). But eventually we shall find that the potato pickers will be there just the same as the horse will be there. But that our ideas will change: we shall have to accept these things. It won't be only a matter of potato picking: it will be picks and shovels and wheel-barrows instead of the mechanical diggers we are using today. Because you can't do things in isolation. It's no good saying: "Can we change this?" Maybe the answer now is No! But these changes will be forced upon us; and the way I'd like to see it going with more use made of draught animals would make it a lot more comfortable than the way it may be forced upon us if we don't take that view.

'I don't think it need be a worse life than we have now. But I think we'd have to rely more upon other things that are renewable, instead of things that, once you've used them, they're gone for ever. Oil is very high on that list! I know very well we're not going to run out of oil altogether. They say we're not going to be completely out of oil in twenty years. But what is going to happen is that it's going to get very much more expensive because we've used all the oil that's easy to extract. I know there's oil in the North Sea and various places that haven't been started on. The oil industry knows about this oil; they've known it for a long time. The reason they've not used it before now is that it is far too costly to extract. We are going to be increasingly driven to using stuff like that which is going to cost such a lot; and I think that's going to be priced out of the market for things like ploughing. The tractor is becoming less and less efficient in terms of cost.

'I'm sure there are a lot of farms now that could very well use a pair or three horses to the great benefit of the farms and the farmers. I'm quite sure of this: there's a lot of 100- to 150-acre farms, mainly grassland, could very well run with a pair or perhaps three horse. It's like an old friend of mine—Walter, an old man of the village—says:

"It's *thowts* [thoughts] on it! You can do it all right if you like. But it's just thowts on it!"

'Well, what he meant—we'd just been talking about a particular time: cleaning muck out of the fold. It would scare a lot of men if you said to them: "There's a heap of muck in the fold and it's got to go into those carts with muck-forks and out into the field." Well, they'd curl up and go into a corner and they'd say: "You can't do that any more!" As old Walter said: "It's only thowts on it, Mister. You can do that if you want to!" And it's true is this. A lot of it is a mental *blocker*. Attitude, if you like, conditioned to thinking that you can't tackle a job of that size just by muscle power. It's something very bad: it surprises me really. They like football, and the Olympic Games have such an enormous appeal to maybe 80 per cent of the population who hero-worship physical prowess, fitness, stamina, strength and the rest of it. And yet in their everyday life they think that physical activity is something really bad, something to be avoided in every possible way. Which I think for true happiness is wrong. I couldn't go and work on a car-production line. I'm not surprised they have so many labour troubles in places like that. It's soul-destroying work in there. But I think you should have a job that you like. Well, there's no point in having a three- or four-day week. Your job should be satisfying in itself. If you work in a small unit you've got a better chance of seeing your own job through instead of putting one screw in one hole day after day, and never really touching the finished product. You've got no sense of achievement.

'You mentioned a great renewal of interest in the heavy horse: I believe it's part of the general interest in anything old; and it's partly a subconscious revolt against the type of technology we are now living with and which supports our modern way of life. People come here—not that they are going to follow our example and work with heavy horses—but they are reassured by seeing that the machine needn't completely take over; that if the machine did collapse life could still go on. By the machine I mean our whole modern way of life that's bound up so much with modern technology and industry. I think that's partly why the general public is so interested in the heavy horse now. They like to see something live on the land. There is a tremendous interest. We run a couple of open week-ends here on the farm every year. We do it because we were getting such a lot of visitors we couldn't cope with them any more, so we thought we'd try that: let them all come at once. We do one at harvest, do all the harvesting and one when we are doing the normal spring work. Three thousand or so people come over the week-end; depends a lot on the weather, of course. A lot of countrymen come, people from all over the country: High Wycombe, Bournemouth, and we get some from Scotland.

'There's a lot of interest and visits from people who want to work with horses: about fifty people who want to work horses write to me during a year. The only good way to learn the skills of driving and working horses is to grow up on a farm like our lads, and to learn without knowing they are learning. But there aren't enough situations available for that type of learning. If we are going to have any marked increase in the number of horses at work on the land we shall also have to have proper training schemes to teach young men. In fact a start has been made in this way. The Agricultural Training Board has had courses running in Dorset to teach people how to work with farm horses—a very simple and basic course to begin with, but I'm hopeful it may get extended to other parts of the country and also to a higher level as well. In Dorset they have a Western Counties Horse Association. They formed that, and the founders were anxious that it shouldn't just be a social occasion and a thing for shows and carnivals but there should be somewhere to learn to work the heavy horse. There was at the same time a demand from the members of that society, from people who were interested and joined the society but did not know a great deal about horses. They provided the original demand; and Charles Penney, a Dorset farmer, approached the Agricultural Training Board and found a lot of sympathy for his ideas. So they started the course running. As it became known that these courses were available so the demand has grown. In fact I think they've run three courses, limited to seven or eight people for each course. This is about the number you can talk to in that kind of subject, well in any worthwhile manner. They run three-day courses. There are plenty of applicants for a lot more which I expect they will hold later on. The A.T.B.'s aim is to provide training for applicants who are farming. They keep out applicants who apply just because they think it nice to know about horses. For the beginning at least they are limited to people who either own a horse or are working on a farm that has horses or are immediately concerned with starting with horses. Supposing, for instance, a man comes round and says: "I would like to own a horse and work him on my farm if you'll teach me something about it"; obviously these are the people that are most in need. It's a means of weeding out the people who aren't suitable. I know from the letters I get, people wanting to come here and use horses: I would make a guess that quite a lot of these people have just got a head full of fairies. They just think it would be a nice idea. Perhaps they'd come for a week and then they'd say: "I've had enough of this. It's a bit muddy, a bit cold. I'm going!" It weeds out that sort of application. But I've been chugging away at this training course business for years because it's obvious to me there's a need for it from the letters I get. If you once had courses running in this district, for instance, there would be an enormous number for people who'd say: "This is what we've been waiting for, but we didn't know anything like it existed!" And I think that having a course of that sort here would produce its own customers if you can call them that. But it's a bad time to start anything new in education because money is so short.

'As I've said these heavy horse courses have been very simple indeed, putting the harness on and yoking them in carts—things like that. Some of them got on to some ploughing; some of them didn't. The problem we've got with that sort of course as it stands at the moment is that we don't really know until the people get there just what sort of a standard they're at. Fortunately, purely by chance, it worked out fairly well: of the three courses most of the people in each course were at a similar level. In one course, in fact, they had all done a bit with horses, and they all got on to the more complicated things quite early; whereas in the other two courses the people were absolute beginners at the job. I think it should work out that way because it would be boring for anyone who is told to turn the collar this way up to put it on—and so on.'

From my own experience during the last few years of the general interest in working horses on the land, I believe that there would be a like demand, here in East Anglia, to learn the craft. It appears also

21

that there are a number of people who already have at least a modi-
cum of skill in handling farm horses, if we may judge from the recent
experience of a Norfolk farmer. He advertised in a Norwich newspaper for someone to look after his Suffolk horses, and he had about
250 replies. Even allowing that a proportion of these applicants had a
few 'fairies in their heads' this is a sizeable number, considering that
the craft of farm horseman has been virtually unpractised for nearly
a generation.

Geoffrey Morton's experience and observations are transcribed here
in full because I believe his opinions to be valuable and often original.
He is one of the few farmers who purposely stood aside when
mechanization was in full swing, and he has observed the progress of
modern farming from an unusual vantage point. He appears to have
arrived empirically at similar conclusions to the soil scientists—such
as Dr Stuart Hill, quoted later[2]—who are questioning the whole
premises of the untrammelled application of modern technology to the
land with its questionable environmental and social consequences. As
a practising farmer his experience has given Geoffrey Morton deeply
held convictions, and his observations over the years since the quick-
ening of the farming revolution deserve careful consideration. His
thoughts, for instance, on the compaction of the soil due to the use
of excessively heavy machinery deserve attention because they bring
out an aspect I have not seen stressed elsewhere. This is the progressive expenditure of energy and capital once mechanical cultivation is
begun: the longer a given area is cultivated by the machine the more
power is needed to bring about an identical result:

'In this district about twenty years ago it was extremely common
to see the little grey Ferguson tractor on the go. They're nearly all
gone now, and the tractor that you see today is a lot bigger and has
a lot more power; and yet it's doing about the same work as the other,
small one did. And judging also by what tractor-using farmers have
told me, and particularly those on the stronger lands, they needed to
get a more powerful tractor because the land is taking more power
to work it all the time. They've said to me: "We could not plough
the land with horses now: it's too hard. It takes too much of a pull."
It is true: when we go to different places to do demonstrations and
things like that, the horses have sometimes to work extremely hard
because the soil is compacted. If you worked it with horses for a

[2] pp. 87–8.

couple of years, it would come very much easier to work, provided you kept the other machinery off. I think that a lot of the power the tractor has is being used because the tractor is *there*—if you understand my reasoning. They are having to use the power because they are putting weight on the land. I am not saying it would be easy for anyone who is totally dependent on tractors to say: "I'm going to sell 'em and start with horses again!" It would be difficult indeed to do it just like that. If a farmer said: "First of January I'm not going to use tractors any more: I'm going to use horses"—in a lot of cases it would be virtually impossible to do it. But I think we ought to make a start: keeping the tractors off the land in the early spring, for instance. There's an awful lot of jobs even if you want to keep a lot of mechanization, there's a lot of jobs can be done with a pair of horses, with great benefit.'

During the course of our conversation I suggested that it would help to promote the spread of the heavy horse on the farms if the Breed Societies compiled a list of their members who were actually working horses on their land. Geoffrey Morton:

'I'm not sure that the Breed Societies are the people to do it. They are usually concerned with pedigrees, shows, etc.; and again not all the people who are using horses are members of a Breed Society. Some use crossbreds and horses that haven't been registered, and they are not particularly interested in pedigrees and so on. You'll not catch them all in one particular net. My experience of the Shire Horse Society is that a lot of the members are not particularly interested in working horses as such. They are interested in horses as show horses and in pedigrees of varying degrees of truthfulness, but not particularly working horses. You could look at most members of the Council of the Shire Horse Society and if you cross out the members who are directors of the breweries (who can be called owners of working horses) only a few of the rest have got horses at work. I keep digging away at this sort of thing, and there are people in the Shire Horse Society who are very enthusiastic towards the use of horses for working, but not nearly enough of them. I would think the time is ripe for a breed society to really push the work horse, I mean the horse at work. If you go back to the days when the horses were in general use I would guess that the Societies—although they were much richer in those days—occupied the same amount of space in things as they do now. Classes in shows: they were a bit bigger. They were the head of

23

the pyramid, if you like, and their purpose was to produce the best breeding stallions in the country. They were hired out in certain districts, and produced—well, maybe a couple of hundred stallions which went out and kept up the general level of the working horse population. We've still got the Shire Horse Society, and the others, of course; but I know more about the Shires. You've got your pedigree, top-ranking stock at the top; but it's got nowhere to go to! There's no bottom to the pyramid now because the working horses aren't there. To my mind it has become top-heavy; and I think all the Societies would do well to try and create, in any way possible, conditions whereby you get more horses at the bottom, *more work horses*. I think this would do good to those at the top; because if you've got a good market down there, the top would take care of itself.

'I feel strongly, too, that the breed is deteriorating through the stallions not working. It's also true that they are not walked around on their circuit as they used to be. But there is no option on this today. The mares are too spread about, they are not concentrated as they used to be. The stallions have to be transported in vans. Besides, you couldn't walk a stallion on most roads today. There's no real answer for this except an increase in the number of horses. Another thing that worries me: I think (again taking the breed I know best, the Shires) that the temperament of the breed as a whole has suffered down the years. This is only an opinion and I might have real difficulty in proving the case. But there are a lot of strains of horses today but nobody could guarantee their temperament in the working conditions because (I don't mean individual horses) all horses of a strain have not done any work for a considerable time. So you don't know what is going to happen. I know—personally know—that horses are winning in the show ring and are well thought of, and I myself wouldn't have them through the gate! I've had some of them through the gate, and worked them out and know what they are like. They are very bad to deal with. And yet they are winning in the show ring; and presumably that is making their offspring valuable. That is not doing the temperament of the breed any good at all. I feel that the temperament needs looking to; we ought to be paying more attention to it by having the animals at work: that's the only way you can pay attention to it. It all comes back to this business of getting more horses working. You know we have Premium Schemes for stallions; quite a useful thing as well, and I've no doubt it's doing some good.

Putting outside money into the breed must in the long run do some good. But I would like to see a Special Premium for every stallion that could be driven round the ring in harness, in a vehicle for single and double. And I would say that if you can get him round the show ring at Peterborough in harness it must prove something about his temperament. I'm not saying that's ideal conditions for judging what a horse is really worth as a working animal. It's not; because it's a show ground, and the animal is got up in high condition—a bit above himself and all that. But at least it means you could drive him round the ring in a vehicle; it means he's "handable" at any rate. And I would like to see a Special Premium for any stallion you could do that with.

'There are plenty of quiet horses about: we've had them here. But I just have a feeling that it's one thing it's obvious we've lost from the days of the old Shire—and that's a good deal of bone. I would suggest that the breed is lighter-boned than it was. It's got a flatter bone, perhaps a better quality limb and a lot less "feather" which might be— probably is—a good thing. But on the way we've lost some bone in the process.

'Is this due to the crossing with the Clydesdale? Well, there's a lot said about this business of Clydesdale and Shire, but I consider there's little difference in the breeds. We know, if we study the history of the two breeds, that we are closely linked. I would think that if the scientists worked on chromosomes and things like this they'd find little difference whatsoever. I know there's a lot of "Clyde" stallions —there are perfectly legal ways of getting Clydesdale blood into the Shire stud book, and a lot has gone in illegally as well. I know perfectly well there are plenty of Shire stallions in recent years have gone up into Scotland putting some *middle* into the Clydesdale where it is wanted. There is also one stallion—going back to early days now— that is in both the Shire and the Suffolk stud books! So it really makes a mockery of the bitterness you sometimes get between the different breeds. *There are good horses in all the breeds.* But I repeat what I said: in all breeds of horses a great danger comes in when you start breeding only for show points.'

Here Geoffrey Morton has brought up a question that is of great importance to the future of the heavy horse of all breeds, especially at this time when in Britain the preponderance of the *hobby* horse over the working horse is so marked: What is your breeding criterion?

25

Do you breed simply to produce an animal that looks spectacular or pleasing in the show ring? Historically, the heavy horse was evolved for a particular function: the destrier for battle, the farm horse for the plough, the transport horse for the road, and so on. The Suffolk horse, to give a particular example—although suitable for road work was bred primarily as a horse for the land; and by the end of the nineteenth century, after over a century of directed breeding, a type was evolved that was ideal for the plough and for traction work in general, possessing qualities that were suited both to its particular function and yet to its distinctive breed: compactness and hardy constitution, along with an amenable temperament; quality and a characteristic colour.[3] The old breeders of the eighteenth and nineteenth centuries had a well-defined objective, and they worked towards it with confidence, attaining in this century outstanding results. If, today, while lacking in general any function other than success in the show ring, breeders aim at various points of conformation in the animal not linked to a definite purpose, there is—it seems to me—a danger of their doing ultimate harm to the stock, for the reason that breeding in a vacuum can very easily degenerate into a "Crufts' Show" exercise, where function is hardly considered at all, and looks and a certain outré quality appear to be at a premium. (Imagine, for instance, a show for sheepdogs or blood horses. The only test of both these animals is not how they would look in a show ring but in their performance in the field: whether the dog has the sagacity and the restraint to work with sheep and the thoroughbred the speed and stamina to win races.) Similarly, without a 'broad base to the pyramid', which implies a definite social purpose, there is a real danger of adopting beauty-parlour standards in default of any other. In the last resort, in no branch of animal breeding is the old adage so much to the point as in this field where the heavy horse was once bred for heavy work: *Handsome is as handsome does.* This by no means eliminates the fine or noble-looking animal: what it does is to suggest that his fineness and nobility is only one aspect, a supererogatory quality, of his fitness to perform the work he was traditionally bred to do.

Geoffrey Morton puts this succinctly: 'You breed for a certain show point, and you get that or something very close or approximate to a Shire, a Clyde or a Suffolk. You start breeding for that particular show point, and you'll obviously select certain animals with it in mind; and

[3] *H.I.F.*, Chap. 11.

over a generation or two, maybe, you'll fix that point. But in the process of breeding those animals you'll have lost animals that have more
desirable qualities; and it's too late because they have gone. There is
tremendous power in the conservation movement (keeping 'the gentle
giants' and all that), but I would rather see the heavy horse stand on
his own feet. I'd rather hear someone say: "I'm going to have a pair
of heavy horses: they will pay me well in the job and compete with
any other system." That's better than someone coming along and saying: "We've got to subsidize these horses because they are worth pre-
serving. They are part of England's heritage and all that." True they
are, and if someone says: "We're having a farm park or an open-air
museum and we want to have horses as a part of it"—well, that's a
good thing. The horses are earning a living there just being seen by the
public. But I'm a little bit wary: I don't want a potential heavy-horse
owner in an economic situation to be put off by a remark such as this:
"Oh yes, those are just things for carnivals, museums and all that.
But they have no real relevance to present-day matters." '

Finally, we discussed the future of the heavy horse. Geoffrey Morton had decided views on this:

'I'm quite sure in my own mind that the horse, draught animals,
will be widely used again in the future. There's no other way open for
us; but it worries me because of the other implications of that fact.
[He meant by this the critical stage society would probably reach before this would happen. In its extreme form it is presumed in Edwin
Muir's poem included here as an appendix (p. 212.)] But there's no
reason why it should happen like this. We should be able to make a
gradual change back again if only we could get people to accept the
necessity of that. Some farmers who are highly mechanized will talk to
me and say:

"You know! Why bother?"

"But what are you going to do when all the oil runs out?"

"Oh, they'll have to find something! What will they be eating if we
don't grow? They can't leave us without oil."

"But where are they going to find the oil if it isn't there?"

'You can't convince them that the oil won't be there. But apart from
this question of the drying-up of oil, there is use and economic need
for the horse now: I'm sure of it. It is more economic to use the horse
to transport goods for small journeys, at this moment. I have friends
who are using horses for delivering coal, laundry, shifting furniture and

so on; and they are running their business economically. I know a dairyman in Lancashire who uses horses—Welsh cobs, as a matter of fact—on his delivery rounds: I am hoping to get some costings off him. But they've done a costing trial with a brewery. Yes, Young's brewery in London. They use their heavy horses a lot further than two miles from their brewery, delivering beer, and they find that it pays: their stables are run economically, commercially I mean. They do have a show team, but they have a working stable with twenty or more horses. They work: they work economically. I know when a costing was done by a firm of time-and-motion, efficiency people into Young's brewery, I understand that John Young said they were not to go into the stables because he didn't mind keeping the horses (he's a good supporter of the heavy horse, John Young): "We're not having them in the stable: they've not need to go in there." But the then head of the stables said: "Yes, we're having them in! We are not being left out of it. They can stand up for themselves!" And, of course, when they went in everybody got quite a surprise. They were pence per gallon cheaper than any other form of delivery. Very interesting. We might never have known that if it hadn't been for that man there who had faith in his horses. And in a case like that there was very little going for them. They are right, slap-bang in the middle of Wandsworth's traffic; go out of the gate and you are right in among it, no messing about at all. It certainly shows that in the smaller cities where traffic problems are not quite so great, they could do a very useful job. Then it comes down partly to the question of men to work them. But I am sure that problem can be solved. When we had conditions when cavalry was still on the go, war conditions, the Army could take men in and make them into cavalry men in a very short space of time; and we could do that with commercial horsemen just the same if conditions were ripe for it.

'Again, there's a great potential for horses at this moment in forestry work, like extracting thinnings. Horses could do this at an economic rate, I should think; and with a lot less damage to the trees that are left standing.'

Geoffrey Morton's last point (elaborated in Chapter 8) illustrates the range of his thinking. His views have grown out of his experience as a working farmer, but he has in addition applied his mind to, and has thought deeply about, the entire problem of present-day farming in Britain and the dead end he sees it running into. Granted that his main preoccupation is the re-establishment of the heavy horse, he nevertheless sees plainly that what is nearest to his own heart is also the measure of a desirable public good. It is this that makes his present contribution so compelling.

# 4

## Hollesley Bay: Suffolks

It would be difficult for a generation born after the horse regime was displaced from the land to imagine a large farm and its complement of heavy horses stabled together—the power centre of a large enterprise getting all the care and attention their importance demanded. The nearest you could get to reconstructing this dated picture would be on a visit to the stable of Suffolk horses still in existence at the Prison Commissioners' Borstal and Detention Centre at Hollesley on the Suffolk coast. There you can see stabled a long line of twenty or so horses in full working condition, standing in a kind of noble placidity, their chestnut coats shining and their sleek, well-rounded quarters imparting an atmosphere of efficiency and latent strength to the scene. The assembled horses in the well-washed stable occasionally gladden the heart of an old farm horseman who is privileged to see them, and he would willingly attest that this is almost exactly as it was in the not-so-distant past.

For though the Colony farm became mechanized at the same time as other farms in the district, for special reasons there was no break in the use of horses, and the colony stables have been in uninterrupted use since the full horse regime. The name Colony gives the clue to their survival as a unit. In 1886 the Hollesley Bay estate, owned by the Barthorp family was conveyed to the 'Colonial College and Training Farms', a company formed under the auspices of the Agents General of the Colonies to promote 'the training of young gentlemen intending to become colonists'. The Colonial College as such had a relatively short life, and in 1906 was bought by the Central [Unemployed] Body for London. This body later transferred it to the London County Council who conveyed it to the Prison Commissioners in 1938.[1] The farm has been worked continuously all through the changes of ownership, and it has been the policy of the Commissioners to retain the stud of Suffolk horses as a vitally important aid in the training and

[1] K. J. Neale, *The 'Colony' Suffolks*, The Home Office, Surbiton, 1976.

rehabilitation of the youths who pass through the Centre. The setting of the Colony on a wide, flat and sky-dominated plain in the Suffolk *Sandlings* with its spaciousness and unique quality of light makes a strong contrast to the aggressively urban environment which is the background of most of the youths who are sent here; and the scene itself has for many of them a great remedial potential, as the authorities rightly believe. On a recent visit I met John Bramley, the estate manager of the Colony. He told me:

'There are just over 1,400 acres altogether. We farm 1,100 acres plus, and the rest is made up of sports fields, woodlands, ornamental areas and that sort of thing; but all come under our jurisdiction. We grow a lot of grass, about 120 acres of potatoes, 100 acres of fruit. 75 acres of mixed vegetables, we have 2½ acres of glass—and of course all the different livestock. We milk at the present moment 350 cows, and we are building that up each year. We find that we can't grow corn or sugar-beet profitably, so we are tending to turn the farm into a grassland farm, and to turn the grass into milk. We supply the whole establishment with milk, and the rest goes to the Marketing Board. But we are installing our own pasteurizing plant and will supply a lot of prisons daily with milk. We supply a quarter of the prison establishments with vegetables daily, using our own road transport. We have our own vegetable preparation plant as well, and a jam factory. The jam factory supplies all the prison establishments with jam. We treat the vegetables—the dirty potatoes, for instance, come out ready for the pan at the other end.

'We have twenty-one working horses. We breed heavy horses and supply horses to the other prison establishments. That is tending to die away a bit. But I have one or two more establishments who want horses for market garden areas. On the whole, we tend to keep them here and work them ourselves. We find we have good use for them. It is being investigated that we should use horses more than we are doing at the present time. Certainly, the market garden areas, especially, use them —ten acres of glass over at Preston: they use horses round there. There are also two establishments in the south-east, and we have to supply two horses to another establishment. Certainly, we hold the view that the horse is to be preferred to the tractor for short journeys —from the cost-efficiency standpoint.

'But we also make big play of the therapeutic value of the heavy horse with the boys: that is our very big point. That is the reason why we keep horses. We attach one boy to one horse; and the boy's character changes: he has now got responsibility, direct responsibility. Most of the boys come from urban districts, and they are all in debt to cities like London. And their attitude changes. I would say that their connection with horses has a very high therapeutic value; the stud is the highest therapeutic place we have on the establishment —certainly on the Estate, anyway. They identify with the horse: a horse is an "identifiable" thing. The boy has got something to look after: he must maintain his horse.'

Ron Wood, a Northumberland man who is stud groom on the estate, confirmed what John Bramley said about the benefits the youths get through working with and looking after the horses. They acquire a sense of responsibility and they are in friendly rivalry with one another to see who can show the smartest horse.

'This is one of the things I've tried to encourage myself,' Ron Wood said. 'This element of competition, and it does develop very quickly. One lad one horse, plus his harness. What I've tried to do is to give them a certain amount of time in the week when they can clean up; and Mr Bramley comes in, usually on a Friday, and has an inspection. And as time goes on a little competition comes into it. It's not too sharp; it's just a friendly rivalry. What I find with these lads, when it gets near to the Friday, is that they'll be asking: "Can I come back tonight and maybe do a little bit more?" But unknown to this one lad, say, he may be the last one who has asked me. So I believe that's a very good thing. They spend as much time as they can with the horses. Admitted, there is the odd one who has not got the aptitude to start with: he just will never make a horseman. How are they selected? Well, I understand that in the first instance they do put in for whatever department they want to come to, and I understand there is always a waiting list for the stud. They are fairly well graded before they come to me, and then I usually take them on a two-week probation period; and I can usually tell if that lad is going to be any use at all at the job. It's no use a lad—if you can see he's just frightened of the horses; and if he's never going to be anything else but frightened, obviously you just have to send him back.'

John Bramley elaborated on the method of selecting the boys when they come in: 'In the first week they are allocated to the different departments on the establishment. The boy can say he would like the stud or whatever other department, and we will have a look at him in some other way first—some sort of general labouring job. If he has an aptitude that is better than his compatriots then he gets a specialized job. So afterwards, if we get him back here, if he doesn't succeed, there are many jobs on the estate and we can move him to something else. We try to fit round pegs into round holes. We employ something like 130 boys every day, so there's plenty of scope to move them around and find different boys to fit in the right section.'

What Ron Wood has to say about his reception and training of the boys in the skills of managing horses is of specific interest in view of the increased number of heavy horses being bred up and down the country, and the need for people to look after them: 'When a boy comes up I usually have a little talk with him: his reason for wanting to be amongst horses; has he had anything to do with horses? I find the chap who has had nothing to do with horses seems to be the best one to work out—here anyway. I then more or less leave him; let him work with another lad for about four days. He then gets the feel of the place; sees what goes on. And gradually I allot him a job. He may do a bit of stable work, sweeping things up, keeping things tidy and clean. He's amongst the horses; he's getting accustomed to it; and that will take about a week. By that time he is leading horses out to the paddock or bringing them in. Then I can size him up and I can say:

"Now I can give you a horse which you'll look after."

The horse is now his responsibility and he goes on from there. Providing he does the job he's set up for the rest of his time here.

'If we do any field work—I'm afraid we don't do a great lot—it is harrowing. We do a bit of ploughing, but it's largely for what you might say exhibition. If someone wants to see a pair of horses ploughing they can yoke up a pair. In the stud the breeding is the first priority. You've seen the mares with their foals this morning. Of course these mares are excused work now, but as soon as the foals are weaned, which will be next month, the mares will be put into harness and they'll work carting or whatever they have to do. If a mare hasn't got a foal—there's one down there with harness on—she'll carry on working. No foal, then you work!'

At this point John Bramley added a note about their policy in using the horses:

'We use them for essential carting, especially in the winter-time because we haven't so many available in the summer when the mares have their foals. But we should like to make more horses available in the summer because we are carting vegetables down from the fields; and it's not economic to tie up a tractor for this job. Again, we find it difficult to find boys to drive a tractor because they have to hold a clean licence without endorsements before they are allowed to drive; and so many boys have these convictions. It is easier therefore to put a boy with a horse than it is with a tractor. And also it's less costly. A £5,000-tractor just to bring vegetables from a field! It doesn't seem very economical. And I would like more horses at this time [August]. We don't have them available because we've got the foals; and although we've had numbers of filly foals over the last few years, we don't seem to get any colt foals to make into geldings. We would like more horses for general carting for the estate, to cart grain and so on. We have three dairy herds at the present time: we'll have another one eventually—four dairy units; and it will be handy to have more horses to deliver to these units rather than tractors and trailers. We want to increase our horses. There's a case for keeping more geldings. We need something for all-the-year-round work. We'd like to have a horse down in the market garden area. Unfortunately we don't have one available. It would certainly help to keep the market garden crops clean. A horse would work steadily [hoeing] between the rows of vegetables—where they don't want a tractor with the big wheels and the compression.'

In addition to acquiring an appreciation of the valuable remedial work that comes out of the existence of the stud, it struck me while learning about the Hollesley Bay experiment that if ever the country was forced to expand its numbers of working horses, units such as this would be invaluable starting bases and exemplars for the expansion. It also occurred to me that to some extent it might also help to meet the difficulty, if horses did return in any numbers, of finding people to work and look after them. None of the officials at Hollesley Bay would claim that they are producing ready-made horsemen, but at least they are stimulating an interest in horses among many of the boys and kindling in a few a desire to work with horses permanently. Both John Bramley and Ron Wood were cautious about the amount of horsemanship they are able to teach at Hollesley:

'The boys,' John Bramley said, 'are here for about thirty-eight weeks; and I feel we don't have enough time with a boy to try and alter his attitude sufficiently. I would like to see them here longer, but that's very much a personal opinion. I think I ought to add, in connection with getting to know the boys, that Mr Wood takes boys to the agricultural shows when we are showing the horses. And I notice it that a boy who goes to a show—when he comes back his attitude has altered a lot. Certainly he'll talk to me more, accept me more than before he went to the show.'

Ron Wood added: 'I usually have six lads here in the stud, but I never take more than two to a show. They know that sooner or later one or two of them will be selected to travel with me to the shows; and this is an incentive for them to keep on their toes; something to work for. They are put on trust. I mean, when I'm at a show, a lad could walk away and I'd just lose him in the crowd; and that would be the end of him except that I would have to go through the normal procedure and report that he was missing. So literally, he's on trust to me; and I try as far as I can to treat them as ordinary individuals. A lad is out with me and as long as he behaves himself everything is all right.

'Occasionally we have a good lad who has the making of a fine horseman. Every now and then over the years there's one individual who keeps coming back in your mind. Only a matter of a month or two back I had a lad here, and he was of gypsy origin. This is another thing: I've found that lads with gypsy blood have this inbred thing about horses. They may never have had much to do with horses. It's mostly cars now, wagons. But it comes out: I've found this. This lad I'm speaking of was exceptional. His make-up, his character—he was very likeable, very polite; he was hard-working and he was devoted to the horses. He would let nothing slip past him. He was an exception.'

During the season a party goes to the shows frequently, and the Colony horses have had a fair number of successes, notably with Parham Rufus, a young stallion that took first prize at the Royal Show in 1975. Naturally these occasions do more for the boys who are lucky enough to be chosen to go than anything else in their curriculum. John Bramley believes this:

'At the show we are all part of a team: the horses have got to be ready on time in the show ring. There's a lot of exchanging of horses, going backwards and forwards, getting horses ready, and parading at the right time: the next horse out of the box ready for the ring when the other one comes out. I think that a lot [of therapy] goes on there: they've got themselves so totally involved in it. They feel they've got responsibilities they have never had before.'

Later I had a conversation with one of the lads, and he gave me the impression that although they are not in the stud long enough to become skilled and experienced horsemen, the sound basic training they acquire easily lends itself to being built upon later. Moreover, the stimulus they have had and an inculcation of the right attitude to the horses add up to a fine usable potential for the future. He is nineteen years of age and comes from the outskirts of an East Anglian city:

'I knew little about horses before I came here. I knew that a horse had four legs and a head, and that's about all. Everything I know I've learned since I've been here. My parents had nothing to do with horses either, but I'd always been interested in farm work since I was small. My mother used to go fruit picking and I always used to break away from her and go to the farm.

'I've been here between three and four months, and all I know about horses I've learned from here, and that's a considerable amount. I come back at night to the stud, week-ends as well. I look after that horse Mallard, one of the black horses [two hunter types, crossbred from the Suffolks]. I used to look after him when we brought them off the marshes. He fell into a dyke and we had to get him out. But he was a bit scared, so I jumped in after him—into the dyke; put a rope round him; and since then I've looked after him.

'You say he's very well groomed. Well, I do the proper grooming with him—a full groom. The feet first, pick his feet out. Then give him a clean up with a stiff brush; then go over him with a smooth polishing brush; then go over it with a soft rag—get all the dust out; go over that; then comb the mane out; brush the mane out with a soft brush and just run your finger through it; tail as well. Then with a damp sponge clean the nose out and the eyes, and the backside; paint his feet up. We do this with oil; it stops the feet from cracking; sand cracks in the feet. If you can put a bit of oil on, that seeps into the hoof. And that's about it!

'Mr Wood taught me how to do a full groom the other day. I'll be tested soon. You learn so much and then you have a Friday inspection. We have a horse each and you have to groom them; do the full groom and then clean all the harnesses up and everything; make sure they're all fitted up nicely.

'I'd like to work with horses, heavy horses if possible. I've developed a new interest since coming here. I was always interested in animals but I've developed it to a state when I know what I'm doing

with horses. But I was a bit scared of them, a bit wary of them before: now I just walk round them and call them and do anything with
them. I'm just not worried about them at all. There are certain ways to
approach them: you speak to them as you approach them, and you
put your hand on them so that they know you are there; and you
won't frighten them then. Talk to them all the time.

'I shall be sorry to leave here. I won't get such a good place as here
to look after horses.'

# 5

# Weyland's Farm: Suffolks

Roger and Cheryl Clark are a dedicated young couple, and the whole of their life is given to the promotion of the heavy horse, the Suffolk in particular. They have a stud of heavy horses at Weyland's Farm near Stoke-by-Nayland in Suffolk. They include Rowhedge Count the Second, this year's (1977) champion Suffolk stallion at the Royal Agricultural Show. ('The Count' also figured prominently during the whole week of this year's 'The Horse of the Year Show' at Wembley.) As well as breeding horses themselves they hire out the services of their stallion and Cheryl Clark is responsible for 'travelling' him.[1] They also break in and train horses of all kinds, many of them after other people have tried and proved unsuccessful—the sort of task that falls inevitably to the lot of real experts. In addition, they are both qualified farriers and they work seven days a week: they are up early and to bed late, and the whole of their life is horses.

The Clarks form a team that is excellently equipped to help the resurgence of the heavy horse on the land. For example, one of the big problems at the moment for those farmers who want to work horses on their farms again is the shortage of horse equipment. Manufacturers in Britain have long since ceased to make the necessary gear: ploughs, harrows, cultivators, hay-machines and vehicles suitable for horse traction. There have been a few suggestions to solve this difficulty. One is to persuade an engineering firm—it would probably have to be subsidized at first—to return to the making of farm-horse gear. Another, is to import the gear from Eastern Europe—Poland for instance—where much of the land is still worked by horses and the implements are still being made on a large scale. Some British farmers have already adopted this solution of importing: Geoffrey Morton, the Yorkshire farmer, has had some of the horse machines he uses sent from the United States. Roger and Cheryl Clark however, are both able to make alterations to tractor gear to enable them to use it with

[1] See Chapter 7.

horses. They have already begun doing this, and they recently showed me a hay-tedder, originally designed for a tractor but which they now use successfully with a horse. Incidentally, the Amish, the Protestant sect who farm in the eastern state of the USA, have never used self-propelled machines; and they met some difficulty in getting horse-gear fifteen to twenty years ago when the majority of working horses disappeared and manufacturers gave up making the machines. But they have since proved most ingenious in adapting tractor machinery and transport vehicles for use with their horses; and many American farmers who are going back to horses again are turning to the Amish and are taking a leaf out of their farming book.

After spending some time in recent years at Weyland's Farm I became convinced that the Clarks are living witnesses to the wrongness of the general assumption of twenty years ago when almost everyone —myself included—thought that the heavy-horse skills and the traditional background lore would disappear with the passing of the old horseman of that time. Roger Clark was born in 1947, and he told me about his early life:

'I've been interested in horses ever since I was a boy of four or five. My father was an engineer: where I get my horse background is from my mother's side—horse doctors and veterinary surgeons right back through the centuries, at Yoxford and Saxmundham. The Wrights of Yoxford, grandfather's cousins, were wheelwrights and blacksmiths. I have got a family tree that goes right back on that side.

'I've done a bit of smithing off and on, but I'm a farrier and not so interested in the iron-work side of the business, only the horses. I really wanted to be a vet but I could never settle down to too much school work, and that went by the board. I started off when I was about fourteen with Stanley Arbon who had a forge at Middleton. I started off taking horses there to be shod, and then I took my own pony and gradually did a bit. Then when I left school I used to go on one or two days a week when he had a few horses in to shoe; and I probably used to do as many horses in a week as what I do in a day now; if you had about six horses a week then that was something outstanding. That was about fifteen years ago. Then when I was sixteen and a half I went to George Coulson's of Long Melford: I went there more or less as a farm horseman. But I was lucky. While there I met Leslie Finch of Martlesham: he is cart-horse shoer for Suffolk. There's no one to touch him. He shod most of the horses in the Suffolk stud book that won prizes for the best feet. And I was lucky enough to get a few hints and tips. I used to help him. We used to work six horses regularly while I was there. With the show horses he used to be there twice a month, and I had plenty of opportunity to get really into the job. We've won the Arthur Pratt Challenge Cup (for the horse with the best feet) for six years with one of our geldings. Leslie Finch shod all the best horses round here. That was his speciality, and that was the job he could do. The foot is important. *No foot: no horse.*

'We shoe as many heavy horses as anybody: we have horses coming here from Dereham in Norfolk. We do the horses at Dedham; we have some come from Essex, plus Adams's and Michael Beecher's. So we do a fair number of heavy horses. We also break in horses for other people. I think we do as many cart-horses as anybody. And the number of horses is increasing. We get more enquiries for heavy horses now than we've ever had. The trouble is—especially with the Suffolks; I'm not saying it's so much with the Shires—is there isn't so much sale. The trouble is not so much selling them as finding them. There's not enough horses to sell. There were one or two private sales in recent years (Charlie Saunders had one): well, there were a lot unrealistic prices there, and that killed the job as far as Suffolk horses were concerned. That put the prices right up, more than they were worth. When someone comes and says: "I want a Suffolk mare." Well, you have to say: "If you want a good one it's going to cost you £1,000." I know about eight years ago when we went to Norfolk —on a marsh up there—we bought one mare for £120, and £130 for another, and 60 guineas for a gelding. We brought the cheaper mare home; pulled her about; got her shod, and sold her to Wallace. And she came out champion; and that only cost him £250. Wisbech sale [1976]—that was three weeks ago; there were heavy horse sales up there. There were twenty-six Suffolks there, a damn good number. And do you know, I don't think there were six of them sold! There was a reserve for a mare: there was one mare went up to 1,100 guineas and was withdrawn. I've seen a lot better mares than her put to work! But there was one that did sell and made between 550 and 600 guineas. That wasn't too bad. I don't know why they put such a high price on the Suffolks.'

In discussing the way forward for the heavy horse Roger Clark said he believes that its future lies with those owners who *work* their horses, who use them themselves and who use them because they are interested in using them. He also believes that there would be plenty of young people who would be interested in working and looking after heavy horses if only they were given the opportunity. And one wonders, in this connection, whether it would be possible for the Government to bring training in managing working horses into their job opportunity schemes for young people. After all something like this was done in the 'Thirties when Sir Arthur Richmond pioneered the Land Resettlement scheme for training unemployed workers and setting them up to work on the land. To illustrate one of the benefits that would be likely to result from getting at least some horses back to work the land, Roger Clark recounted the following experience he had:

'An interesting thing happened just at the back here. I wanted to practise ploughing for a ploughing match. Well, we're on an estate here: and they are very good: I've only got to ring up a man and say: "Can I do a bit of ploughing in such and such a place?" and I can carry on. Well, there's a piece on this corner, about three-quarters of an acre and it's very wet. I ploughed that with horses, not very deep on the *stetch*[2]—made narrow stetches of it, and finished it to the end. Later the tractors came along and started ploughing where I finished. Then they pulled that field down and drilled it; and when the corn was so high [about six inches] and you looked at it from the road, the bit that was ploughed with horses was far greener and denser and taller, and looked a lot better than the piece that had been done by the tractor. You could see where the horses finished and the tractor started. It was not only my observation but also the farm foreman—a rare mechanized man, and a good chap too. It was really outstanding when you got up on to the road and looked down.

'There are plenty of jobs for horses on the farm—there's no doubt about that. It must be more economical to use a horse to cart about and to cart fodder for cattle. One man can do it with a horse where you want two with a tractor. This is where we find a lot of our trade with heavy horses is: this is what people want them for. And the funny thing is you can sell an old horse for that job a lot easier than you can a young one.'

Following his early training as an old style of farm horseman who, in Suffolk, was as skilled in cultivating the land as in looking after and training his horses, Roger Clark is an expert ploughman and takes almost as much interest in the exercising of this skill as he does in

[2] A 'land' or 'rig', a section of ploughed land.

managing and shoeing his horses. For six months of the present year he and his wife have been taking their horses down to Dedham Vale Heavy Horse Centre which is open every Sunday. Roger Clark also takes one of his horse-ploughs, and during the course of the day he gives a demonstration of ploughing the land with a pair of horses; and it is an indication of the novelty of demonstrations such as these, and the interest taken in them, that until horse-ploughing was renewed in this way during recent years, many young farmers, even, had never seen a pair of horses ploughing, so effectively had the tractor driven the horse off the land.

Leslie Mills, the owner of the Centre, has ten Shire horses in his stables there with all the harness and gear necessary for their showing; and the Clarks bring down ten of their Suffolks each week-end to make a sizeable complement of horses on display. This autumn, on one of the last days of the season, my wife and I went down to spend the morning and afternoon at the Centre. It was a day following an unseasonably warm October day, and there was a thick fog all the way down on our journey to the Stour valley. We saw nothing of the countryside farther than the hedges and about forty yards of a hazy road in front of us. When we got to the Centre, just before the official opening time, the pall of fog had not lifted. 'There won't be many people here today,' was the verdict; but presently, towards midday, the sun showed wanly through, tentatively as though undecided whether it could repeat its performance of the previous day; and soon people began to arrive in their cars and to look for places to eat their lunch. By two o'clock there were hundreds of cars in the fields used as temporary car-parks, and they were still coming in. By mid-afternoon the fog had lifted completely, revealing the beauty of the Vale of Dedham and the green, undulating pastures of this particular farm, bathed in a pellucid light that was in dramatic contrast to the myopic fog of a few hours before. While we were waiting for some of the horses to parade it occurred to me that in spite of the uncharacteristically crowded farm, and the hundreds of people who had flocked to the nearby village of Dedham, drawn to the famous places and basking in the resonances of a name, Constable was still present: his genius was still there in the glowing scene to be given its meed and its bright vindication.

Leslie Mills explained to me that he got the idea of the Centre from a similar one at Maidenhead. But he wanted the Dedham Vale

Centre to have a greater involvement of the visitors and more variety in the things for them to see. He appears to have succeeded, for here are the chief activities that we saw during our visit: the shoeing and grooming of heavy horses, the viewing of the glittering gear in the harness room, braiding up the mane and the tail of one of the horses, the feeding of the horses and the cleaning out of their stalls. We saw a pair of horses being harnessed to a wagon, a young girl of nine or ten grooming a huge Shire horse, another leading a seventeen-hand horse about. There were side-show activities like the plaiting of corn-dollies and the details of the plaiting of the horses' manes with bast and with ribbons.

The Clarks were there from early morning as they had to bring their horses the four or five miles down to the Centre from their farm. As soon as the gates were open Roger Clark was busy shoeing one of his Suffolks, watched intently by a crowd of people of all ages. This activity was in spite of his very full day just before. Late on the previous night he had brought two horses and his plough home after competing and winning first prize in the contest for ploughing (using a *swing*[3] plough) at the Southern Counties Horse Association's Show in Hertfordshire. After he had finished the shoeing, he later took a pair of Suffolks with a Ransome's Y.L.[4] plough onto a field and demonstrated the soothing *swish swish* of the soil over the mould-board, and

[3] A plough without wheels.

[4] *Yorkshire Light*, made by Ransomes of Ipswich. It first appeared in 1844 and in that same year it won a 'double first' at the Royal Show at Southampton for the best plough on both light and heavy land. But Ransomes evolved its final design a short time before this as the result of a complaint by a customer, a Yorkshire squire farmer. The local blacksmith, a Ransomes agent, had supplied him with one of their ploughs and he had complained that it was no better than any other. The smith, not wishing to lose a good customer, got in touch with the Ipswich firm giving them some suggestions for improving the plough. After numerous experiments on their trial fields the design was perfected. Tradition says that on receipt of the plough the smith decided to use a method of his own to impress the squire. He chose one of the squire's worst fields; took the Y.L. with a team of horses and ploughed an acre of it *by moonlight*. The squire was very angry on finding that someone had been making free of his field. But he was also very impressed by the standard of the ploughing. Who had done it? Someone hinted that he should visit the smithy. He took the hint and that morning gave his blessing to the very first Y.L. plough. No customer has ever complained to better purpose: it still holds the record among British horse

the equable, unfussy progress of the pair of well-trained horses. In the meantime his wife had been grooming the horse she was to use in a wagon. She then harnessed it and hitched it up before going out to attend on a group of children who were waiting to be taken on rides around the big pasture.

The cars were still coming in well after mid-afternoon. Earlier we had watched them with Bruce Sutherland, a Scottish veterinary surgeon from the nearby town of Hadleigh. He had been there for some time tending one of the horses. 'Look at them,' he commented on the stream of people. 'Their own life now has so much unreality that they are searching for a glimpse of another kind of life. They sense the heart-power that's in living animals, and they come out here to see it.'

---

ploughs both for long life and popularity (see *The East Anglian Daily Times*, 1 January 1908). A Norfolk farmer, James W. Seely (born 1894), of Mundham, recently confirmed its popularity: 'Every plough was a good plough until the Y.L. came out. Then you couldn't find a better.'

# 6

## More Working and Hobby Horses: Percherons and Suffolks

The number of farmers working horses on their farms is at the present time very small, although more are now looking around for a heavy horse or two to do marginal—chiefly carting—jobs about the farm. The cost analysis of using a horse for short haulage distances has persuaded many that it would be in their interest to keep a horse if only they could find someone to use and tend it. But the demand for heavy horses that can be used as an additional attraction to a stately home, to an open-air museum, or to a farm that already houses a collection of old farm implements and vehicles in its old barns is now considerable, if we can judge from what has been happening during the last two or three years in East Anglia. The 'hobby' horse is flourishing: more and more people are buying Suffolk Punches not for the purpose of drawing furrows or loaded tumbrils but for drawing people to their farms at week-ends or special occasions when they throw open their collection of tools and so on for the public to inspect. In fact there are a great number of people ready to be attracted to view a parade of farm horses or horses doing some mild ploughing or harrowing, or even just pulling an old harvest wagon loaded with children. These are chiefly the Sunday afternoon motorists who take the family out and are looking for some kind of diversion. These horses may be kept chiefly as crowd bringers, doing only the occasional carting job mostly during the winter, and they may also be exhibited in the agricultural shows where the heavy horse classes are always a great focus for the attention of the crowd and the television camera.

One of the few Suffolk farmers who still work horses regularly on their farms is John Utting of Mettingham. Although he now does most of his ploughing with tractors he has never been without horses since he started farming. It would be best, however, to let him tell his own story; yet it would be as well to point out here that apart from its immediate relevance to our present purpose the account is important

45

for his being one of the last men in this area to start his farming more or less from scratch and through unremitting toil build himself a sizeable farm. In this respect the account is a historical one for the reason that the time when a young man could with the minimum of resources carve out for himself a holding simply from a singleness of purpose and sheer hard work already seems aeons away. He started his farming career exactly thirty years ago (1947)—a short interval of time, barely a generation, but during it the whole farming structure along with its social context has been turned upside down:

'I was born in 1932 and when I left school I was fifteen. I went to work for a man and I was with him for a year. Then I left him and went to my uncle's: I was with my uncle four years and from my uncle's I went to Mr Le Grys of Flixton (farm work all the time). I was there for one year then I started on my own. When I started on my own I was twenty year old. When I worked for a master I started in such a way that I was working [for myself] before I went to work: I was doing my own jobs; and then again after tea at night when I left off. I done some more jobs on Saturdays and Sundays. That's how I got a start. Then I hired a little place, thirteen acres, off my father for £25 a year. My father had just these thirteen acres. He was a shop-keeper, manager in the International Stores. The farming was on my mother's side—all round Ditchingham, Denton and that area. My father's people came from Norwich.

'Well, I kept adding to these thirteen acres, piece by piece, and five or six years ago I bought this farm, and I still got the other farm lower down there where I keep the cows. I gave up the regular job because I was starting at a quarter to five in the morning, and I was milking three cows by hand, then I'd to get the milk on the road, and get to work by seven. That was about as much as I could do. One night I come home and had these cows to milk, and my father said: "I had two more heifers calve today," so I got five to milk. Then I gave my notice in at the job; and I started working [on another system] not doing a full day's work but at 3s 6d an hour, which was goodish money. That covered my holiday pay and my insurance stamp and everything in those days. Then I helped people—casual, like harvesting and pulling sugar-beet and that sort of thing, working, "taking to do" [contract or piece work]. I was on my own for nearly a year before I employed a boy. Then he had to go into the Forces and he left. That's how I originally started and one thing led to another: I

46

got a tractor and I started doing a bit of contract work. I already had a horse—well, I've never been without a horse. I was seventeen when I bought my first horse: £42 that cost. Never in my life have I ever been without a horse—since then, seventeen year ago. I sold that one: swopped it with Mr Munning's. I started young! and I have 250 acres belonging to me now—all due to hard work.

'I was very keen on horses, and although it was more profitable later to use a tractor I sometimes think it was an excuse for people to have an easier life. It's the general nature for a man to go the easiest way, isn't it? Most things—if you see the easiest way to do it, you'll do it that way, I think that's a lot to do with it: a lot of people would rather ride than walk. Politicians are all to blame: they create the situation where they encourage the lazy man and burden the men who do the work—with taxes and things.

'If you count the ponies I've got eleven horses and two foals now. The working horses are Percherons: five working horses and a three-year-old that ain't broke in: I haven't had time to do it yet. I've got four tractors as well. The horses all live off the farm and they don't cost any money—only indirectly. They breed foals we produce ourselves, and we can sell them. They'll do a lot of jobs which I class equally as quick as a tractor. (I think people get lazy sitting on the seats of tractors.) For carting all sugar-beet and things like that about the yards horses are much better. I'd rather have them at any rate. We also drill with the horses some of the time: when I got labour to do it I prefer drilling with horses because it [the seed] go in better behind the horses' feet than behind the wheels of a tractor. If I had time and labour I'd do it all with horses. It's a job to get everybody interested in that sort of thing: they—the young ones were brought up in a different time. There are two men with the cows, an old-age pensioner, and another chap working with me—four all told. Some of them will use the horses when the jobs arise. It's medium land, a bit hilly on this farm. We use two horses, sometimes three: there's some places where there's a good tidy pull. The job is to get the horses all to pull together: if one stop it shove the load on to the others, you don't want. Of course, they are not as regular as they were years ago when they had to do everything and keep going every day.

'There's a bit of difficulty in getting men to work horses, too—to get them when you want them. Years ago everybody on a farm didn't know anything different from a horse. I used to do all the carting and it wasn't a hard job to find an extra man because he needn't know anything about tractors, and they didn't want to know. The more skilled jobs were put out to the head man, the head horseman, and the lesser skilled jobs—well, nearly anybody could do them because all could use a horse; even if they only been carting about in the town, they could still do harrowing and that sort of thing; and carting about on the farm because they'd been used to harnessing up a horse.

'It's true, you can get your drilling done earlier with horses. I drilled a piece of grass seed into this barley out here for that reason—with horses because it was so bad on the headland where I had to turn. If I'd ha' done it with a tractor I'd ha' chewed all the barley up. I drilled that overwart [athwart] with the horses. They turned round better, you know: where they came up into the headland they turned round better where it was so wet; they turned round and set into their work. That didn't make no mess when I finished. Is it more economical, you ask, to do it with horses? Well, they are all produced on the farm, ain't they? That's no use having a £100, if £99 belong to someone else, is it? It ain't the man who earns the most but the one who finishes up with the most is the one who's doing best. It's no use your cows giving more milk than anyone else if it's going to cost you a lot of money to get it. If it costs you £99 to get a £100 out of your cows, you are better off getting £30 if £20 belong to you.

'If you get a good man and he's horse-minded you can save a lot of money on a farm; but if he's a bit of a dozer and slow in his thinking—well, he won't get by either way. It depends on how you think: most work is done in the mind, isn't it? If you think: "Oh, Monday morning: I've got to go to work!" then you're beat before you start. If you enjoy your work it isn't a hard day, is it? I'd rather be over there digging in a ditch there than on Yarmouth front wandering up and down—any day! Tractor driving ain't work at all. You are sitting on a seat going up and down the field. If you were playing football you'd be burning up a lot more energy, wouldn't you? Some of the men like having a break with horses: some don't. Some do it because it's an order: they don't particularly enjoy it. One or two of them do it because they like doing it. The people who don't like it have been brought up since mechanization.

48

'You ask me about the breeds of heavy horse. Well, there are good and bad ones among all sorts of breed. When I worked for my uncle we had Friesian cows and Suffolk horses. That's what all I ever knew and continued to have. Then I bought a Percheron horse and the Suffolk mare died, and I bred from the Percheron. That's how I came to have Percherons. I won't say I prefer one from the other: it's just what I got now. I don't think one breed is better than the other. You get good Suffolks, and a lot of people didn't like the Shires years ago because they used to have greasy old legs. But they are better now.

'My wife often says to me I was born fifty year too late: I should have been born fifty year sooner: she means I'm old-fashioned in my ways. Had I my choice I think I'd go back to the old-fashioned ways. If I was the sole power to decide I would swop everything back to the old ways because there wouldn't be the rush there is on the land today. You got to rush over this and rush over that to get it done in time. There was plenty of men and they let the horses feed. It was peaceful. They worked when they had to work. You take the land. How long will it stick the treatment it has had over the last generation or so? They're now using up the richness the old-fashioned farmers put into the land. Sometimes I think about those things and I wonder if it will harm the land so it won't produce so much.'

Margaret Utting, John Utting's wife, as well as bringing up four children, is interested in showing his horses; and she prepares them and takes them to the agricultural shows, chiefly in East Anglia.

'We had them at Soham in Cambridgeshire last Monday [6.6.77], at Outwell in May, at Loddon in June, and we had them at Cottenham last year. They are all working horses off the farm—Percherons. We have a thirteen-year-old mare that we work: we have a colt foal. But we haven't a stallion. We generally take the mares to where the stallion stands—Peacock's at Wymondham. We're pleased with what we've done in the show line. We've had second prizes. The mare that's thirteen, she took a second on Monday, and her foal took a third. We combine the two: the working side and the show side. There's a lot of those horses we compete with that are kept just for the showing; and it's nice to think that our horses can do the work as well. Whereas the majority of those—I don't think they've had a collar on. It makes you think when you go to these shows. We went last Monday and there

49

were horses galore: Shires, Clydesdales, Suffolks, Percherons, and when I looked round the ring—there was a grand finish and all the horses were in—it just crossed my mind as I looked round: how many of those horses could you take to the drill or the plough? To be 100 per cent genuine about it! The working of the horses does help them. They seem a stronger animal for the work. We see it in the horses themselves: when they've just been trained they'll sort of jib at a job, but when they've been worked, the muscles are there and they'll do anything. Quite a number of people came to the thirteen-year-old mare last Monday, and they said straightway: "She's done a lot of work!" —which she had. She could work the rest of them on that field into the ground; and you could tell just by looking at her that, compared with the other horses, she was the horse that had done plenty.'

Harry Burroughes (born 1908) is a retired farmer of the generation previous to John Utting. He lives at Chediston Grange near Halesworth in Suffolk, and has five Suffolk horses which he keeps as a hobby. He does no farming himself now, but he has kept a pasture out of his old farm for his horses. He spends most of his time renovating his extensive collection of machines that were used in farming before the coming of the tractor. He often has open days at Chediston Grange, and his horses and farm vehicles have appeared in films and in demonstrations at agricultural shows and county museums:

'I left school at thirteen and went straight on to a harvest with a scythe. I was thirteen on 15 July, and I left school that very day at dinner time; and I went with a scythe cutting hay, and then I went during harvest—not much of course because my father only had a small farm; it weren't really big acres to do, but I did some. Then as a teenager I went with an old professional thatcher. I did a harvest with him, helping pulling out the straw and taking it up the stack. A very good few weeks with me, because I learned the art of thatching, and I always did my own thatching. I've realized since retiring one of my boyhood ambitions. When I was a lad I had a great desire to be a blacksmith—horse-shoeing because I always loved horses. So, owning a small farm and working on the land, I never did become the blacksmith I wanted to be. But since I retired I've now bought my own forge and anvil and I shoe my own horses now. I've learned through watching. I've not actually made my shoes; I bought some from an old blacksmith. I heated them up and burned them on, and I did very

1 Sudbourne Hall. Horses in a double-breasted road wagon

2 Charles Saunders and Jennie Caldwell with some of the Suffolks
at Oakley Park

3 Jennie Caldwell with two Suffolks

4 Horses at work in the Liverpool Docks

5 Sowing on the Cotswolds: a two-horse seed drill

6 The Suffolk Show: Felixstowe, 1908

7 Hollesley Bay. A stable of 'Colony' Suffolks. One of the lads 'picking' a horse's hoof

8 Ron Wood, the head groom at Hollesley coaching a lad to plough: a Ransome's Y.L. plough and a pair of Suffolks

9 Roger Clark ploughing at Dedham

10 A pair of horses with an old Norfolk 'gallus' plough. The photograph is by Emerson, the nineteenth-century Norfolk master

11 Jennie Caldwell with eight Suffolks 'in hand'

12 Cheryl Clark exercising the Count

13 Cheryl Clark
unclenching a
horse's shoe

14 David Brown at the Royal Show, Shrewsbury, 1884

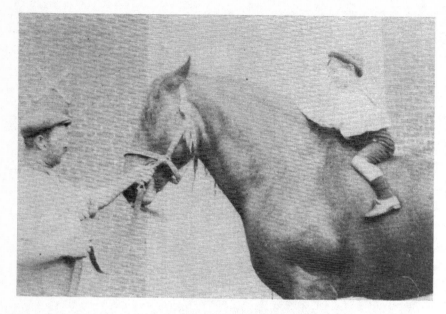

15 Arthur Brown and his father Thomas Brown (born 1885)

16 Horses about to raise a log on the tripod prior to lowering it onto the drug

17 Coal horses 'doubling up'

18 Cart stable at Chilstone Madley, Herefordshire on the farm of Price Addis (churchwarden). On 1 May each year his wagoner cut a young silver birch tree: decked it out with coloured rags, and clamped it to the stable wall. The purpose: to keep witches out of the stable, otherwise the horses would be hag-ridden. Photograph taken by A. E. Bixby, *c.* 1931–2

19 'Professor' Henry Miller

20 Ida Merry (Mrs Sadler) with wounded soldiers during the First World War

21 Sharpening a scythe in a Norfolk harvest field. Another Emerson photograph

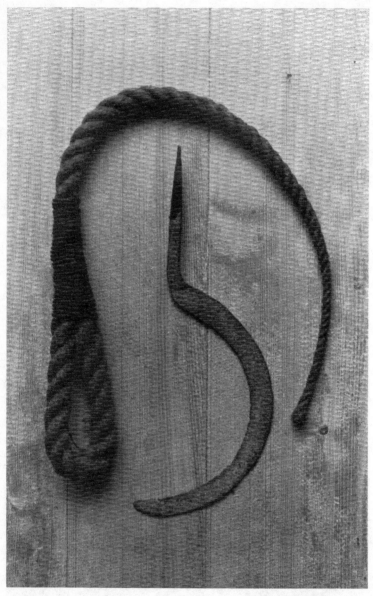

22 A whip-line; and a hook made from a blacksmith's rasp

well. Because when I went down to him and told him I was doing some shoeing—after I'd shod the first one, three weeks after—he said:

"How did you get on?"

"Oh, all right."

"Did your shoes stop on?"

"Of course they stopped on. That's what I put 'em there for!"

'Honestly, I was very pleased. It started when I took the horses to the blacksmith years ago: I used sometimes to take the old shoes off for the smith. I'd got the idea of getting the horse's foot up and working on it. And the smell of the burning shoe on the foot, I think that's marvellous. It's got a lovely smell (my son thinks it's horrible!) The old smith I used to go to kept—swept up the filings from the horse's foot, and he used to give them to his hens. He reckoned they were full of protein and were the best thing in the world to make the hens lay.'

Harry Burroughes then went on to tell me about his farming career and his involvement with horses. His account is given in fairly complete form for the reason that it illustrates a not unusual pattern in farming careers during his generation, and points to the dilemma they were faced with, and the ambivalent attitude to change that bedevilled him and many of his contemporaries. They were compelled by economic forces beyond their control to alter drastically their system of farming, but in doing it they were not entirely at ease in their minds. And in Harry Burroughes we perhaps see this dilemma working itself out in a token return to the old system which he and many of his coevals gave up with such misgivings.

'I'd been farming since 1929. My brother and I took a little farm of forty-five acres in Michaelmas '29. Our first harvest was in 1930 when we sold barley for 11s a comb. When the merchant said it wasn't up to sample he had the generosity to give 11s a comb—which was 5s 6d the hundredweight; no comparison with today's prices, of course. It seems hard to believe anything was such a price. But that's what it was! Wages were 28s a week then (they had been £1 and even lower than that in earlier years). We had one old chap who used to work for us, and his wages were 28s: I suppose the insurance was 1s 6d. Farming was at its lowest then. We hired this little farm for four years, and during those years I said to my brother that if things didn't improve within those four years, I would find something else to do, because there was nothing but starvation. You just couldn't make

51

money anyhow. But going on to about '35 it did improve a bit. They started the subsidy for sugar-beet and that helped quite a lot. We had forty-five acres and we worked, of course, with horses. We had a pair of horses. My brother was horseman and I was cowman, stockman and general labourer and so on. We did most of the work between us.

'Well, then a few years after that we hired some additional land so we were able to buy what was our first tractor. From then on we progressed a bit. We were both single when we took the farm; then my brother got married in 1936 when I hired another little farm. The County Council had bought up a large farm and split this up into small-holdings. We had one of these, and we were still in partnership: we had the two farms within a mile and a half of one another, and we worked the two together. It worked out very well. We used the same capital and the same machines for the two farms. We got a little herd of cows together which was a great help in those days. That was in 1936.

'The war helped the prices quite a bit; but the only hold-back was the introduction of food-rationing. You couldn't keep as much stock as you'd like because you couldn't get the feed for them. We could get the rations for the dairy cows because milk was important; that was essential. But for other things we had to make do. We had a few rations such as sugar-beet pulp, and what you could grow yourself. We had five or six horses then, as well as our first tractor—a Fordson. We used to do our ploughing with that. All the other work—drilling and all that—we did with horses. As time went on we sort of phased out the horses more and more till twenty years ago we didn't have any horses at all.

'It was only in '72 after I retired that I bought one horse, just for old times' sake; and from that I developed. I've now got five, and of course I bought all the old machinery and all the implements and everything to go with them. So, as I've told different people, I'm a little bit unique among collectors because several got machines; some have got horses without the other, but I've got them both, and I can harness the two together and make them work in the old original way. We've got all the harness, the drills, the reapers, horse-hoes, ploughs and an elevator with horse-gear; everything for horse farming: tumbrils, harvest wagon, miller's wagon, road wagon and so on. We've got the old rack-reaper;[1] then the next step, the old sail-reaper which de-

[1] F.A.V., (illustration in first edition).

52

livered the wheat in a sheaf for a man to tie up; and then of course the binder which tied the sheaf itself. From then on they went to the first combine. I used them all except the rack-reaper: I never did use one of those rack-reapers.

'We came to Chediston Grange with no horses at all. I didn't do any farm work there with horses until I bought the ones I have now; and we've done a little with them, just enough to keep them so that they know what work is. But apart from that we don't do any general work with them. But I would think that if I were farming now there would be an advantage in using them, because there are a lot of small jobs a horse could do very economically provided a farmer could find somebody who could use them. Because, as I've told different people, a horse is an individual; it's got life, and therefore you always have to keep your mind on your horse. With a tractor, you can stop a tractor and you can leave it for a week for that matter. It should still be there when you come back. But with a horse—when you're working with a horse you've got to have your mind on your work, never forgetting that you've got a horse at the other end which is liable to do anything. Anything could come and give it a fright, or if it were a restless one it could decide to walk off—all sorts of things. You've almost got to have split attention: some of it on the work and some of it on the horse.

'Besides, a horse is great company. When you are using horses you feel they are part of you: you commit yourself with a horse. He understands what you say and he is definitely company. And it's amazing really how the older horsemen—as I travel about they like to come back and renew their acquaintance with the horse, to just get the handle—the feel of the plough-handle. It brings back something to them and really is to them their life. When I was at Stowmarket Museum, an old chap there said he was eighty-six. He said:

"Do you think I ought to have a go?"

"Well," I said, "I don't know your condition. But just to say you've had a go why not go a few yards up the field?"

'So he went twenty yards holding the handles which he had done in years gone by; and it really made his day to feel that there was still the life he knew, a little of it still surviving. He was delighted.

'I think the young generation would be willing to use horses on the farm. The men about thirty-five, I don't think they are keen about horses: that age that have got established with the new way of farming, they don't seem to be keen. But the younger ones, the teenagers, they seem to be the ones that are most keen. I believe that with this age the mechanical things have become so familiar that it has lost the attraction it once had. There's something always new about the horse, and there's this link between the horse and the man who is working him.

'I believe there's a chance of the horse coming back in some degree. I don't say that it will come back—not to regularly plough in the field, but there's a chance that it might come back around the farm, marginally. Talking to—I was talking to some young farmers when the petrol scare was on. They said:

"Well, of course, you couldn't do it with horses now. You couldn't get through the work."

"Well," I said, "if the oil dried up it won't be a case perhaps of you couldn't do it, you'd have to do it. It would perhaps be going right back not only to ploughing with horses but to ploughing with bullocks. For without the oil what would you do?"

'I sometimes think that it wouldn't be a bad idea if there was some sort of grant just to keep the horse as a stand-by because you never know how the job is going to work out. Apart from the oil, in these days of the terrific price of machinery, the horse is very economical. The cost is very marginal as compared with machinery. How important the horse is *directly* to the land, I don't know. Because in the old days they didn't attach much importance to the horse manure that went back to the land. It was the bullock and the pig manure that were the best. They were corn-fed, you see, heavily fed on corn, and the manure was always that much better. Of course the horse manure helped a bit: it gave some body—humus to the soil, especially if it were stacked up beforehand, so that it heated and rotted down well. Then that would work much better: otherwise that would tend to dry out. That sort of manure is essential to the soil; it must be because it creates new soil; that is the point. Everything can be bought these days from the bag which feeds the soil I suppose and breaks it down artificially; but it isn't putting back anything into the land. Time will tell (time is young yet, I suppose) what it will actually do to the soil. But this type of farming where they grow white straw after white straw—it's not perhaps now but in thirty, forty or fifty years' time when there'll be a possibility that it might break down. They're very concerned during the last few years with this compaction as they call it, especially when you get a wet time. It surely must have an effect on the land. Yet you couldn't think of going back to the old system as things are: the overheads are all against it today. The overheads are so much today that you got to have something that will get over these acres quickly. On a farm of this size—300 acres—where you used to have ten men, today it just wouldn't stand that. It wouldn't stand that expenditure in wages.

'But it would be wise to think ahead. Horses are things that take time to produce. From the time you *sow a mare*, we'll say, it's at least five years before you get a horse that's capable of doing a good day's work. The horse has got to be four years old. You can gentle them at two year old, but you can't do much with them. Then at three year old, they can do some jobs—something like a "threequarter man"— you want at least a four-year-old to do a good full day's work. From four year old to ten year old are the best years of a horse's life. I firmly believe that it would give some little sense of security—not much perhaps—if there were more promotion of the breeding of heavy horses. A cushion of self-sufficient farming, for instance, would be vital in the case of the oil drying up altogether.'

Harry Burroughes mentioned the Museum of East Anglian Life at Stowmarket in Suffolk. Demonstrations of old farm processes with horse traction are held here occasionally, as they are at the corresponding Museum of Norfolk Life at Gressingham. In both counties there are other, private ventures along these lines: in Suffolk at Easton Park where there are farm livestock—notably Suffolk horses and Longhorn cattle—on display against a background of a model dairy and a group of nineteenth-century farm buildings which were the nucleus of the home farm of the Duke of Hamilton. In Norfolk, Richard and Judy Fairbairns, who farm 230 acres of medium sandy loam at Church Farm, Martham, near Great Yarmouth, are incorporating a museum, with demonstrations by craftsmen, into the activities of a conventional arable farm. They started this spring (1977) with regular open days, attracting crowds similar to the other museums of this type. Next year they plan to open all the year round, inviting the public to view the conventional part of the farm as well as those acres they are setting aside for working solely with horses.

This 'horse portion' of between twelve and fifteen acres is devoted to market gardening, and the Fairbairns plan to sell the produce in the shop attached to the museum. They have three working Suffolks, a filly foal, and one of their mares is now in foal. The horses have already been working on the market garden acres (they intend to work this section entirely with the horses) and also on the conventional part of the farm where they plan to use horses for certain definite tasks, mainly transport. They are building up their stock of working horses to this end. They have already proved invaluable in the cultivation of one of their main crops: an amount of potatoes are grown on the farm, and Richard Fairbairns uses irrigation to carry the crop on through the dry periods of the summer and sometimes the spring. This year the horses transported the irrigation pipes on to the seed-bed with little or no damage either to the land or the crop, certainly much less damage than a tractor would have done; and the horses have undoubtedly done the job at a much smaller cost. He has also experimented with feeding the horse-manure back on to the market garden section; and already the soil there is beginning to come up more friable, less brittle and 'lumpy' than on the rest of the farm where artificial manures have been used almost exclusively. He has no problems with cultivation gear and horse vehicles as the museum is well stocked with these; and the horses have already justified themselves during the short time they have been on Church Farm by their usefulness in transporting material on the farm and in collecting the harvested crops—cauliflowers, leeks, carrots and so on—on the market garden section.

During one of my visits I got into conversation with Lew Passant, a craftsman who demonstrated regularly at the farm museum. He is a harness maker, and when I met him he was having a break from working on a horse bridle. In the flow of the talk I asked him why it was there was so little lore connected with the harness-making craft as opposed to, say, smithing. He answered without hesitation:

'It's not difficult to find the reason for that. The job I'm doing now needs all your mind and you can't let a bit of it be concerned with anything else. I couldn't listen to anybody talking to me.'

He then showed me what he meant:

'You see the shape of the awl [lozenge shape in section]. Well, the point has to go into the leather not only dead in line but to make sure that the shape of the holes the awl makes lies regular. You see there [he pointed to some of the stitching on the bridle where it was not quite even]: that's not really a mis-stitch. The point went in on the line, but the awl didn't go into the leather in the right way.

'That there, [he went on pointing to the unevenness] is where my wife asked me if I'd like a cup of tea!'

# 7

## Women and the Heavy Horse

Since the last war it has been noticeable how women have become more involved with horses than even before—horses of all types, and extending right across the scale of uses: racing, jumping, pony riding and trekking, breeding, showing and training, and especially horse-keeping or grooming which was formerly regarded as the preserve of men. It is certain that those women who went onto the land during the last two wars helped to widen the scope that women developed in this field. During my former researches in the late 'Fifties I did not meet one woman who was directly concerned with the heavy horse: during the last two years I have met at least half a dozen women who in varying degrees are concerned with the breeding, tending and, occasionally, the working of the heavy horse.

One of the best-known of the women who are linked with the heavy horse in Britain is Jennie Caldwell who is stud-groom for Charles Saunders of Hoxne, Suffolk. Miss Caldwell is a familiar figure in all the chief agricultural shows, and can be seen driving a team of Suffolks in the rings of at least eleven shows up and down the country each year. She is probably the only woman in Britain who can handle a team of six or eight horses each weighing about a ton and harnessed to a wagon. But she is too modest to claim this as an absolute distinction. She said: 'I don't know of any other woman driving eight-horse teams: I've never seen one. But a lady came up to me once and said she used to drive six in Australia.'

Here is an account given by a knowledgeable bystander after watching Jennie Caldwell harnessing up her team before going into the ring at the Royal Norfolk Show a few years ago:

'I stood there for an hour and a quarter while she harnessed up those eight horses to the wagon. She did it all herself. She may have had a little help to put the collars on, but all the rest she did herself. And when she had got those eight horses harnessed up, she went round slowly and examined everything, but especially the billets [the buckles fixing the reins to the horses' bits]. If there were three holes in the leather of the rein for fastening the billet, the identical one—say, the middle one—had to be used in every case. This is very important, as it means that as soon as the handler touches the reins and the horses get the signal, they all respond together, at the precise fraction of a second; and then they move off together as one horse. They all pull at once.

'While all this checking and re-checking was going on the horses stood as quiet as mice, their heads down as though they were in contemplation. But as soon as she got up into the seat and took up the reins, up went their heads like a well-drilled squad of soldiers. And there they were, all alert and ready for action! Then she spoke to them in a small, quiet voice, and those eight big horses moved off as one. It was pretty to see: no fuss, no hurry, like a mother who was in full control quietly shepherding her bevy of children off to school!'

John Cossey, the blacksmith at Brooke, Norfolk, first drew my attention to the success of women in handling horses. A smith more than anyone can estimate the character of a horse (and his handler!) when they come to the smithy; and John Cossey has found that on the whole young girls are much better with horses than men: 'They are gentler with them, and the horse is much easier for me to handle. Men usually are rougher: the old type used to break a horse's spirit rather than get round it. They get worse results that way. Did you notice last Sunday at the Badminton Horse trials women took the first three places?

'But they sometimes make it difficult for the men. There's a stud of Arabs not far from here, and there's not a man on the place. They are mostly young girls looking after the horses; and I and the vet are the only men who go near there. And we don't get a very good reception. Those horses don't like the smell of men. I've tried everything to make my job easier when I go there—even to sprinkling some of my wife's talcum powder over my clothes. But even that doesn't seem to answer.'

J. S. Rarey, the American horse-breaker who stood out against the brutal treatment that was commonly given to horses in his day, was also in favour of women's method of handling:

'A good education, either upon man, horse or dog, will never be thrown away. The horse, the most beautiful and useful of animals to man, is seldom sufficiently instructed or familiarized, although certainly capable of the greatest attachment to his master when well used, and deserving to be treated more as a friend than a slave. It is a general remark how quiet some high-spirited horses will become when ridden by ladies. The cause of this is that they are more quietly handled, patted and caressed by them, and they soon become sensible of this difference of treatment from the rough, whip-and-spur system generally adopted by men.'[1]

The response that women and young girls get from horses is also in line with what we know of the regard that women were held in as horse handlers and tenders among those peoples who have been historically identified with the horse. Frequently, gypsy women were extremely skilled with horses, and I have recorded one example (p. 74) during my present researches. The Arabs relied on their women to bring up their colts, and the Bedouin entrusted the first three years of his horse's life to the care of his women. In North America the women and children of the Plains Indians are reported to have looked after those young horses that their men would later ride on warlike expeditions. Goddesses, moreover, rather than gods are traditionally the patrons of horses; and it is essential, as Virgil suggests,[2] that in breeding horses it is of first importance to choose a good dam.

But to return to Jennie Caldwell: her active interest in horses began during the last war:

'I started with heavy horses during the early part of the war. I was a bit young for a land-girl—I was seventeen—but I joined with my sisters at Egmere, near Fakenham in Norfolk—with Mr Keith. There were about 1,300 acres on that farm, and we had to work those. Not ploughing them: I ploughed at the next place. But there was harrowing and rolling, horse-hoeing and things like that; and I've been with heavy horses ever since. But I remember even before that, when we used to go to Anglesey for holidays we had to cart water with a horse and cart: we used to love it. After Egmere we went on the land at Hethersett, and then I went down to Devon; used horses down there. Terrible the hills were down there, about 1 in 5 sort of thing. We used to use a turn-over plough—those are the ones that turn over sideways.

---

[1] *The Art of Taming Horses*, p. 104 (see later, p. 67).

[2] *Georgics*, iii, 49–51:

> Seu quis Olympiacae miratus praemia palmae
> pascit equos, seu quis fortis ad aratra iuvencos,
> corpora praecipue matrum legat.

On those steep hills you turn over once, and it would go halfway down the hill. Start again! For corn carting we had a long, two-wheeled cart and we had to cart down a hill about 1 in 7, I think it was.

'I came back to East Anglia just after the war was finished. I came to Mr Saunders. I think I got wrong with the Land Army because I got the job myself and they thought they ought to get it for me. But shortly after that they disbanded the Land Army, and they were quite happy about it. I liked the Land Army: there was plenty of company, of course. But I'm quite happy on my own: I like being on my own. I had two sisters with me at Keith's, and then one of them came with me to Hethersett; then I was on my own after that. Mr Saunders had four horses down here when I first came here because he had some at the top stables when Bob Smith was in charge here. Then he left after about two years. He used to drive a team; and then Mr Saunders said: "Come on. You'd better drive a team!" And that's how I started. Then he had more horses, young ones, and mares breeding, and colts. And one or two he used to break in for other people. He kept one or two of those, especially a big horse called Short. He used to keep heavy horses at the top stable as well as the racers—four of five of them. Then they came down here when Bob left; the harness came down as well.'

The bottom stables to which she refers are a huge, fort-like structure, a central space or yard bounded on four sides by the stable buildings, with two impressive-looking arches given entrance on opposite sides. They are all that appears to be left of the complex of the big house which has given its name to Oakley Park and the stables themselves. The top stables are a less ambitious group of buildings higher up the hill about a quarter of a mile away.

'When I came here I had about thirty horses in my charge. He kept steeple-chasers as well, but I had nothing to do with them. They're too flighty for me. I prefer the heavy horses. I used to get up about 4 a.m. and start feeding. There used to be eleven or twelve horses in boxes (the boxes were up the hill) and we used to feed those right early. Then we'd have breakfast and then feed the ones outside. Then the yearlings used to go out till dinner-time. The geldings used to come in for dinner. Then after dinner we used to train them or put them in the wagon, mess about with them. The others used to come in at night-time. Then we'd start on our way home, about six, or sometimes later. We feed them on chaff, cut-straw, oats, sugar-beet pulp (we had it in nut form and we had to soak those well). But we used to have several colts out on the top meadow there—about eight —there in the park, two- or three-year-olds. It was a seven-day-a-week job. We had to groom only the ones that were working, not the other ones, the outside ones—just the team ones, the ones that had to be showed.

'When I first started we used to show them *in hand*. In hand is when you are leading a horse round the ring on his own. A *turn-out* means a single horse in a tumbril, or a team of two, four, six, or eight horses drawing a wagon. I break them all in myself. I like to be on my own rather than have two or three people around. I bit them up at first, and then put a surcingle[3] on; and then we'll do that for a day or two. Then start driving them about with long reins, and keep doing that for a week or a fortnight. Then put them on the logs [getting the horse to drag a log along the ground]; let them pull back a yard and keep moving round a bit so they can feel the trace, and then take them out again. Then put them on a bit longer the next day. Then the exercise to put them in a cart. I get a longish pole and tie one end of it to the tees on the *sales*[4] and hold the other end and let the horse feel it against his side so that he won't find the shaft of the cart strange when he comes to it. Next I fix up the cart by placing a pole under the shafts. Then I drive the horse back one step and perhaps take him out again; and I take him back a bit further the next day, and the next. Quite often they'll turn round and back in on their own. I keep praising them up! I enjoy working with horses: they enjoy it too, the horses—especially when they get into the ring. Sometimes when they go out on this meadow here they are as lazy as anything; but as soon as they get to the Show they're up on their toes. They're very conscious of being in the ring. We had one horse, Jock: he knew exactly when he got into the ring. He'd go strolling up; but as soon as he got into the ring, away he'd go. As soon as he was out of the ring, he'd go strolling along again. You notice the character in each horse. When we had Jock he was a very good leader but he hated being behind. He always knew which way you went into the ring, where the gate was, and as soon as you got to that gate-way again he would try to get out!

[3] A belt or girdle fastened round the horse.
[4] The metal or wooden attachment on the collar; hames.

'And they know where the grandstand is. (You've got to stop at the grandstand.) We got one now—Emperor: he knows where you have to stop at the grandstand. He'll keep going round and when he gets to the side opposite the grandstand (you have to pull in that way, pull into the grandstand) you have to watch him or he'll quickly come

---

### PRIZE SUFFOLK CART COLT,

*For a limited number of Mares this Season,* 1859,

**At £1. each Mare, and 2s. the Groom,**

# CHAMPION,

WAS BRED BY AND IS THE PROPERTY OF

## Mr. C BARNES, Kettleburgh Hall, Suffolk.

HE is a bright chestnut, rising 3 years old, with short legs, and exceeds 16 hands high, plenty of bone and substance, excellent temper, and a very rare constitution, and must make a first-class horse.

He took the first prize at the Suffolk Agricultural Show, at Bury St. Edmund's last July (the only place he has been shown) and against 13 competitors, including 2 colts which took the first prize at Ipswich and Chelmsford, also the one which a few days afterwards carried off the first prize at the Royal Agricultural Show, at Chester.

Was got by "Boxer," a horse well known for great power and substance, and who left an unusual number of superior colts, he was the property of Mr. T. Crisp, of Butley Abbey, his grandsire was sold by the late Mr. Catlin, to the Duke of Manchester, for £300. and from a favourite chestnut cart mare.

*Will travel during the Season as follows :—*

*Mondays.*—Will leave home at 7 o'clock, through Monewden to the White Hart, Otley, the Crown Inn Clopton, and return home that night through Debach and Charsfield.

*Wednesdays.*—Will leave home at 7 o'clock, through Earl Soham, and be at the Horse-Shoes Inn, Tannington, from 11 to 1 o'clock, and return home that night over Saxtead Green.

*Fridays.*—Will leave home at 7 o'clock, through Framlingham, Cransford, and at the White Horse Inn, Swefling, from 10 to 11, and return home that night through Farnham, Stratford, Marlesford, and Parham.

At home the greater part of *Tuesdays, Thursdays,* and *Saturdays,* and no business on *Sundays.*

Money to be paid the first week in June, to W. Maulden, the Groom, who is accountable.

N.B. Perhaps it will be well to add, that although he has been offered for sale, the owner now pledges himself to refuse any offer until the season is over. (J. LODER, Printer, Woodbridge.

A stallion leader's card, advertising his horse

---

round before he should do. He knows exactly where you have to go. And some will stand in the place opposite the grandstand, and stand well, but if you stop anywhere else they'll get excited, as much as to say: "This is a bad place to stop!" They know the procedure. The first time they've been in the ring even, they seem to know where they should stop!'

Apart from looking after and training the horses, one of the biggest jobs is keeping the harness in good trim:

'It's non-stop during the period of the shows. It really takes two days to clean the harness properly. That's the harness for a team of four horses. The harness we have here is very valuable: it costs—well, thousands of pounds, I should think. We use harness with a leather trace for heavy horses, leather and just a short iron trace at the end. We paint their hooves with neat's-foot oil. The harness keeps all right in the winter-time. You just clean it up at the end of the shows and you keep the fire in throughout the winter. If you don't it gets a little mouldy as it has done this year because of the damp weather. I give it a good clean up before every show and then do it again after each show, and also during the show probably. If you've got the team on the first day of the show, and the pairs on the second day, you have to clean the pairs' harness and the rest of the team, ready for the pairs the next day. And if you have the pairs on the first day you have to clean that ready for the team the next day. We use chromium-covered chains or traces usually, but if we have steel chains, we'd put them in a sack. Then one person holds one end of the sack, another person the other; and we keep swinging the sack backward and forwards until the chains, through rubbing against one another, clean all the links. We are busy non-stop while at the show ground. I used to drive the horses to the show myself. We had two boxes and another lorry to take the wagon at one time. We took six horses—three in each box. If we took four we had a bigger lorry, and you could get the four in there, and the harness and the grub to eat—the tin stuff. And you had the wagon, the hay, corn and granary stuff on the big lorry. As I say, I used to drive the horses: now I drive the wagon lorry not the horses.

'When the show is on a wet day it creates some problems, especially for the Shires. They have to wash them. They were a bit dubious about going out into the ring at the Royal Show one time because it was so wet—mud splashing around. With our horses, the Suffolks, you can let the mud dry and brush it off; but with the Shires they've got to wash them and spend the rest of the day drying them. They wash them and then they dry them with sawdust. But with the Suffolks we dry them with straw, and next day you can brush the mud off. We usually bed the Suffolks down with straw, but the Shires are bedded with wood shavings. The manes and the tails are done differently in the Shires from the Suffolks. In the Suffolks they do all the mane in the pack: in the Shires they just put a little in. And the Shires' tails: they are not allowed to dock them, so they shave the ends of the dock and just do the top bit. It's horrible! We use bass to do the mane: six points. We also use wire—bell-wire—as well as bass to make these points. They have about ten when they are just in hand without the collars on: if they have collars we have about six.

'How are a team of six horses harnessed up to the wagon? Well, the first two horses, the *wheelers*, are harnessed to the pole attached to the wagon; attached to the end of the pole are two whipple-trees, and the *middle* pair have traces from these, as do the *leaders* or leading pair. I remember various incidents in the show ring. I remember Short, for instance, that big horse that was sent to be broken in and we kept him. He was a character. We put him in the lead of a team at Blackpool. Then Ted Williams came out with a horse he'd been jumping—came into the collecting ring; and he gave his horse a good hiding. It upset Short. He never was the same since. He used to hate the band, too. During the band's playing the Musical Ride he was terrible. One time we had him in a single at Cambridge Show. We had no space to let him loose. That was quite near the band, and when the band started up Short started to go up in the air. Well, they had to stop the band in the end. I don't think the conductor *could* stop it (it must be a job once they get going), and it was ages before it stopped. He was marvellous in a turn-out but not so good in hand. He used to go wild behind the others: he always wanted to lead.

'I've learned that if something goes wrong not to panic. I once had six turn round like that [an unrehearsed movement]. I think it was the reins came undone and the two leaders came round here. Once up at Blackpool, too. We had two lovely leaders, but they were a bit nervous, and the ground at Blackpool is between the hangars and there were horse-boxes on one side and something happened on the other side. The near-side horse saw that side and started going that way, and the off-side horse got scared and went back round that way. We turned round, and luckily it was concrete and the wheels skidded round otherwise we would have been tipped over. I think we cracked the pole: otherwise everything was all right.

'I laughed after an experience I had at the Norfolk Show! My sister sent me a little model, a wagon with horses in it. It was on there, on the shelf, but just before we went to the Norfolk Show on this occasion it fell off and got into the biggest muddle on the floor. Well,

65

things went wrong at that Show; and when we got into a right muddle I suddenly thought of the broken model and had to chuckle. But as soon as I got back I put it straight. Superstition!

'You ask me whether I think the heavy horse will come back in any numbers. I don't think so, not to work in any great numbers. One of the difficulties is, if you have working horses, in order to keep them fit you have to work them all the year round. I used to do a little demonstrating, ploughing and so on: I demonstrated at Ipswich a couple of years ago. Well, when I first started to prepare the horses they were weak; and their shoulders were soft; and it took seven or eight days to get them into the kind of fitness that was needed. That is why I think it is no use thinking that they can be used occasionally (on heavy land, for instance): they have to be kept working.'

In June 1977 I met Mrs Lilian Cater whose husband and son figure in later chapters. As the wife of the head horseman on a large estate she became involved with farm horses to such an extent after her marriage that she became almost as expert as her husband in certain branches of horse care. Yet she had no tradition of horse management in her family. Her father was a carpenter and she knew nothing about horses before meeting Walter Cater:

'I often used to go down to the farm to take my husband's food; and one day there was a molecatcher there, and he said to me:

"You could make it a lot easier for your husband, you know."

It happened at that time that Walter had to come back to the stables every four hours—perhaps he'd be working way out in the fields—to feed a young foal whose mother had died. I thought about this, and when my husband came home that night I said to him: "What's this about the foal?" He told me what had happened, and I agreed to look after it. So they brought it up from the farm and put it in a shed at the back of the house; and I fed it with milk and water in a bottle every four hours. Apparently, the vet had said that it had to be fed every four hours right throughout the night.

"But even my babies don't need feeding through the night!"

"But this baby does."

'So it was quite a job. It went on for weeks. At one stage Walter said:

"This foal is constipated."

And the vet advised changing the proportion of the milk to the water. Before, it was one part milk to three of water: now it was to be three

66

of milk to one of water. That was natural: like a baby it wanted thicker food as it grew.

'But I got a shock over that. People can hurt you! When I explained to the farmer that we wanted more milk, he looked at me queerly and he said: "I can't understand that." He thought, I'm sure, I was trying to get some extra milk for ourselves. People can hurt you!

'I brought up a lot of foals for my husband and I helped him with the brood mares. Sometimes a mare had twin foals, and then I'd take one of them. We called these foals by a special name—Moon. There was Half Moon, Full Moon, Crescent Moon and so on. I remember once when a mare wouldn't take her foal. (They sometimes don't: they turn against the foal.) But Walter said: "We'll go and get the sheepdog." And as soon as they brought the dog into that loose box that stirred the mother's instinct: "That's not going to have my baby!" And she took the foal there and then.

'But Walter used to have a terribly hard time when the mares were foaling. There would be seven or eight brood mares at a time. And he'd be setting with them for weeks. He was working a twelve-hour day, 6 a.m. to 6 p.m.—and he'd be up most of the night for weeks, having only cat-naps. I recollect them coming up here for him one night. He was sleeping at home as he didn't expect anything to happen that night. Well, they came up from the farm: they wanted him down there as a mare was going to foal. He was so tired that he could hardly stand up; and I said to them: "Can't you together see to it?" But he went down; and the mare was just lying down comfortably: she was days off foaling!

'We used to go down to the park on Sunday afternoons, taking the children down when they were very young. He'd whistle and all the horses would run over to us; and there we were surrounded by these great horses, and we were holding up the babies to them! It scares me now just to think of it. But they were very gentle. My husband was ploughing once and he told me: "Stand in the furrow." And he set the plough, let go the handles and walked alongside the horses as they ploughed. The horses drew right up to me before they stopped. On another occasion I was sitting on a bank with my feet on the headland, and Walter was coming along with his horses. I drew my feet in naturally to let them pass, but he called out: "No, leave your feet there!" Sure enough, the horses stepped gently over my feet without touching them.

'There was an understanding between my husband and my son, Mervyn, over the horses. He took after Walter: he took to the horses. But my eldest son had no interest in horses. He became a carpenter after being apprenticed to a wheelwright. He took after my side of the family.'

Cheryl Clark, wife of Roger Clark, is a young woman who spends most of her waking hours with horses—heavy horses particularly. Like her husband she is a registered farrier; but in recent years she has rarely had time to help with the actual shoeing of horses since most of her days are filled with her many other activities: leading a Suffolk stallion, breaking in young horses (both light and heavy), preparing heavy horses for showing at the agricultural shows, tending the harness and the other gear and transport that all this involves, using the horses for carting on the farm; and finally, preparing the horses and implements for a weekly display and demonstration of farm work (ploughing, harrowing and so on) at the Dedham heavy horse centre. The name of their establishment near Stoke is Weyland's Farm and it is appropriate that this particular farm with its evocative traditional name should now house two skilled, working farriers.

Mrs Clark told me about her life and her present routine with horses on a recent visit to Weyland's:

'I remember three working geldings on a farm near my home in Stoke when I was about eleven. But I'd always been interested in horses—since I was born, I should think! I used to cry to be taken to the farm (my family, by the way, had no connection with farming, on either side: they were town people). But anything connected with animals interested me, not just horses—animals. I always wanted to be a veterinary surgeon, but it was a long, long process. I had my first pony when I was eight, and I've been with animals ever since. I used to help on the farm with those three heavy horses: clean them down and I'd ride on them. I'd always had a colt to ride and drive, and when I met Roger we started up with heavy horses—Shires to start with. Then we went over to Suffolks. That was—well, we've been married ten—eleven years now.

'We had a couple of Shire mares which we used to breed from, and we gradually got Suffolks, until we had a pair to show; and then a four-horse team, and this year we had a six-horse team. All the heavy horses in this area years ago were Suffolks—no Shires. When we got

68

married we took on horses to break, to earn some money; and we've been breaking horses ever since. Now we've got five geldings and a stallion; and three youngsters coming on; one is three year old so he'll be ready for the team next year. But we are booked up for two years breaking in horses: we can't take on any more. Roger does nearly all the shoeing now and I break most of the hunters in and the cart-horses as well. So once we get going with the breaking in we put them to work and Roger ploughs with them. All the horses we have here now go to work on the farm—straw carting, ploughing (we are getting them ready now to plough down at Mr Leslie Mills's place at Dedham for next Sunday).

'I am involved in everything connected with horses. When we first got married we had only one or two horses to break in; then I used to do the shoeing all day. We used to go out together; and that was our main living. But now we've got so many horses that I only do shoeing when I have to. My main job now is breaking in and looking after the horses. I also travel with our entire horse—Rowhedge Count the Second. Yes, I suppose I'm the only woman travelling a Suffolk stallion. I travel him by myself; I put the horse in the lorry; take all the gear with me; drive him there, to the farm. Then they get the mare out, and we *try* her and we use the horse. Some people are embarrassed when I go, but they're getting used to it now. One chap he said—I got the horse out, and he said:

"You're not going to use him, are you?"

" 'Course I am! There's nobody else, is there?"

'They're not used to a woman doing it, are they? But they're getting used to it now, and they don't worry. The farthest I've been with a horse is King's Lynn. But it's a lot better if they bring the mares to us here. The trouble is you get to these places and there's nowhere to try the mare, and only old iron gates and so on. It's a job. And they'll leave the foals on the meadow with the mares; and the mare won't let the stallion go near her because of the foal. It's a job. It's far better if they can bring them here, because we can shut the foal[5] up and somebody can stay with the foal; then bring the mare out to the *trying bar* we've got out there.'

Trying a mare involves seeing if she is properly in season (or *in song* as some old horsemen say). For this a *trying or teasing bar* is

[5] A mare is more likely to conceive if she is served during the period after she has foaled, usually about nine days.

used. On Weyland's Farm this is a structure of five railway sleepers laid edgeways, one on top of another, and clamped by two massive steel girders at either end, sunk into the ground to form a stout fence or partition about five feet in height. The mare is led to one side of this partition and the stallion is held at the other. He then *teases* the mare by playfully biting her neck or rubbing his head against her.

'If the mare is not right she kicks: she won't take the stallion. So we let the stallion tease the mare over this bar to get her ready. But if you put the foal—if the mare has got a foal with her, she won't let the stallion near her because she's protecting her foal. If you shut the foal up and bring the mare right out of the way she doesn't worry about the foal then. I've had this teasing bar built, and now a stallion can charge up against it and it won't come down. When you take the horse anywhere there's no facilities like this. Years ago, there was always a proper place to try the mares on a farm because the stallion used to walk from one farm to another—regularly. And without a bar like this it's sometimes dangerous for the stallion. These mares will kick if they're not ready; and I've even seen them kick through the teasing bar, smash through it. And when you got a stallion worth anything around a couple of thousand pounds that sort of exercise doesn't pay. He could easily get damaged.

'We start the season in March: then we start covering the mares. If we're lucky we get them in foal first time. But we have to travel round all the mares every three weeks to try them. But if they're not in season you cross your fingers and go in another three weeks. Well, after you've covered them the first time I don't return any more: you can get them tested in 42 days after they've been covered. Then if they're not in foal you start again. I do everything in my power to get them in foal; we've even had them all stitched up (if the air get in, you know, it kills the sperm): we do everything we can, and then we have them tested and we can tell whether they're in foal or whether they're not. There's a lot of work: weeks, weeks of it! To give an example: there was one mare, we got her in foal. We started covering her in March. We got her in foal and then she lost it; *slipped* it. Then she came in season; and we did it all over again: it took us ten weeks to get her in foal. But eventually she had a filly foal, so we were quite pleased. It's very time-consuming work. We charge £50 if they're in foal and £20 if they're not. It probably takes more time and more effort if they're not in foal. This is the trouble. There's no money in it! But there were nine foals born this year, eight of them fillies. So it's worthwhile: it's carrying the breed on. But whatever mare you have, if she's not in foal they always blame the stallion. And it's not the stallion. He has proved himself.

'He has an extra diet during the season. He has corn and boiled food while he's covering mares; and he's kept fit. I lead him out every day, walk him for about three miles to keep him fit. Then he goes up to the meadows, and has about seven feeds a day to keep him fit. The difficulty is I've got to keep him in condition to cover mares and fit to show as well. This is a job especially at the end of the season. He covers six mares a day. But he'll cover a mare then I walk him round this piece of ground out here, and he'll go straight and cover another one. This stallion, Count, got out one day (someone pinched the electric fence during the night), and he went and jumped a five-bar gate and got in with six mares. Luckily they all came to him, all Suffolk mares; and he was covering them one after another; and he got them all in foal. They all came to him. He was having a helluver time.

'The Americans want Count: they'd give anything for him. They want him for over there. There was some talk about having his semen sent over there. They went into it. Freezing it is all right: it's exactly the same as a bull. But it's unfreezing it doesn't work. It *can* work but it's such an expense. You've got to have real experts. The people from Newmarket would have to go with it; and it would be such an expensive process that they've called the whole thing off. It's a pity really: one service from him would cover no end of mares. Besides, we don't want too many Suffolk horses to go to America. We want them here. We could sell no end of geldings here to go to work. You can't get 'em: there are no geldings about; but they're coming on.

'The Count has won a number of prizes again this year: champion at Woodbridge Show, champion at the Norfolk Show, and champion at the Royal. He was supreme champion at the Norfolk, champion of all the Suffolks. We won the big cup at the Royal; we won it last year as well. It goes right back to 1911. (Look at the number of names on it. There's Arthur Pratt, 1911. He was the breeder who gave a prize for the Suffolk horse with the best feet. Charlie, one of our geldings, has won that for the last six years at the Suffolk Show.) The Count travels very well. He's no trouble to get into the horse-box. And at the show I have a *stallion bluff* over his head. I've got one here. It's a

71

kind of bridle, hood, or mask that goes over his head, with two leather guards over his eyes that allow him only to look downwards. If he's got that on he's perfect. If he's not got it on he'll smash the box down! If horses go by and he can see them he'll charge at the door. But with his bluff on he's as good as gold. With that on it's safe to put mares behind him. I take him over to Mr Mills's at Dedham every week, and I always put that on.

'But you've got to be the master with a stallion; and Count is a horse you've certainly got to be the master of—well, any stallion is. But Count really has the best temperament I've known in any stallion. (A stallion I had before had a very bad temper: he was all right with me, but if a stranger went in to him, he'd have him!) But Count, even children—as long as I'm with him—can go in that box with him. There're not many stallions you can do that with even with the best temperament in the world. Stallions are tricky things: they're like a bull, you can't take your eyes off them. But Count is a lad! He's a horse with high courage. He really enjoys parading in the ring. He shows off. He'll slouch up to the parade ground; and I'll think: "We're not going to do anything with this horse today. He won't win!" But once he gets into the ring, up goes his head. He knows. He really enjoys parading in the ring. He knows he's the champion: when the people clap he knows it. He pulls me about like a bit of paper. I've got to hold him: as long as he knows I've got him he's all right. He's quite good really, but he weighs a ton. Stallions are funny things anyway. A stallion will kill a gelding. If he got out and got in with those geldings he'd kill 'em; he'd really fight. I did have two stallions at one time: Rupert, who is now in our team, and Count. I couldn't have Rupert cut because he was a *rig*[6]; so we had to leave him until he was four. Of course, at four he was feeling his feet a bit. And they got out one day, and the two of them got together. If we hadn't have been there there would have been a real fight. You see, according to Rupert these were his premises: according to Count they were his. So each of them was trespassing—like in the wilds. There's only one stallion, the leader of the pack. When they fight they bite one another behind the knees, so they have to go down. Then they get the master of him. They'll get hold of the crest and keep him down and kick him.'

The philosophy behind the Clarks' enterprise at Weyland's Farm is that the heavy horse has a bright future, not simply as nostalgic spec-

* A horse with an undescended testicle.

tacle for week-end crowds who want to see something living and colourful but as potential source of power, making a contribution to the nation's economy. Its future, as Roger Clark says, is with those owners who put the horse to work that is economically productive in one form or other. Cheryl Clark said:

'The heavy horse is coming back; there's no doubt about that. I think the Suffolk will go ahead now and increase in numbers; and once all this young stock that's now two and three year old—when they get to four year old and go to work, then people will go ahead. There're a lot coming on but they're not the right age yet. Classes have started to teach people how to use heavy horses, so there shouldn't be any difficulty in getting people to work them. And there's still horsemen about, and great interest in the heavy horse. This has been shown over at Dedham: about 2,000 people come every Sunday: none of them horse people. In the shows you've only got to rattle a chain and they just come about you like flies from nowhere: you can't move for people. Just rattle a chain and put the harness on a horse. And people want to see the horse being worked. They don't want to see it being led around: it's being worked that they want to see the horse, doing things that they used to do years ago.

'There's nothing nicer than having a horse to work with: I'd never have a tractor. We've got a horse—Becton: you can put him in a cart and he's like a tractor. You can come in and have your dinner and he's still there when you come out. Becton is an exception, though: you can cart muck with him and he'll almost do it himself. But if horses are worked every day—it's use that makes them quiet. It's the same with colt breaking: once you start you've got to do it every day, and twice a day. If you miss him for two days you have to go back to the beginning. There are no short cuts to colt breaking. It's hard work; and every horse is different. We break in between fifteen and twenty horses a year; and no horse is like another one. There'll always be some difference. It's a challenge each time; and it means hours of patience.'

One of the first objects I saw when I visited Weyland's Farm gave prospective corroboration to what I later saw and heard. It was a life-size straw guy with obscenely wide and bandy legs, leaning bibulously against the wall of one of the stables. Mrs Clark explained that it was a figure she had made herself—a kind of wildly dumb jockey —to break in a young hunter. The horse had been sent to her because he would allow no one to stay on his back. But Cheryl Clark had

ridden him to hounds that morning. She was able to do this only because the bibulous and bandy-legged guy was the horse's first and innocuous rider at Weyland's: after he had become acquainted with the
guy over a period, only then was the horse ready to take a real, live
rider on his back. This is an example of the Clarks' sound dictum for
careful preparation *before* putting a horse to real work or action:
*Make a horse ridable and drivable before he is ridden or driven.*

To return to an earlier theme: that in primitive tribes or communities, or communities living close to the earth, women were deeply involved with horses and expert in their use. Here is an example, from
the oral tradition in Suffolk, of the skill of a gypsy woman with horses.
Mervyn Cater (see Chapters 10 and 11), the son of Walter Cater, a
farm horseman, recalls his father's account of a gypsy woman who
had a local reputation for her horse-skills. It illustrates particularly
the undoubted empathy some women possess in their handling of
horses.

'There was an old gypsy woman called Mrs Silver, and she always
told the age of a horse from its behind! Always used to, never its
teeth. Father said she was more accurate than those horsemen who
looked at the horses' teeth. She often bought horses and ponies from
him; and of course he knew exactly when these were born. He said she
was very accurate with the age she put on them, a lot more accurate
than the men who gave the year of birth: this old girl would give the
month of birth—she was that accurate.

'I remember him telling us one night that she used to come to a
public house in the village: they used to buy and sell ponies at this
particular pub; and this is something he'd seen her do several times.
My mother also mentioned her several times. She was the same lady
that my mother and father moved near to when they went out Hoxne
way (he was horseman out there for a time). She was very clever, and
the gypsies lived at Denham at that time. Now one of their boys was
taken ill and he'd got to be in Norwich hospital as fast as possible.
And she rung—or one of her boys rung some gypsies that were relations. They were on Mousehold Heath; and within a few hours one of
them had come down with a trap and a mare. This mare had had a
foal a very short time before; and when they turned her round she
went back to this old Heath flat out all the way. There's a lot of
psychology there, isn't there? She knew which horse to pick: she told
them which horse to send with this light trap. They had to force the

mare to come away from the foal; but once they laid that boy in the back, left the doctor's care here, the shortest period of time possible was between the doctor's care here and Norwich Hospital. She was running back to her foal, and she was flat out all the way to Norwich. Luckily, my father said, the gypsy knew too much about a horse to let him kill her. The mare could easily have killed herself going back if she was allowed to. And the gypsy said afterwards he had to hold her back all the way to Norwich. I remember my father saying that this gypsy woman knew more about horses than most of the horsemen in this area.'

# 8

## Timber Hauling with Horses

It has been suggested that one of the jobs a horse can still do efficiently is the extraction of felled timber from a woodland. There is a
long tradition of this craft in most areas of Britain, but I have found
in the memories of the older generations in East Anglia, that as well
as a straight description of the actual techniques, there was a fair
amount of migrant labour involved in the practice of felling timber
and hauling it with horses either to various saw-mills or to the nearest
railway station. Two Suffolk farm workers I met had worked about a
half-century ago with men and horses that had come down—one from
Scotland, another from Yorkshire—on timber-felling contracts.

William Bailey was born in 1891 at Orford (Suffolk) where his father
was a policeman, but he spent most of his life at Hoxne near the
Suffolk-Norfolk border. After serving as a shepherd's page, and later
as a butcher's boy, in 1915 he joined the Royal Welch Fusiliers, and
spent most of the war on the Western Front:

'I came home from the Army after finishing up in Egypt, and I had
three weeks' leave, then I started going on this timber job: they were
here at Hoxne carting the trees. They had eight horses, and there were
six men. This man, James Wardley, who came from Scotland, owned
the horses and he wanted an extra man: he wanted me to go with him
to Ixworth (Suffolk) for two months' carting trees from there to Thur-
ston station. Then we came back to Hoxne to cart trees out of Hoxne
(Slade's Wood and the Farm Wood). We carted to Diss or Eye stations.
All these trees went to Mr Langley's of Worsborough Dale, Yorkshire,
to his saw-mills. James Wardley carted for Langley of Worsborough
Dale: he used all crossbred horses. Then we went off to a place
near Brandon and carted to Mildenhall station for six weeks. From
there we moved to Thetford Chase, and the horses were always fed at
Thetford Chase Tavern, and we laid up just up the road. And we carted
all the large trees to Thetford Chase station which is done away with
now. We carted these large fir trees in there, and these went to Lang-

76

ley's of Worsborough Dale—a mining area close to Barnsley, four or five miles from Barnsley and eight from Sheffield.'

It is clear that the Yorkshire firm was taking timber of two different kinds from Suffolk and from two different areas of the county. Timber like oak, elm, beech, ash came from the central strip of the county, from the area called by the eighteenth-century writer John Kirby the *Woodlands*: here the heavy clays—often boulder clays—are natural tree-growing soil; and the oaks from here were in great demand in the seventeenth and eighteenth centuries for building ships for the navy. Brandon and Thetford are in the part of Suffolk which Kirby designated as the *Field*: on the whole this was much poorer soil; and although parts of it gave good corn in Kirby's time it was chiefly used for sheep-walks. In modern times it has been planted with conifers which were largely used for pit props until steel became the commonest support for underground roofs.

For hauling the timber the main equipment the teams used was: a *drug*.[1] 'The Drug is composed of two axletrees and two pair of wheels

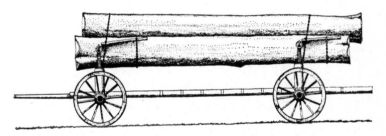

A loaded timber-drug

—the hinder pair movable nearer to, or more distant from, the fore pair on a pole.' A *jim* (in Norfolk *jill*, and the drug is called a *jack*) is made up of an axle and a pole for moving timber *under* it. The timber is laid on *top* of a drug; *skids*, stout ash poles were set against the drug to form a ramp up which the timber was dragged by horses pulling from the opposite side of the drug. The *tripod* was used as an alternative method of loading the timber on to the drug; various pulleys, or snatch- and sheaf-blocks were also used in the woods along

[1] *Suffolk Words and Phrases* (1823), Edward Moor. Reprint, David and Charles, 1970.

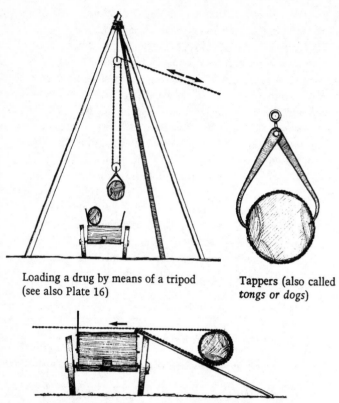

Loading a drug by means of a tripod
(see also Plate 16)

Tappers (also called
*tongs or dogs*)

Loading with *skids* (stout ash poles)

with differing lengths of rope. William Bailey describes the process of
loading with a tripod:

'But in the woods, instead of us rolling the trees on to the top of
the drug (some call 'em *timber-trucks*) we used what is called a tripod
(Plate 16). We used to lift up all our logs with this. We had a three-
sheaf block at the top and a double-sheaf block at the bottom, and a
pair of *tappers*,[2] knocked into the side of the log. Then we had one
horse or two horses or more, if it was a big timber, to bear on this
line that was attached to the log, to pull it up and then drop it on
to the drug. After they'd hauled it to the top of the tripod the horses
would hold the log there while the drug was moved under the tripod;
and then the horses would back slowly, easing the log into position

[2] Also called *tongs*.

78

on the drug, helped by a man who stood against the drug. The size of
the drug was adjustable according to the length of the timber. A drug
has four wheels, and you could lengthen them out to any length you
wanted by moving the wheels along the pole. In some of these timber-
drugs they got holes in the pole so that they could move the end
wheels up, and a bolt goes through the holes to fix the pair of wheels
in position. A timber-jim has only got two wheels. You take a jim into
the woods if it's bad to get the timber; and you just hang the tree up
underneath it (see below), just so that you keep its nose off the ground

*Transporting a log by means of a timber-jim*

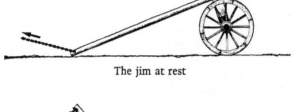

The jim at rest

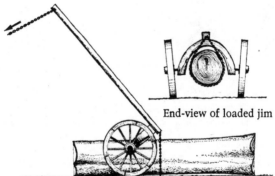

End-view of loaded jim

The jim with beam, up-ended and chained to log, ready
for horses to pull down

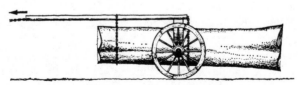

The jim loaded near balance; rear slightly heavier

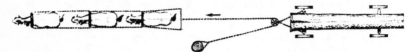

Dragging a heavy log out of the woods using a snatch-block and the 'double-purchase' method

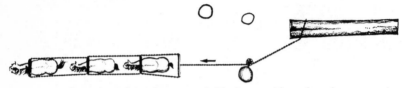

Dragging a log using a snatch-block to avoid an obstacle

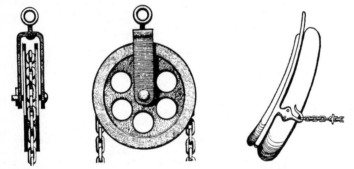

(*left*) A snatch-block
(*right*) Wooden sales or steel hames, attached to horse-collar; short steel chain (called *tees*) which is fixed to the horse-traces by a cross-piece

so that the horses can pull the timber to where you want it. We didn't often use a jim. We'd put a lot of horses on to the logs and drag 'em out of the woods and save a lot of work—drag 'em like what they call *over the collar*. We used to take the full eight horses.

'We had a special tackle—snatch-blocks—for this. We had a 100-yard rope, and if the horses couldn't pull a log "over the collar", we used to fasten this 100-yard rope to a tree, and put a snatch-block on with a chain on the tree—put a snatch-block on there, and then hang all the horses at length and pull the log up to the end of the 100-yard rope. This gave double-purchase. But we only did this in the worst places.'

Timber hauling must have been a traditional occupation in Hoxne,

William Bailey's home; for Major Edward Moor, writing in the early 1800s, culled the following epitaph from Hoxne churchyard: [3]

> In memory of William Catling who departed this Life August 16, 1802, aged 20 years:
>> I was on my journey returning home,
>> And little thought what was to be my doom,
>> So as the rolling *Jim* did me control
>> The Lord above have mercy on my soul.
>> Short was my stay, the longer is my rest,
>> God took me hence because he thought it best—
>> Therefore, dear friends, lament for me no more.
>> I am not lost but gone awhile before.

'There were usually three men and eight horses on a job. We stayed in lodgings. The farm worker's wage at this time [*c.* 1919] was about £2 a week; then it dropped shortly afterwards. I got £4 a week when I started at Ixworth, and after we got so we had to pay a little more for lodgings, we were getting £4 10s. The head man got £5. Of course, we had to pay for our lodgings out of that.

'We started work at 7 a.m. and finished at 5 p.m., sometimes later depending on the distance we had to go from the wood to the station or saw-mills. We fed our horses on hay, crushed oats, bean meal and a little chaff—straw chaff, a little wheat-chaff (whatever you could get), and a little bran. They took nose-bags for midday; and at night, oats and bean meal and a fair amount of chaff before racking them up for the night. We did our own doctoring. We used to pay great attention to cuts and bruises, sore shoulders—rub grease in them, vaseline. If you didn't do this you would get had up by the police. Our youngest horse was about seven, the oldest about fourteen.

'When we were carting on the road, we had three horses: one in the shafts and two in the traces. We used to go in for three loads a day—two threes [logs] and a two. We went up to Doncaster once, and owing to the bad weather we didn't cart the logs to the station but straight to Langley's saw-mills, carted them there every day, three loads a day. We had four miles to go to the woods (we used all that wood up what was there), four miles back and four miles from Barnsley to Worsborough Dale. So we had a good day's work because the horses go slow, especially when they are loaded, and when we came out

[3] *Suffolk Words and Phrases*, p. 185.

of the wood we had to come up to Barnsley. There was a long hill there, went up like Hoxne Church Hill. So the horses couldn't pull the loads up there, so we had to help one another up. Put all the horses on one load; and these horses what we took out of the shafts had what they called belly-belts on them. We'd got some spare traces and we put these shaft horses on them. Then we left one drug-load at the top of the hill; and then took the shaft horses down with the others and put them back into the load at the bottom. All the horses would then pull up the second load.'

William Bailey's account of 'doubling up' on a steep hill calls to mind the once common practice among coal-merchants of sending out their carts in pairs, so that if they came to a steep hill they could dispense with the help of an extra trace-horse. In metropolitan areas, special trace-horses were often stationed at the foot of a steep gradient, with a man in charge: for a fee he would help any loaded vehicle up the hill. Here is a vignette of the practice by Sanders Watney: [4]

'I well remember these "trace" horses being used to help single heavy drays up the hills from both Knightsbridge and Grosvenor Place. . . . I remember a magnificent and well-turned-out Suffolk Punch standing in readiness near St George's Hospital. It wore a white quarter-sheet inscribed "Our Dumb Friends' League"—the horse being the property of this Society. Apart from the useful work it did, it must have been a magnificent advertisement for the Society.'

William Bailey:

'We used to load 'em up so they'd take a "level load"—on the level, about a ton and a half for each horse. Eight horses were needed to pull the load up, sometimes six, sometimes five; it all depended on the weight of the tree. We had many little incidents while carting timber. Once the drug sunk into some soft ground, and we had to cut the shaft horse's harness to release him.' [To the horse collar were fitted the wooden *sales* or steel *hames*, to which the *tees* or short chains, that fitted to hooks on the shafts, were attached. The sales or hames were fitted to the collar by leather thongs at the top (the *top latch*) and at the bottom (the *throat-latch*). These thongs could be quickly cut with a knife and the horse released if they 'got into a muddle'.]

'Then we went from Barsley and came to Beverley, and carted a lot of timber there. We used to take the timber into Hull—eight miles

[4] *Country Life* (letter), 24 February 1977, p. 449.

from Beverley—and it made it a very long day; took it to Lambert's and Goddard's saw-mills in Hull. They used the wood for buildings and furniture: elm, ash, beech, oak: we never carted any poplar there. A lot of woods were cut down during the First World War, and the woods weren't left very big. Where I finished up with them that was Hornsby, the other side of Beverley, close to the sea. They still wanted me to go with them, but I say I wanted to be home here. I got a job at Mr Edward Saunders's at Chickering Hall; then I helped my father (he had retired to a public house here) when he was busy. Charlie Saunders's father, I worked for him for four years and then the poor old chap died; then for Charlie—the man you are talking about—for about twenty year, off and on.'

Another farm horseman who has had extensive experience of timber felling and hauling is Arthur Brown (born 1913) of Belstead, near Ipswich. Like most farm horsemen he comes of a long line of men who worked with horses. His grandfather David Brown was horseman for Manfred Biddell at the time Herman Biddell was compiling *Volume One*[5] of the Suffolk Horse Stud Book (Plate 14). Arthur Brown's father, Thomas Brown (Plate 15), was stud groom at Wherstead Hall, Suffolk, and he himself was brought up early to the craft of horseman. One of his early memories is of coming back from Colchester Market with his father and the stallion he was travelling. They were living at Thorpe le Soken in Essex at the time:

'My father, prior to travelling the horse he was in charge of, took it to Colchester Market to show it to the farmers who wanted the service of him. I went with him; and on coming back the train stopped at Weeley station where we were to get off. My father went to the office to see about it. But the train set off, leaving me with the stallion from Weeley to Thorpe. They telephoned to say what had happened, and my father walked along the railway line to join us. As I was only ten years of age I was a bit young to be alone with a stallion.' Another incident he recalled from his 'prentice days concerns Ipswich: 'It was one Friday afternoon, and I went from Bourne Hall to Cobbold's brewery after wet [malt] grains. On the way I met a man coming along with an elephant. He had walked from Harwich and was going to Christchurch Park where there was to be a circus on the following day. It was a strange feeling for the horse and me to meet this

[5] In 1880; p. 14; 1884 David Brown was at Luck's Farm, Playford.

elephant, for as that passed us there was no noise at all only puffs
of wind from his feet.'

Arthur Brown spent his working life at Wherstead Hall, near Ipswich,
and he was awarded a long service Premium at the Royal Show in
1972, and another at the Suffolk Show last year when he completed
forty-nine years at one farm:

'I started at Bourne Hall at the age of fourteen: 10s a week, a 50-
hour week; finish midday on Saturday. My father was head horseman,
and the second horseman got laid up so I was asked to go and help
my father mornings to bait. I used to get up at 5 a.m.; stop there till
6, helping him to bait; 3d overtime extra for the 5 to 6 clock; for
six mornings a week (3d for each morning; 1s 6d extra for the week).
When they reckoned my time for the week-end, I used to do one hour
Saturday afternoon, two hours Sunday morning, an hour Sunday afternoons: 3d an hour that was. I was with horses as long as there were
horses on the estate; but I did more or less everything on the farm,
looking after pigs, hedge laying, ditching. But you asked me about
timber-felling and so on: well, I'll tell you.

'I was along with the Head Forester for several years. We used to
go into the woods, cut down the trees and take them to the saw-bench
and saw them—whatever we want: gate-posts, or fencing-posts, or
different other items. And after we'd done that we'd erect whatever it
was. We used seven-pound axes at first to fell the trees; then a mechanical saw. And the old sawpit was replaced by the saw-bench. We
used our horses for pulling out the timber from the woodland, but
later the tractor.

'That photograph of the horses at length on the tripod (Plate 16):
they were Yorkshire horses, came down from Yorkshire—to the Wherstead Estate in 1928. That was for Squire Dashwood then; went all
over the estate after trees with these horses. If there was an awkward
tree beside the road they had five or six horses at length; tell them to
hold while they were felling it so that it wouldn't fall back onto the
road: they used to pull it down with them. And when they wanted to
load up with the drug, they used to drag the timber to the tripod.
They'd put the horses on the pulley and pull on it up; hold it in the
air at the top of the tripod. Then the other horses brought the drug
right under the tripod. And they'd tell the horses that were at length
to go back slowly, and it would drop right on to the drug. These horses
were trained to it. They were mostly Shires. They'd also come after

some chestnut poles out of the woods at the top of the hill; and they brought them down and laid them on the edge of the River Orwell. And there used to be a barge come from Maldon, named *The Twilight*; and they loaded these chestnut poles up on this barge and they'd take them to Maldon for May and Butcher. They used the poles for chestnut fences; split 'em down and wire 'em. They are the people for fences. The timber-contracting firm was called Green, from Yorkshire. They brought the horses down. They lasted very well; treat the horses well and they last. That's just on fifty year ago.

'The timber-jim had just two wheels. You lay the tree out on the ground first; put the jim over the top of it with the pole up in the air. You bring a chain down from the pole; and the horses will bring that pole down to the tree, and they'd fit the chain round the tree and hold it on the balance.

'As you know, a timber-drug has four wheels; and the beam is made with holes, and you can adjust the length of the beam to the tree you are going to carry. If you got long trees, like light trees—little oaks or long firs—you had it at full length. But if you got some oaks —big oaks and short—you hauled the wheels up along the beam or pole and then you'd peg it. The spare part of the pole would then stick out at the back.

'When we had the horses I used to sit up with my father when a mare was due to foal. The mares couldn't do much work on the land for ten days before they foaled, so it was my job to exercise them, take them for exercise. And after they foaled I used to look after them, clean them out and see if they were all right. Then after so long, when the sun was shining brightly, we'd work them for about one or two hours. Yes, I saw the milt when a mare foaled, but not always. Father used to keep it, and he scented it with something. There were one or two mares when they had the first foal, they didn't take to it very well. So very often we had to put the foal in the corner of the loose box, with a gate; let it out when it had the milk and then put it back again.

'Yes, I think that horses could do a very good bit of work on the land still: I do. Well, you see, horses haven't quite as big a foot as a tractor! Not so much weight on the land. They would leave it nicely.'

Horses are still used in small numbers by the Forestry Commission in Scotland, Wales and the north of England where the ground is less suitable for tractor work. They are also used on private woodlands. As for the future of the horse in forestry work, there appears to be no danger that his work will cease altogether. On the contrary, if we can judge from American experience the horse in this kind of work will have something of a revival. In the USA logging with horses is not un-common,[6] either using a sled with steel runners or rubber tyres, or just by looping a rope or a chain around the timber and attaching it to a whipple-tree for the horse to drag out. One advantage of using a horse, according to the Americans, is that he will do less damage to the woodland than a tractor will: the horse is less likely to harm the young, self-set saplings which promote the natural re-generation of the plantation. Another big advantage is that a horse can work in con-ditions such as thick mud or snow that would defeat a tractor. Two American operators in a woodland stressed an advantage that is not obvious, and at first sight might appear trivial, but undoubtedly it could be a considerable boon to workers employed in an echoing forest: 'The woods are quiet and there is plenty of time to talk while the team rests.' That is, there is no machine to set a relentless, ineluctable pace.

Statistics in Britain[7] show that the horse in forestry suffered a sharp decline during the same period as the farm horse but at a slightly slower pace; and its replacement, moreover, was not as complete. In 1960 horses were the most important means of extraction of timber from woodlands, and were responsible for 53 per cent of the total volume handled. By 1969 this had declined to 14 per cent for the Com-mission and 12 per cent for private estates. The compilers of the Fores-try Commission *Census* (p. 4) wrote: 'Though reduced, the volume handled is still appreciable (particularly in contractors' and mer-chants' working) in East Scotland, the Border and Wales. Displace-ment of horses has been most rapid in mountain country, where double-drum winches have taken over. How long horses can continue on the more "tractorable" areas will probably depend less on econ-omics than on difficulties of finding men to work them.'

This census was published before the sudden, drastic rise in the price of fuel oil; and although the Commission have no plans for pre-venting the decline in the use of the horse in forestry, it must remain in doubt whether economics will eventually induce them to change their policy.

[6] See *The Draft Horse Journal*, Waverley, Iowa, Winter 1976, pp. 35–7; and Spring 1977, p. 5.
[7] *Census of Harvesting Equipment and Methods*, 1969, by A. A. Rowan and T. R. Sawyer, The Forestry Commission, 1971, pp. 4, 21–2, 48–9.

# 9

# The Future of the Heavy Horse

It will be seen from the preceding chapters that the revival of breeding and active interest in the heavy horse has taken two forms. The first and by far the greater category is the keeping and breeding of horses for what can be loosely classified as *hobby* purposes: that is solely for exhibiting at shows and public occasions, for their keeping as adjuncts to rural or 'living' museums, for the adorning of stately homes and as an animated and added attraction to the general public who on the whole appear to have taken even more in recent years to the heavy horse than to the show jumper or the riding pony. The other category is the very small minority of farmers who are actually working the horse on their land; the few commercial firms that are using the heavy horse on the streets; and the breeders who supply users with their stock or give the service of their stallions, and also raise horses for export to the USA, Canada, Argentina, Pakistan and other countries.

We should, however, resist the temptation to label the one form as socially and economically useful and the other less so. In any case, the two categories cannot be entirely separated for the reason that those few farmers who are cultivating their land with horses are drawn almost inevitably into 'show business': they find the hire of their horses by film and television companies a useful and acceptable supplement to their income. But above all, both categories should be looked at against the background of British farming in the next half-century. It will then be appreciated that the present use of the heavy horse is secondary to its continued existence as a pool of potentially valuable stock that could be put to direct economic use on the land, if this is needed—as some believe it will be—at a time in the future.

The prospect of the world supply of fossil-fuels drying up within the next couple of generations if consumption goes on at the present rate—or even, if not failing completely, increasing in cost to a level where their use will become limited and economically inefficient for some purposes—has provoked many agronomists to anticipate a crisis. They talk of a *post-surplus society* and forecast a *post-industrial agriculture*. This view has been put forward in convincing form by Dr Stuart Hill, a Canadian scientist[1] who also says that it is not only the shortage of fuel oil that is the cause of unease among informed observers. They are equally concerned with what they claim is the wrong direction that modern farming has taken. It evolved in a period of over-confidence when phrases like 'the conquest of Nature' were loud in the air; and, following the tempo of the last war, when there developed a narrow concern for production at all costs, for quantity rather than quality, ultimately giving agriculture a self-destructive bias whose effects are becoming increasingly apparent. In addition to its dangerous reliance on the continuance of a usable oil supply or on the discovery of a practical substitute for oil, modern farming has two great defects: 'It is no longer directed at trying to create human health. It is directed towards productivity and profit which compromise the objective of nutritional quality and health; [and secondly] it is damaging the environment.'[2] To say that this is inevitable under the present system and that the farmer could not otherwise survive, is not to invalidate this bald statement but merely to underline the deficiencies of the present economic and political context of agriculture. This is the farmer's dilemma: to stay in business, that is to produce sufficient *quantity*, he has to use up expendable resources: the land itself, the fuel oil he uses to cultivate it, and also the inorganic fertilizers and pesticides whose manufacture largely depends on oil.

The inevitable limitation in the future use of artificial fertilizers (either through increased costs or actual shortage) will be no bad thing because these, it is claimed, contribute to the second great defect of conventional farming, the damage to the environment. Nature, far from being tamed, has already shown unmistakable signs of restiveness. Within the last few years she has presented a clutch of invoices in the shape of decreasing yields, the cost of damage to the soil structure, and the side-effects of indiscriminately used chemicals. As time goes on, with the present direction unchanged, it is not inconceivable that she will present the full bill.

[1] *Conditions for a Permanent Agriculture*, The Soil Association, Vol. 3, 2 June 1977.
[2] *ibid.*, p. 1.

Considerations similar to the above have caused Sir Emrys Jones, Principal of the Royal Agricultural College, Cirencester to say:

'The time has come for young men in farming to rethink agricultural systems evolved over the last thirty years. . . . Students now being trained will have to realize that they could be farming without fuel-oil by their fiftieth birthdays. They will also be without inorganic fertilizers, and most of the insecticides and pesticides we now take for granted, unless the scientists come to the rescue. If I were a young man I would certainly not bank on them coming up with the answer. I would accept that I would be in a very different ball-game in thirty years' time.'[3]

A micro-biologist, Bernard Dixon,[4] has given damning evidence against two of the accepted practices of conventional farming:

'Suffice it here to say that the folly of neglecting the natural, microbial activities of the soil is nowhere more apparent than in our crude misuse of fertilizers in recent years. To the blinkered chemist, replenishing the earth with large doses of chemical fertilizers can more than replace the natural contribution of the soil microbes. To the agricultural engineer, intent on boosting productivity, the use of heavy machinery makes technocratic sense. In practice, the combination of both techniques has conspired to damage soil structure almost irreversibly in many parts of the world. Just as important as the chemical composting of the soil is its physical organization and its flourishing organic life. Humus, a rich mixture of plant and animal remains being slowly degraded by microbial action, is crucially important. This soft, brown, spongy material is vital to the structure of the soil, making it friable. It holds water like a sponge and also acts as a reserve store for slowly released food for both plants and microbes. If this dynamic zone, or that round the plant roots, is destroyed and if the soil becomes compacted by heavy machinery, then however rich it may seem when assessed by chemical analysis, the soil will become barren. In December 1974, research was reported showing that a delicate microbial balance exists in the soil, in which anaerobic bacteria producing ethylene gas play a crucial role. If disturbed, soil structure and nitrogen availability are impaired, and root disease increased.'

Another big defect of conventional farming here in Britain has not been mentioned. This is closely linked with its comparatively recent

[3] *The Soil Association*, Vol. 3, 2, June 1977.
[4] *Invisible Allies*, Temple Smith, London, 1976, p. 45.

industrialization. Farming was the last sector of our economy to be transformed by the Industrial Revolution; and in one important respect it has emphasized the tendency of all industries under our present system to move towards fewer and larger units. The mechanization of farming and the consequent engrossment of small farms has caused a drastic revolution in the techniques of farming and also in a social upheaval in the countryside. How drastic I was reminded when on a visit to China a year ago (1976). We were taken around some of the countryside within thirty or forty miles of Peking. There we saw people working in the fields and walking or cycling along the roads after work, chatting to one another with animation. I got the impression that here was a countryside that was being lived in. It is true that there had been some mechanization; but we also saw men following teams of bullocks and occasionally a mixed team of a horse (or mule) and a bullock. The countryside was alive, and I couldn't help thinking of some of the remoter parts of East Anglia where one can travel for long distances and meet no one who is not in a motor-vehicle. In parts of this region I have called at a farm house and found no one at home and no one visible in the surrounding fields: similarly in the villages, I have seen no one in the street to ask for a particular direction and it seems that in two houses out of three no one is at home to answer a caller. Consequently one has the depressing feeling that the countryside has been completely dehumanized. For the great part of the day, at least, huge tracts of it have the appearance of being a social wilderness.

With this picture in mind I visited with my daughter a Chinese commune not a great distance from Peking. This was the People's Commune of Nan Yen, embracing a population of 41,000. After we had been introduced to the leader of the commune and two or three officials, the leader explained the composition and aims of the commune, through an interpreter. He then invited questions and one of the questions we asked was this: if they mechanized agriculture—as they intended to do, at least to some degree—how would they escape some of the negative effects we had experienced in the West: a displacement of the working people of the countryside, massive drift to the towns and all the ill-effects that arose from an unbalanced concentration of people in large conurbations? He replied that mechanization as long as it was controlled would cause few problems. Displaced workers would have no need to go to the towns for work or to the cities. For the commune was not solely a farming unit: there were small industries within the commune's area and under its jurisdiction, and they would be able to absorb displaced labour. (We visited one of these later: they were making hand-tools and parts of machines that were being assembled elsewhere.) The commune was also responsible for stock-raising, fishing and forestry enterprises and was therefore diversified enough to escape depopulation arising from changes in the method of production. This appears to be an excellent solution for the Chinese who are profiting from the painful experiences of the industrially advanced countries. But how unrelated it is to our present difficulties in Britain with the revolutionary change of direction such a solution would entail! And the realization of our powerlessness to apply an effective remedy is deepened when we recall that the social evils following the engrossment of small farms have been emphasized for us in an historical object lesson that could well have been heeded. I refer to the land crisis in Italy caused by the growth of the Roman State and the scale of her foreign conquests. Numbers of war captives were brought back to the mother country and became slaves on the land; and gradually the employment of slaves displaced the small peasants whose holdings were taken over to form large, commercial enterprises—big estates called *latifundia*. The country dwellers flocked to the towns—notably to the City itself, Rome—eventually contributing to the instability of the later Roman Empire. A perceptive Roman summed up the process in a well-known aphorism: *Latifundia Italiam perdidere*—The big estates put paid to Italy. The new slave population was the instrument of change at that time: the machine has been the slave *par excellence* in ours. It has given efficient labour but we still have to add up the social cost of it; and in so far as the machine tends to direct the speed and the course of its own development it has ceased to be a slave and shows signs of becoming our master. This, however, is to put the blame where it cannot fairly be apportioned: it is not the machine that is at fault but its indiscriminate use regardless of the social effects. The difference is one of degree—the difference between mechanization and hyper-mechanization where over-use of the machine causes more problems than it can solve. Barbara Ward in a study of this problem[5] poses a question: Is mechanization worth the social cost if a corporation invests, say, $10,000 in a plastic sandals factory, thus providing jobs for forty operatives, yet at the same time

[5] *The Home of Man*, Penguin Books, 1976, p. 56.

puts 5,000 traditional [African] shoemakers and their suppliers on the scrap heap?

It is to be hoped that the return of the horse to farming, even in small numbers, will help at least to define the nature of the crisis if not to solve it. In talking to men and women concerned with the heavy horse, I found that the young people among them are reacting strongly against the over-mechanized state of industry and the increasing abstract and faceless quality of life in present-day society. They believe that life itself has become spiritless as though the iron of the machine has entered its soul: they sense that the direction of conventional farming is leading to an inescapable dead end. Their reason also tells them that there is no place for them to make a full career on the land since entry to farming is closed or at least bleak unless a man possesses a massive amount of capital. The enthusiasm of these young people for the horse and their readiness to become involved in promoting his return to farming is a true expression of their dissatisfaction with conventional farming and the kind of life it implies.

But the older generation among heavy horse owners and breeders are on the whole very sceptical: they cannot see the return of the horse in any numbers, even though there may be a place for him on many farms and for many jobs on the road, always provided that there is someone to look after him at week-ends. Indeed, their caution appears on the surface to be justified because the new interest in the heavy horse can be put down, at least in part, to the diffuse, generalized interest in the immediate past that has given rise to a host of activities and organizations, from the collecting of old engines, old motor cars and farm tools to the digging out of multi-shaped and multi-coloured bottles from the middens of half a century ago.

Yet it could equally well be argued that all this looking back is an instinctive reaction arising out of a feeling that in trying to make a complete break with much of the past—as we appear to have been doing in the last couple of generations—we have thrown out the seed-corn with the chaff and the cavings.[6] The heavy horse has become a symbol of this reaction, apart from the likelihood of its becoming of great use in an energy crisis. This partial return of the horse, moreover, is not confined to Britain. There is a great interest in the heavy horse both in the USA and in Canada. A recent report from the United

[6] An East Anglian dialect word: the refuse from threshing corn—unripened ears, etc., usually fed to fowls.

States[7] claims that 'draft horses are ploughing their way back into the agricultural scene'. The energy crisis, high fuel costs and a growing interest in organic farming have combined to send farmers back to 'the original form of horse power'. 'In 1968 the 14 registered breeds numbered 139,000. They reached 212,000 by 1975. Among the heavy breeds, particularly, there has been a tremendous increase in registration: not only are there more horses but the quality of the stock has been increased enormously.' We have already mentioned one aspect of the revival of the 'hayburner', as they call the heavy horse in the States: this is the intense interest in the Amish[8] of Ohio and Pennsylvania. These descendants from a sixteenth-century Swiss Protestant sect have always used horses on their farms; and for that reason their equipment and their ancillary craftsmen have been kept in top working form, and are now being eagerly sought after by the farmers who are bringing horses back on to their land.

[7] *The Christian Science Monitor*, 31 August 1977.
[8] *The Draft Horse Journal*, Winter 1976, pp. 4–7. See also *The Fields of Peace*, M. Brand and G. Tice, Doubleday and Co., New York, 1970.

# Part Two

---

## MAGIC

# 10

# Walter Cater

*Magic* here stands for all that traditional horse-lore—empirical as well as irrational—that I had tried to collect twenty years ago. At that time I thought I had got the body of it. I was mistaken; and it was a meeting with Mervyn Cater of the village of Redgrave on the Suffolk-Norfolk border in April 1976 that persuaded me to make a reappraisal. For some time before this I had the feeling that a great deal of the tradition bound up with the pre-tractor-farming, and the life that went with it, was still fleshed in the people of the countryside and that important sectors of it were probably unrecorded. As it turned out, I discovered that in spite of the passing of a full generation the tradition was still vigorous, although attenuated. It was, moreover, still of absorbing interest not only for the fresh discoveries that were possible but for its further confirmation of the authenticity and the historical worth of material I had already gathered in different areas of East Anglia during the preceding generation.

But when I was first recommended to visit Mervyn Cater, who was born in 1936, I was doubtful that he would have much that was fresh to tell me about the old horse regime on the farms. The idea was fixed in my head that I had done my stint on this and had already recorded the rich lore at the best possible time—when the horse was finally displaced, almost entirely, by the tractor; and when the horsemen (many of them in the full vigour of their manhood) were themselves free and ready to spend long hours talking with me about the old system that was just going under. At that period I had spoken with and had been instructed by dozens of old farmers and farm workers who had been born in the last half of the nineteenth century. Surely I had already got the essentials. And what had a youngish man to add to the lore that men of his father's and even his grandfather's time had already told me?

Yet as I listened to Mervyn Cater unfolding his experiences with horses and horse farming, reaching back to his early infancy, I realized how ill founded was the preconceived idea I had held about the stamina of a tradition that is founded in the basic historical work of the countryside, the farming of the land. The words of Dr Iorwerth Peate, formerly Curator of the Welsh Folk Museum at St Fagans, came back to me with an invigorating force: 'It is never too late to collect the authentic tradition.' That Mervyn Cater had this tradition was apparent during the first few minutes of my meeting with him. Like all the men I had previously come to recognize as its fruitful carriers, he came from a long line of Suffolk farm horsemen who had purposely trained at least one of their sons to carry on their craft. Mervyn's father, Walter Cater (1904–73) was an outstanding horseman who had only one or two counterparts in the farming district: he was one of a very tight phalanx of the elite who had the 'real know' about horses and who cherished the tradition in its richest form. Walter Cater had spent forty-seven years on the same farm, and he and one or two other men (one of them a smith) were recognized as the king horsemen of the district. Although I had never met Walter Cater I had a good picture of him from his son who very closely duplicated his father in appearance. He is about five feet ten inches in height, powerfully built and weighing about fifteen and a half stones.

'He was heavily built, and I'm glad to say us boys have taken after him. But he was very very powerful. His forearms were about half an inch further round than mine. When I was—I remember when I was twenty-one, I'd just got married, he came to the door of our cottage, and he stood with his arm just round the door; and my wife said: "Look at your Dad's arms! They're further round than yours!" And I said: "I don't think they are." And he heard us and he said: "Give me a tape measure." He was half an inch bigger round the forearm than I was. He was a very powerful man.'

The son's schooling in horsemanship began at a very early age; but here in this chapter I have concentrated chiefly on that part of his testimony that relates to the secret, 'underground' methods used by the rare, inner-ring horsemen: the drawing oils, the jading substances and the supposedly magical means of horse-control that I have discussed in previous books.[1] I do this because I believe them to be from the deepest level of a tradition that has rarely been recorded with anything like a full understanding of what is implied in the practices, or of their real provenance. They are of great significance because they

[1] *H.I.F., P.U.P., D.T.W.H.S.*

demonstrate how such practices can be concealed as craft secrets for centuries; and this being so, it follows that they are of value in illuminating documented accounts of magic, 'witchcraft' (*deception* in plainer terms) of much earlier historical periods. More about this in a later chapter. Here now is a transcript of my first meeting with Mervyn Cater:

'I was three when I started going down to see [his horses]: my mother took me there and set me on a horse's back, and I started from there riding between the saddle and the *sales*[2] [the hames] on the collar. I held on to the sales. The horse was Pansy and I grew up with her. My mother and father both said that the minute they set me on her back, her back never swayed any more. She walked very carefully because she knew I was there. That mare Pansy was there all my working life with the horses. She was my mother's favourite mare: she was the big one. She had several foals—well, one every four years. It wasn't necessary for her to have a foal every year because they had so many horses. Normally there were fifteen in the stable and nine colts in the meadow, so they'd always got a pretty big stock. I remember my father got seven and sixpence for every foal born alive, on to his money which was then thirty-seven and sixpence (when I can first remember) to keep the lot of us. He used to take myself or my older brother down in the middle of the night to sit on the corn bin, holding the lantern while the mare was foaling. We were sound asleep at three o'clock in the morning while he was foaling. He always was there when the foal was born. He very rarely left the horse, and he'd spend a fortnight often, sleeping down there, because he'd got so many foals coming on at the same time.

'From the time I was three it was just about a permanent thing: I lived with the horses and with him. And if I did miss a day, if I was ill—he was a very patient man—he used to come to my bedroom and tell me just how he'd been doing: what they were doing and which horses they had. I knew all the horses by name, and I knew exactly —one horse, for example, was awkward. He had a horse called Smart: she was an old devil. The awkwardest man on the place had her (that was Mr X: he lives in the village here now), and he was very awkward, and the horse was just as awkward. The two went together. My father

[2] The attachments on the collar to which the traces are fixed. In this district *sales* is the name given to the wooden attachments, *hames* to the metal ones.

used to say he always had that horse purely for that reason: two awkward ones together.

'As I said, the idea was to teach me to control the power of the horse by my hand and voice. You very rarely heard my father speak to a horse because he spoke so quietly. But if he did shout, they really jumped. I was frightened of him when he raised his voice. And one of the things I remember very well: I had a horse—Brandy her name was. That was a small horse, about fourteen hands, no more: I had to run to keep up with that. I was about eight or nine. I was hoeing between rows of strawberries. She was a little thing. She'd lost one lung— well, she was born like that; her tongue was hanging out of her mouth most of the time. Well, that one played up all day. That wouldn't turn round at the ends; that did everything wrong. And my father was about two fields away, and he must have seen her playing me up. He came over about half past two, and he said:

"Take her back to the stable, and I'll have a talk with her."
And I went with him, and he locked the stable door and I stood outside, and he was in there about twenty minutes. I could just hear him talking all the time, but I couldn't say what he said; I couldn't hear a word but I could hear him talking in the distance.'

The son tried to see through a small hole in the stable door but could make nothing out of what he saw: 'There was a piece of board nailed just above the hole where the latch was—a piece of board on a nail that swung down over the hole. And I got my eye as close to the crack of that to try and see what was going on, but I couldn't see anything or smell anything. Because I'd heard the men say there was a strong smell of brimstone, but I never smelled anything.

'But when he came out that horse was quivering all over, frightened to death. "You'll have to stand and talk to her for a moment," he said.

"Whatever have you done to her?"

"Only had a talk to her. She'll be all right now."

'I stroked her neck and I took a piece of sack and wiped all the sweat off her as I was taught to do. I took the harness off. (I remember I had to lead her up against the feed-trough because I couldn't reach her otherwise. I had to drag the harness into the feed-trough.) I wiped her down, put it back on and took her back to the field. And she never put a foot wrong! If I spoke to her she jumped; and she was all right for the rest of the day.

100

'I said to the second horseman: "Father had her and talked to her this afternoon. She was suthen scared when he was done. What did he do to her?"

'He said: "I don't know, boy. Anyway," he say', "it ain't for you." He meant I wasn't supposed to know. I had a feeling that the second horseman knew more than he'd tell. But one of the men said:

"Did you smell anything strange?"

I said: "No, only the horse's sweat."

"You didn't smell anything like brimstone?"

"No."

"Well, I did when he had a talk with my old gel!"

'Another asked: "Did you see flames?"

'Mr Bedwell, the owner, always said he would talk them to death once he took them into that stable. He said that is what it was—continuous talk that nearly drove the horse mad. But I don't know what it was. The men always said that if they had a horse playing up, they used to go to the head of it—I've seen men go to the head of the horse—and say: "I'll have Walter to have a long talk with you if you aren't some careful!"'

The pattern described here—the horse and the man locked together in the stable—has been related to me many times and has also been described in the literature of horse control. The low, mumbling talk that was heard came to characterize the operator as a *Whisperer*: the technique attributed to Sullivan, the Irish horse Whisperer is similar to the above. It is certain, however, that the operator did something else as well as talk. For talking, or whispering, was one of the 'covers' or distractions that misled bystanders while the real 'control' trick was being exercised. An example is later given by Mervyn Cater when on another occasion his father explained to him what he actually did to obtain what to the onlookers seemed an almost magical effect. But he himself was involved on one occasion when his father carried out what people at the time—including, it appears, the farmer—believed was some kind of magic:

'My father had to leave the horses because he had a thrombosis in his leg. He was in bed, and the second horseman was left to take his job of head horseman. But the second horseman had just taken a job elsewhere. In fact, it was a place just outside Newmarket. I remember my father saying at the time; this horseman was a huge man and my father said he was going to the wrong place—Newmarket, because he weighed about sixteen stone. Woodrow his name was. He left, and the next to him was this chap who had been in the 1914–18 War with the cavalry, and he was vicious with horses. He'd never stop for a rest at either end of the bout. He worked 'em from morning till night: no stops, no rests. That went on for about a week; and the doctor came and told my father he wouldn't be back to work within a month. So the next night father said:

"It's getting time those horses had a rest. If I know that chap, he's working 'em into the ground!"

'So he sat in bed and told me to get a hand-cup[3] and some soot from the chimney-sweeping during the winter, and some of the stuff you put on cricket bats—linseed oil! a glass of linseed oil. And I took them to him, and he said, "Now send Kenny up." (That was my older brother.) And Kenny came up, and he got so many things towards this mixture. That was all mixed up in the hand-cup while he was sitting up in bed. And my mother was ordered to get the other two things. None of us knew the complete recipe. And he told my mother to dilute it with clear water and to mix it up in a pail. And the two boys —the two older boys, myself and Ken—were to take it down to the meadow—well, to the park gates where the horses were and paint the two posts. And the horses never came off the meadow for five days! The men kept saying, "That's Walter!" They knew it was Walter, my father, and kept saying that was Walter that was holding them horses on the meadow. In the end Bedwell's pick-up shooting-brake pulled up outside our cottage; and he come up to Dad's bedroom, and he threatened to sack him unless the horses were at work the next day. Of course, we were in a tied cottage!

'So that night it was the washing-up water that we took and tipped over the two gate-posts; and the next morning the horses came through. That was the only time that I can ever say I saw what could in any way be considered black magic; and to someone who didn't know what had really happened that must have seemed a bit strange. But that was purely smell. I knew it was playing on the horses' sense of smell. None of us knew what the others got towards the mixture. Most of it came from the corner cupboard. My father had a black corner cupboard out in the shed with all the things that he would normally need. It was never locked—mainly I suppose because no one ever bothered to go to it. We were never told. Father was never the

[3] or Jet: a galvanized iron bowl with a short handle, like a large ladle.

strict one in the house. Mother was, and she was always there. To be honest, my mother knew a lot more about horses than any of the men on the farm. I don't think there's any doubt about that.

'Dad used to get the stuff he used from different places. He used to hate this biking around on a Saturday during the winter when there was not much else to do—to the chemist's. He'd hate it, because Mother used to say: "Your poor old father has been biking to Attleborough because he didn't want to go to the chemist's in Diss." He'd been there once and would only allow himself one visit to any chemist. He got his ingredients from all the way round as far as Attleborough and Walpole. I've known him to bike to—what is that station? Halesworth, that's it! About twenty-five miles away. I don't know where he got them, or what they were. But I knew he got nicotine because it was in a little tiny tin in his weskit pocket. He showed it to us and he said to me: "Don't any of you touch my weskit!" '

Many instances of the above type of trick of stopping or jading a horse so that no amount of force or persuasion would induce him to move forward have been given in the books already cited. To the uninitiated the men involved were considered as witches, dealing in black magic. But the principle behind all of these incidents was the playing on the horse's hypersensitive smelling power; the substance used was so obnoxious to the horse that he remained immobile. One of the simplest methods of stopping a horse entering a field or a stable was to rub the post or the lintel down with a dead mole. A horse could also be prevented from approaching his manger, in spite of his hunger, by rubbing the edge of the manger down with the skin of a dead mole. Many horsemen who did not know or would not stoop to use this trick maliciously, knew exactly what to do if the trick was played on them. As one of them told me: 'I knew how to get a stopped horse out, even if I wasn't interested in stopping one myself. The thing to do was to wash down the doorpost, or if that didn't serve, to wash the horses' harness, because they sometimes put the stuff on that.'

The drawing oils which attracted a horse through their pleasant odour were also used frequently. But in recent years the true drawing oils—many of which were imported from the East—have been impossible to get through the usual channels as they are no longer in the shops. Substitutes have been sold in their stead, but these have usually no effect at all on horses. This was the experience of a blacksmith friend, Hector Moore, who had about 400 light horses on his books, and could not afford the risk of being pulled about the trav'us⁴ by an unruly colt. He tried to renew the particular oil he had used for years but was given a substitute by a chemist who assured him that it was the genuine oil. If he had used paraffin it would have been just as effective. I therefore contacted a very old farm horseman, Albert Love, who had a small bottle of the oil left from his working days. He agreed to let Hector Moore have the oil as he had no further use for it. From the very first time the smith tried it he had no misgivings about its value. He had an appointment to shoe a horse at 11 a.m. on this day. The horse was being brought some distance in a horse-box. It did not arrive at the smithy until 12.30. The owner apologized, saying that they could not get the horse into the box; and now that they had arrived she thought it better not to get him out as they would have the same difficulty in getting him back in. The smith said that as the horse was there he had better shoe him; and he would probably be able to help in getting him back into the box. He shod the horse without any difficulty, and handed him over to the owner who proceeded to lead the horse out of the trav'us. As soon as the horse got outside and saw the tail-board of the box down ready to receive him, he bolted across the road and tried to get through the adjoining hedge. The smith said: "Leave him to me!" and after going inside to get his jacket, he asked the owner and the bystanders to hide themselves out of the way. He then took hold of the horse's headstall and led him quietly up the ramp into the box. One of the bystanders was rash enough to ask the smith: "What did you use?" The answer was short and sharp: "Cat's piddle and pepper!"

It was the stopping of a horse that caused the most comment and speculation, however, at the time when there was little except horse-drawn traffic on the roads. Here is an example from the beginning of this century when a Suffolk horseman went to work on a Yorkshire farm. James Knights (born in 1880) had served his apprenticeship on a farm in Debach, Suffolk:

'But I had some funny horses about there in Yorkshire. We used to keep sixteen or eighteen pair in a stable. I'd been there about five or six year and the boss said I'd got to take some corn to the station. He was a chapel man; and when I took the first load (the pubs

---

⁴ The annexe to the actual forge where the shoes were made. The horse usually stood and was shod in the trav'us (trave house).

were open all day at that time o' day) I called at a pub to have a pint. Well, he happened to come by in his trap; and he said to me, he say:

"I won't have my horses standing outside public houses," he said; "I don't drink beer and I don't see why you should."

"Well," I said, "if you don't like to see your horses stand outside public houses, you want to take 'em home. I'm not ready for a quarter of an hour: I got my beer here to drink."

'He say: "That's what I will do: I'll take 'em home."

'So when he got into the wagon and got hold of the reins to go, the horses kept backing and stamping; and at the finish he got 'em turned round, so instead of going home they were going back to the station again. So I stood in the passage looking out of the pub door: "Take 'em home," I say.

"But they won't go home!"

"They will when I'm ready. I learned my horses to stop where I am."

'The old man he couldn't make it out. He jumped off the wagon and was going to lead 'em, and they wouldn't go. When he got hold of the first horse to lead it and call it along, it went up on end and was going to hit the old man on top o' the skull.

"Well," I say, "best leave them alone. You can't get 'em home, and they'll be here all night."

'So a little later I said: "I'm now going. I'm ready!" So I got on the seat and got hold of the tapes, and I said, "Come on, old boy!" and away they went as right as rain.'

Although the old horseman would not admit when questioned that he had used a jading substance, this is a classical example of its use, and similar incidents occurred many times outside public houses in Suffolk.

The stopping of a group of horses in a most spectacular manner is one of the highlights of Mervyn Cater's memories of his early days working with his father:

'But I saw what I can only consider to be an example of black magic; so did my father, and he said afterwards he never knew for the life of him how it was done. There was an old chap from Thelnetham, a village near here: he'd got the worst bloomin' horse you ever seen in your life—a bone sticking out everywhere. He was a tall, thin old man, and he wore a hard hat which was superior in itself at that time; and he would dress very much as an old gentleman. He was just a horse-dealer: only he had this top hat. Of course, the men— every time he went past—took the mickey out of him. He went past every Friday to Diss. And I suppose on this occasion he'd just had enough. I know there were six pairs of horses standing there along the headlands, having their *nineses* as we call it in Suffolk (*dockey* they call it in Norfolk), having their bait.[5] I was there: it must have been during the Christmas holidays, the end of the Christmas period. They were all ploughing, and I was with my father. I must have been nine or ten: I was old enough definitely to remember everything that happened. I know that he reined his pony (well, I don't know whether it was a pony or a horse: it was a cross between a donkey and a mule! Well, I'd never seen anything like it, a frightful looking thing). He pulled it up and he said:

"Well, together, you've had your little laugh. Now I'm going to have mine. You won't do another stroke until I come this way again."

'And he just touched the reins on that horse and trotted off to Diss.

'They finished their breakfast, and just kept laughing and making a joke of what he said. They walked to their horses and not one of them could move them. And my father went off home and got out that book [his 'horseman's note book']: he left his horses and got out that book. But he couldn't find anything there to help at all. He took dirty water and poured it underneath the horses and did everything he knew. But he couldn't move 'em. At half past eleven the boss had seen these horses standing there, and he come up. And Father told him in front of me what had happened, and he said: "Well, there's nothing we can do!"

'And they stood there till a quarter past four that night. And the old man came back from Diss; and Bedwell the boss was there—not too happy. And the old man explained quite honestly that he'd had enough of his men making a fool of him every time he went past. And he said: "You can goo now!" And they just came on and turned their horses and off they went. And the old man never got off the trap!

---

[5] The mid-morning snack in the field. It is also the usual word in the stable: *to bait the horses*, or *to give the horses their bait*. Icelandic, *beita* = food; *beit* = pasture.

My father said the old man "had been to the river".[6] That was the only thing.'

I have recorded a similar incident that happened not far away from Redgrave,[7] and it seems to me that there is no need to postulate anything 'magical' to explain it. The old horse-dealer had evidently used one of the jading substances or liquids, probably an immensely powerful one unknown to the others; and he had chosen his occasion very carefully. Undoubtedly, he must have been galled many times before by the scorn of the men, but he had evidently waited until conditions were right before attempting to get his revenge. The main condition was that the wind should be in the right direction: without their knowing he could then easily drop his jading substance after he stopped to harangue his tormentors. Just as easily he could pour out the neutralizing or cleansing agent at the same spot before he stopped on his return, removing the obnoxious odour and releasing the horses.

Mervyn Cater, like his father, believed, however, that there was something in this incident more than the usual method of stopping or jading a horse. He could not understand it:

'The old man must have "been to the river"; that was the only thing. Normally, even at that time if there was a horse that wanted moving [after some trickster had jaded him in the pub yard], and we often had it because we lived beside the Redgrave Half Moon, a real horseman's pub! and we often had it. Ponies wouldn't go home at dinner-time after being left outside on a Sunday. Well, they would come to next door, which was of course our house, knowing my father was a horseman, and ask for a bowl of dirty water. Even then I knew as a boy if you throw a bowl of dirty water underneath the horse's feet or in a ring around it and killed the smell that was there (that was purely smell, that's all it was) the horse would move. But when they drew that ring round it [with a substance the horse didn't like] you couldn't shift it. Even I knew that! But this incident with the old horse-dealer was something beyond my father; and his family had been horsemen for generations. But he had never gone in

---

[6] Through the toad's bone ritual. This involved the bones of a dismembered toad (sometimes a frog was used), and casting them into a gently flowing stream at midnight. One of the bones so thrown floated upstream against the current. This bone was believed to give its possessor 'magic' control over horses. *D.T.W.H.S.*, pp. 29–33.

[7] *ibid.*

for this black magic as such a thing: he never messed about with the toad's bone.'

But my experience over many years of trying to find the pattern of these so-called magical practices convinces me that there was in fact nothing *magic* about it at all. The old horse-dealer had used a similar principle but he was more knowledgeable, perhaps had a more powerful jading substance or liquid than was generally known. Therefore, when Walter Cater was non-plussed by a man who evidently knew more than he did, it is likely that his phrase, 'he's been down to the river' was more of a face-saver than a true indication of what enabled the old man to trick them.

In June of this year [1977], a year almost exactly after Mervyn Cater had told me the above story, I called on him at his home. He had recently had an accident at work: a piece of steel had fallen on his foot and he was partially immobilized. We discussed the incident of the old horse-dealer again, and he eventually volunteered to show me the exact place where the plough-teams had been stopped. The field they were ploughing is called Pye's Hole and is approximately fifteen acres in extent and adjoining the road that runs due east from Redgrave to Diss. Mervyn Cater told me that the only changes in the scene since the incident occurred thirty years before were that the big pit situated on the other side of the road (it had probably given its name to the field) had been filled in, and the high hedge that had screened it had been cut down. He showed me where the six plough-teams had stood: all in a line parallel and close to the road itself.

Seeing the exact location appeared to me to make the explanation, that the old man's main concern was to ensure the wind was in the right direction before attempting his trick, was the only correct one. The time was early January, and the wind therefore was likely to be in the east, blowing against him as he went on his way to market. He confronted the men, told them he'd had enough, and what he was going to do. But they had laughed at him and had dismissed him out of hand as soon as he started his horse up again. He had then continued a short distance on the road to Diss right into the wind before placing the jading substance on the side of the road. Immediately, the obnoxious smell would have been carried towards the horses. The fact that the road was screened by a high hedge enclosing the field opposite to where the horses were standing would have helped to channel the wind towards them. Then later in the afternoon when he returned and considered that the men had been given their lesson, the old man could easily have placed the neutralizer over the jading substance, dropped it from his trap, before the men waiting in the field had noticed his approach.

Mervyn Cater and I both agreed that anything *magic* had to be ruled out, and it was only some such explanation as this that would give any sort of clue to what had actually happened.

Yet I must confess myself completely puzzled by another incident that Mervyn Cater relates about his father. He infers that it is not in the same class as the incident just described, and that it was simply a trick that Walter Cater knew how to pull off in order to confound the people who saw it, and to impress on them his power as a 'master horseman'. I had first heard of this trick in the Battisford-Barking area of Suffolk. It was described to me by an old farmer, Charles Bugg. He did not claim to have the inner-ring horse knowledge himself: he merely described the performance to me as something inexplicable he had once seen. It was this: a horseman stuck an ordinary four-tine fork into a muck-hill or manure-heap. He hitched the traces on the horse to the fork handle and gave the horse the command to pull. The horse appeared to exert all his strength, and he could hear the harness and the traces creaking: the fork, however, remained upright where it was. Mervyn Cater saw his father perform this trick on more than one occasion. I asked him to describe it:

'Well, he simply hung his horse on, as a rule the first time by the traces; hooked the traces onto the handle; and the horse laid out trying to pull the fork over. Nothing happened: it was simple as that! And then the other men tried if they could pull the fork over. Yes, I've seen the men walk up onto the hill; thought there was something attached to the fork through the muck-hill; and pulled the fork out and examined it themselves and put it back again. And then they horses could pull it over! But he [his father] had to pick the fork up and walk up on the muck-hill and put it—always in a different place. He never simply touched that fork: he actually walked across the muck-hill and put it in a different place. But whether it was—I don't know; it's impossible to know what happened. To me it was something I was just proud to know that my father could do. But the other men went to hang their horses on, and as I said you could hear the chains [traces] creaking under the weight: they were pulling all right but they couldn't shift it.

109

'There was always that particular weather when it was done, *sny*[8] weather, usually frosty, snow, often snow. I've seen him do it about five times, and there was often snow on the ground so that anything put on the ground would have been visible, unless it was put on the night before they went in. In which case they didn't have a guarantee that they were going to feel in the mind [to do the trick], because they would all have to agree that they were going to try something like that. My father always agreed, because he always said he didn't like the horses standing too long without putting them into harness, especially in the winter-time. He thought they should come out to work every day, even if it was only light work. And I took note: I don't think for one moment that was the reason he did it so often. I think he was like everyone else: he liked to show his skills as much as anyone else. And especially, I think, at that time if he'd got a few new chaps on the farm since the last year or two: that was a good way of showing his dominance. And from then on their respect would be gained. I always had the feeling, even as a child, to watch the faces of the new men (the older men took it for granted). But the new men—some of them had seen it done before on other farms—but some of them were a bit frightened. They thought: he's a lunatic or a witch or something ridiculous. But I'm sure this was the reason it was done as much as anything. That's my own personal opinion. You got the few fresh men on the farm then: there were often thirty-five men on the farm with cowmen and everybody; and he'd have a big audience, sometimes even the boss. He would walk out, and I have known him to bring his friends locally; and give them a 'come-down'; and maybe there'd be something else by the time they got there. But I'm sure that was to prove to the new men that "I'm the boss, and I know my job!" And no one ever questioned him.

'This was done for the men's benefit especially in really *sny* weather when there was very little to do. And sometimes they used to set in what they called *The Smokey*.[9] That was an old shed where the boss smoked his hams. They all set in there round that scrubby fireplace. They had to set there all day: they'd got to be on the premises to get

[8] 'Probably a derivative pronunciation from earlier forms of *snowy*', Dr John Widdowson, Department of English, University of Sheffield.

[9] The sixteenth-century writer on East Anglian farming—Thomas Tusser —called this small building where meat was smoke-cured *The Smokey House*.

their money. And the boss would sometimes—because he was a reasonable boss—come out and either tell 'em to go home, or they would come to an agreement who would take the cowmen's place for half a day to give them a break. It was the time of the year when my father did the *tricks* (I don't know what you'd call them) which us boys used to go down there to see.

'I've no theory myself as to how it was done but as I said I've never seen it done when there wasn't a frost. There was always a frost and snow—that kind of weather. I've never seen it done in the summer or the spring. It was always that period in the winter when horsemen and the men could all be in the same point at the same time, and when the horses were free. And it seems to me that there was that one thing all over the country: you would never get the horsemen plus horses, free, plus every man in the farm in one spot at the same time, with time on their hands, unless the weather was bad—frost and snow. (They couldn't plough, for no one would plough snow in. This was one of the things you learnt when you were four: no one ever ploughed snow in.)[10] This is the only connection I've ever been able to see: it always had to be the same weather. Somehow or other the frost had got some connection with this in some way; but how, I just don't know!'

This purposeful exhibition of his skills—almost a staged exhibition —by one of the horsemen, usually the head, must not have been uncommon in this area of Suffolk, but this is the only occasion I have come across it. As suggested by the son, the father's purpose was to establish his authority as head horseman. He elaborated on this in another context when there was a kind of trial of strength in the barn —again probably when the pace of work was slow.

'My mother used to go on to my father about lifting weights that were too heavy for him. Because he was a very strong man. He used to lay flat on his face on the barn floor in winter-time—again just to show how good he was—and they used to lay a twenty-one-stone comb of beans across his neck, and he could get up. He'd put his hands underneath him and do a press-up: his own weight plus the twenty-one stone of beans and get onto his knees and get up with

[10] Not an invariable rule. I saw a man ploughing in the snow (January 1977) at Trowse, Norwich. And an old horseman from the Saints, south of Bungay, once told me that he had a good crop of oats from land that had been ploughed in the snow. But in both instances the land was fairly light.

this comb of beans. The idea was for someone else to beat him. That was a winter-time thing—for show. Three or four stone weights on a shovel, that was another little thing. If you could do that you were supposedly as good as him: put three or four stone weights on a shovel and pick the shovel up in the normal way. Well, he used to say to my mother [when she protested about his weight-lifting]:

"Look here, gal! If I ain't the cock o' my own muck-hill, how can I be good anywhere else? Time I'm down here I want to be the boss!" '

---

# Mervyn Cater

The main reason for concentrating on the farm horse in relating some of the recent history of an arable region such as East Anglia is that the horse was at the heart of the pulsing life of the farm, and by extension of much of the life outside it. He supplied most of the power that such a farming area needed; and without this power the raising of crops on any large scale would not have been possible. The horse, moreover, solved the transport problems in the countryside, even after the coming of the railways, because the railways serviced the bigger population centres, primarily, rather than the countryside; and even where there was a good rural network the transport from railway station to the farm was all provided by farm horses. The horse was truly in the centre of the economic life of the region; and in addition he was also the focus of much of the social and folk-lore of the countryside. Around him a great deal of the life of the region was constellated; and this life, moreover, was in the mainstream of the history of the region since at least the time when horses were first used in farming—from the twelfth century, as we know from Suffolk evidence, when the horse is recorded as making up 'mixed' plough-teams with the ox. Incidentally, it confirms the remarkable historical continuity linked with farming, the traditional work of the region, when we know that these mixed plough-teams were used within living memory in East Anglia. Examples are given in Appendix One.

Much of the richness of the less publicized life associated with the horse and the farms is recorded here to indicate that a study of the farm horse in this particular region presupposes looking at the tradition, the folk-life of the region, if only to illustrate unfamiliar aspects of the continuity just mentioned. This tradition comes through the farmers and the horsemen themselves; the horsemen, especially, being the conscious transmitters of an immemorial lore, son following father and grandfather and so on as horsemen, and each generation being

113

assiduous to train, and to pass on their secrets to, at least one of the sons who were following them in their craft.

Walter Cater's schooling of his sons—in fact almost the only kind of schooling his son Mervyn obtained—is an excellent example of the way this was done: learning not by precept alone but by example and doing under the eye of a man who was a master of his craft in all its aspects. Mervyn's schooling started when he was very young, at the outbreak of the Second World War. By the middle of the war he was doing many of the farm worker's jobs, chiefly those in the stables and the small jobs about the farm such as leading the horses in wagons or in tumbrils. Workers were so scarce at this period, exactly as they were during the First World War, that child-labour was usual on the farms in Britain. He related one incident that tells exactly how young he was when he started doing responsible tasks in the stables:

'A funny episode I had when I was seven. When a horseman walked to the back of the horses with the feed-bin under his arm they always opened and he walked through them; and they always opened where he seemed to walk up behind 'em: they parted, moved apart. Well, I did this. I simply—I realized that it was a fact that you had to have the courage to keep walking at 'em, and if you got close enough they'd part. Well, I did, but I picked the wrong place. I didn't know there was a certain place between the horses, but apparently there was; for both these horses stepped the wrong way, and I got my head between 'em. And they got me off my feet. I couldn't reach the ground; and my head—I could feel it being squashed. I couldn't shout: I tried screaming, but nothing come out. And I suppose Father must have seen me hanging there, because he just spoke to the two horses, and they parted and I went crash down. I'm sure my head went a different shape: it felt as if it was going to burst!'

About this time he also started doing active work in the field. The old narrow *stetches* or *rigs* (with the water-furrows at regular and frequent intervals) were being replaced by wider stetches more suitable for the various types of machinery that were coming on to the farms; but here and there on the Redgrave farm, where the land was very heavy, extra draining was needed in spite of the increased underdraining that replaced the narrow *lands* or stetches.

'We used the ten- or twelve-furrow work where the field needed draining so that the furrows laid the right way for the water. After we'd done this we nipped 'em back again up to fifteen-yard stetches. That was where I was allowed to take a plough. That was too wet to really keep it straight anyway. By this time, I was working all day although I was still at school. During the war you had a little card, a little coloured card to allow you to work during school time. (In fact it was against the law for me to be at work. But what happened was, we had these cards—country boys did anyhow—and they allowed you to go to work when you were still at school—at harvest time and the times when the sugar-beet needed to come off, that kind of thing.) And Father used to come to the school to get us. But the reason I was pushed into it (I was legally too young) was this: he took one or two boys from the school, and at night their mother and father were at our door: they didn't want their children working on the farm when they should have been getting educated at school! So Father suggested that I went. Well, that suited me! I was no good at school, anyway: I was dreadful at school, and would much rather be with the horses. So I went with him [unofficially] when he wanted me even though I was about eight years old: I was too young to be there really. The other boys who went were fourteen, or nearly fourteen, very close to leaving school. But he would rather have me, simply because he wouldn't get wrong [with the parents of other boys]. So by this time I was learning quite a bit from him, being with him all day. He used to *clod* or *stone* me if I was leading the horse-hoe and went to sleep. I used to lead the horse-hoe for him all day, and I used to go to sleep, walking. And he used to dig up clods and throw them at me to wake me up. Most of the time I was drowsing; I just couldn't keep my eyes open.

'Then I got to the point where the beet got big enough so he would allow me to take Pansy, the big mare I had grown up with. And if I took Pansy, she would walk up the rows of beet without anybody leading her. The plants were three or four inches tall, and she seemed to be able to see 'em plain enough to walk between the rows. Then he used to give me a hoe, with just eight hoes on, and I was allowed to go horse-hoeing alone. This was good for me. The thing was, I was so poor at school: I'd got no interest at all, and I was put on the garden while I was at school because they couldn't teach me anything. But the minute I got down there with my father, I knew; I sensed that I probably knew more about horses than the rest of the men did. At least, I thought I did which was enough to give me a lot of confidence.

And the fact that Father would allow me to take his own horse, that in itself was a thing of pride to me. When I took her back to the stable at night, I made sure I wiped her down till she nearly shone before she was allowed to go into the horse-box. I made a lot of fuss of her because that was such a rare thing: braid the tail, I always used to do that, used to go early enough. I knew I wasn't going to school and I used to get up at quarter past five and go down with him. He always had his horses in the horse-pond which was just below the farmer's window and he could hear those horses in the pond every morning. And they'd got to be there at quarter past five. They always were: I used to go down with him to give me time to braid my horse's tail if it was winter-time. Summer-time he liked to have them free. If it was wet and muddy we always braided them. I wasn't very good at it, but I used to braid mine up. And my mother would iron my piece of ribbon, usually a red piece; and I used to put the ribbon just because I had the horse: that was my horse! But what was so valuable that Pansy, that horse—no one else was allowed to use it; and if I was allowed to take his horse, say in November, horse-hoeing beet, well, that was great. He did it probably for me; and I knew he would do anything for me. At the same time I liked it. My mother said to me: "You won't do any good at school." I was never going to do any good at school, and he knew where my interest lay, and I went with him.'

In recounting his early lessons on the farm Mervyn Cater illustrates what a high standard of craftsmanship meant, not only in horse matters but in general work on the farm; and what kudos and local reputation the highest standard gave to the horseman. His father had decided while his son was still very young to give him instruction in using a steerage-drill, a machine to drill or sow the corn: this was an operation that demanded a high degree of skill and also care not to jeopardize one's own reputation because any mistake one made in the drilling would be visible to all when the crop came up. It was a Smythe drill, and his father took him on some 'short work', a piece of land where no one could see it. He was allowed to drive the drill backwards and forwards for a couple of dozen times. His father walked beside him, behind him, leaned on him, did everything he could to teach him to drill. One day, after he had been having lessons for some time, his father was called away by the boss: there was a horse in the ditch; it had gone to sleep on the edge and had rolled upside down into the ditch and couldn't get out. They came and took his father away to help with this horse. Mervyn was left with the drill:

'I stood beside the drill and kept looking up at this line we had just made; and it was like a gun-barrel. It must be easy once it was straight! (I got a bent line if I did it on my own, but here was one to follow.) It looked so easy to walk along that straight line; and of course it was a long field right to the road. In the end I had to have a go! I walked round the back of the drill put the lever on and let the corn run, and I driv those horses across the field. When I looked back that was dreadful! That was inches out. I turned the horses round, kept them on the headland and didn't drill any more that day. When my father seen this he was hurt—not angry, he was hurt!'

He was hurt because the reputation he prized, perhaps most of all, of being an all-round expert on the farm would now be jeopardized; and when Walter Cater met the horseman he admired most in the district, as he did every Sunday morning, he was asked quite seriously: 'What! Were you taken ill, Walter?' And although his father said: 'It was thet boy o' mine!', the bent drill-furrow was always a source of leg-pulling between the two friendly rivals: 'You're not a'going to tell me a tale like thet, Walter Cater. You fell over! Course you did.'

Mervyn went on to explain that this other horseman, Cook, who worked for a farmer at Rickinghall, was on a par with his father. Walter Cater respected his judgement: 'I knew by the way they talked (Father rarely talked to other horsemen) but whenever he met this chap, well, there seemed to be something between them. They knew. I didn't know what they knew, but whenever we met this man Cook, we could guarantee it would be a two hours' stop. And on Sunday morning you would see my father biking out towards Rickinghall and the other chap biking this way.

'There was only one other man he respected as much in horse-matters: that was the blacksmith, Mr Rous, at Wortham. He had been a blacksmith there all his life; and I suppose he was a pensioner when I went there. And you could see the respect between the two of them. I'm sure that old blacksmith knew more about horses than the ordinary smith. I often heard Father say:

"Tell Alf Rous, when you get there, to look the mare over; see what he think."

'I've never heard him say that of anyone else; and old Rous would

117

look her over; and he'd go and scribble something on a piece of paper and stick it in my pocket and say:

"You leave thet there, boy, and see the owd chap git it."

'I didn't touch it because first of all I wasn't man enough to read it—and he knew or he wouldn't have given it to me. The fact was, there was something that was built in, long before I started to be *taught*, I would take Dad's place someday; and I knew by the way he treated me and the way I was made—made! well, encouraged—to handle horses, and the way the horses respected me. Because strangely enough they did. They would come to me. There were fifteen horses on the farm plus nine colts; and if I walked in the park alone, they'd all tear towards me; and I must admit when they were about thirty yards away and doing about twenty miles an hour coming towards me I was terrified. But they all skid to a standstill round me. Even if I went for a walk on my own through the wood, they all reacted the same: "He's a friend"—let's put it like that, rather than, "Here's the boss!" They would come to me, and they knew I would make a fuss of them. This was the thing Dad always used to say:

"Never touch a colt. Let the colt touch you." '

This is a true observation and it appears that it is equally relevant to very young children. A friend of mine who spent a lifetime teaching infants bound herself by a strict rule: 'Never approach too close to, or touch a child you are meeting for the first time. Hang back until the child comes to you.'

Mervyn Cater: 'That was a thing he used to do with his horses. They'd all gather round him because he always used to walk across the park and count his horses on the way home—every Sunday. That was when he made a fuss of the colts. He handled them and they pushed him about, and they'd play with him. I've seen one or two of them nearly knock him down—swing their neck up against him as if they were playing with another colt. He'd throw his cap and his jacket down, and he'd play with them for about half an hour, the sweat streaming off him. He'd play with his horses just like a big kid. But my mother took it seriously. She'd never seen Father play with horses. He handled horses: there was something between him and the horses, mainly because they worked together they should play together. I don't know what it was. My father used to say: *"Farm workers are not made: they're born."*

'I was very much the learner. The things he did teach me—in fact

118

he never taught me as such: I saw—were usually for medical reasons. For instance, I went down and helped him take a horse's tooth out. Now he did explain that to do this he must use a gate-hook, and it must be drawn from the post, never an old one. I got the job of holding the rope on top of the beam.'

It should be explained at this point how a horse's tooth was taken out. The horse was made to stand in the stable or out-house with his head under one of the tie-beams. A rope is looped in his mouth and his head is pulled up towards the beam to reveal the tooth that has to be removed. The boy sat on the beam holding the end of the rope that had been firmly looped round at the required point. The operator then stood on a pair of steps or a ladder holding the gate-hook (one of the hooks on which a gate is swung) in one hand, and a hammer in the other. He knocked the offending tooth inwards.

'I was frightened to death by this business. But why it had to be a gate-hook drawn from the post—I had a feeling that there must be some chemical in the wood that kept the hook sterile. Father said he'd never seen a jaw that was done in this way go wrong after a tooth had been knocked out with a gate-hook, but he'd seen it go wrong with other things they used. This gate-hook or *pin* is on the hanging side of the gate: the gate swings on it; and you took two hammers and you hit it on either side at the same time; and you could then draw it out of the gate-post. He impressed on me that it must be a gate-hook; nothing else would do. It would cause infection in the jaw with anything else. The gate-hook being buried some way in the centre of the post, he never touched the end of the hook. When he drew it he always held the end and that would normally be standing out in the air. He never touched that end of the hook until after he'd used it. It was sterile, maybe something in the wood; the oak had quenched it with the years. That was what he always used. I only had anything to do with it twice in my life; and in both cases I was shown and helped to draw the gate-hook. This is the way you can draw a gate-hook: if you hit, not necessarily behind the bulge, the ring on the hook, but simply here on the side, that will draw; and it don't matter how tight you knock 'em in or how long they've been there, if you hit them both sides at once—two hammers, one in either hand—that will draw. Usually the second horseman would come and help as well, but I usually got the job of sitting on top of the beam, sitting on top of the rope. And I could see the horse; and I

119

could see what he did. Whether I was put there because I was the smallest to sit on the top of the beam or whether in fact I was there to watch. Of course, he was enough of a psychologist: so maybe there was no way of telling quite what my purpose was in being there at all; because often as not the second horseman was just standing there at the bottom of the ladder just in case of trouble—but I never saw him do anything.'

A description of a process such as the above shows how much subtlety underlies much of the apparently crude methods used by the old community. In this respect I am sure that many of the skills and processes used with profit, and proved by their long continuing, have been grossly undervalued during the last half-century. The example that comes repeatedly to my mind is the old horseman's knowledge of the curative property of the moulds they used to clear up an infection. Long before penicillin was isolated Suffolk horsemen were using various moulds on their horses,[1] and as many anthropologists—notably Levi-Strauss—have remarked, how detailed and subtle is the knowledge of the primitives of South America who have built up over countless centuries a corpus of empirical knowledge through their deep familarity and concern with plant and animal life that was necessary for their survival. A Cambridge botanist, Professor Richard West, once pointed out to me an example nearer home: the crofters of the Hebrides by reason of their use of vegetable dyes in the finishing of cloth have— or did have until recent years—a remarkable knowledge of the range of plants that would supply them dyes.[2]

Therefore in setting down in their context details such as are in the above incident we are salvaging a piece of lore that could conceivably be of use in the future. Mervyn Cater was himself aware of the attenuation of the lore he had gained from his father. A lot of it had already been lost since the horses went from the farms: a great deal of it had become vague and inaccurate. For example, people would report such an incident as the 'stopping' of horses or containing them in a field, as described earlier, dramatizing the whole incident without knowing

---

[1] F.A.V., p. 114.

[2] Professor West cites a work listing the Gaelic words for plants and animals in South Uist and Eriskay. It was written by the Rev Fr McDonald (1859–1905): *Gaelic Words and Expressions from S. Uist and Eriskay* (Ed J. L. Campbell), Dublin Institute for Advanced Studies, Merrion Square, Dublin, 1958.

the essential clue to what had happened. He said: 'Nowadays you talk to people about things as they were when the horses were on the farm, and they don't want to know: they're not interested. But I have kept a lot of the knowledge. In all probability it will never be used. Yet I like to think so as I enjoyed working with horses.'

In the following anecdotes he shows how craft knowledge, occasionally secret knowledge, was so useful in the working life on the farm:

'You may never have heard that on this 180-acre Redgrave park, where the horses runned on during the time the estate was rich, the problem of fencing was never one that concerned the horseman, because the estate carpenters and his helpers kept the fences up. But by this time it got to the point when Father was responsible for keeping his own horses in. We used to have horses running about the village here several nights during the winter; and he went to Mr Bedwell and asked him whether he'd mind if he bought a donkey and put it on the park. So us kids thought: "Marvellous, we're going to have a donkey!" So one night—this was during the time when we had lamps—oil lamps, no electricity, Father said: "I want you children in the kitchen tonight, before you go to bed: I'll have a talk with you." We all set round this big round table that Mother had: three boys and one girl; and, in fact, there were a couple of Londoners as well because this was during the War. He said:

"The donkey is not for you. It's for the horses." And none of us could understand, but he said: "Those horses will never be any trouble once I put a donkey on the park. A horse never leave a donkey."

'And he put the donkey on the park, on the meadow with the horses; they never got out again. If the donkey won't go out, the horse won't go. If the donkey lead 'em, everyone will come out. But a donkey in the normal way don't try very hard to get out: it's fairly content to be in an area as big as that. We never had any more trouble after he bought the donkey. That was his all the time he was there: it was stabled in the shed at the back of our house and he looked after it and fed it. And it was purely just that he had to get the boss' *say* [permission] to put the donkey on the meadow. It was there for about nine years. And when he finished as horseman he took the donkey and sold it; and the next bloke had the problems! By that time the fences had deteriorated more and more, and they just couldn't keep the horses in. But my father lived for his horses. He had a very strong love for them; and if there was one ill that was just like one of his children; and he worried as much as if it was one of his children —just as much. It would worry him if one of us was ill, but if one of his horses was ill it would worry him just as much. The whole family, not just him: my mother would go down with him at two or three in the morning to see one of the horses; and if there was a foal, he'd bring him home, if its mother had died or anything like that; and we kept it here in one of our sheds.'

The following not only makes the point about handing on of useful knowledge but illustrates the conscious, purposeful way in which the lore was preserved in the traditional horse-families. There was little sentiment about it: every scrap of knowledge relating to the farm horse was an atom of power which the holder could use to his best advantage to make his job easier, or even to retain his job at the time of the farming depressions. For no farmer in an arable area would get rid of, or even treat with anything short of respect, a horseman who had the knowledge in his bones, had been born with it into a horse family of long standing. Therefore Mervyn Cater could say about his father: 'Well, again, my father was in a position where he could not, of course, ask for whatever money he wanted, but he could certainly pick his farm, where he wanted to work—without any doubt. Not all the farms, because some of the farms had horsemen that were his equals, perhaps better; but he could pick his farm within reason if he wanted to.'

He then went on to discuss a topic that has a very old historical provenance: the identification of the district or place a horse comes from by an examination of his shoes. (Prince Charles—later Charles II —to give an example, while escaping after an unsuccessful battle during the Civil Wars betrayed his identity to an astute Dorset smith who was replacing a cast shoe on his horse. 'The prick-eared blacksmith Hamnet' recognized one of the shoes as coming from Worcestshire): [3]

'Diss area was supposed to be a good area for horsemen; and one thing which my father told me in preparation was that if you were a good horseman you should be able to pick up a horse's hoof on any street in this area and tell where that horse had come from and who had shod it. He knew it, because I remember one chap coming down to the farm with a load of grain—a complete stranger: this was new grain—and Father lifted the near hind foot and he said:

[3] P.U.P., pp. 179–80.

"That's recently been shod," and he showed me: "There you are! That was shod near Newmarket"; and he knew the bloke's name. He reckoned you should be able to tell where the horse had been and nearly on what farm he came off, just by looking at the shoes and the way the horse was equipped. I would know a shoe from this area, had I been in any other part of the country because they had a very high front to stop the gravel cutting into the hoof. In other parts of the country especially in Lincolnshire (I was up there for a time with my father) the horses had hardly anything round the front of the hoof. But the Suffolk had a very high front to his shoe to protect the hoof against the flints. We didn't get sand-cracks here on our land: that was something out of the ordinary here. But some of the horses from Thetford and East Harling—on the sandy soil—had to have plates screwed to the hooves to hold them together. I never did get to know everything about the shoes as my father did; but the knowledge was there for the taking had things carried on, and the horses were still on the farms.'

A useful piece of stable-drill was practised in the Redgrave area, and it is the sort of custom that is forgotten and dies out after a few years. Mervyn Cater mentioned it while we were ruminating on a previous visit I had made to his village: 'I often wondered since I talked to you before why every horse *staled* [urinated] before he went into the stables. But this was common practice. While the horses were standing outside the stable just before going in, the men just simply whistled; every horseman did it. The whistle was long drawn out and the horses would stale. This was the usual practice to get the horses to stale outside and not to mess up the stable.' But this reflex conditioning was not confined to horses. Having been brought up in a household where there was a succession of small boys, I well remember the gentle, rather inexpert whistle that was presently followed by a more assured tinkling in a resonant earthenware pot.

As we talked for long hours on my second visit Mervyn Cater kept reverting to the tricks his father played to establish and keep up his reputation of a *master-horseman*: sometimes they were purely a self-conscious exhibition of his skills, but occasionally they were played for a more immediate advantage. As he told me some of them he appeared to be filling in the details that were hidden to him when he witnessed the tricks as a young boy, and was now enjoying a fuller rehearsal with the satisfaction of making the whole performance—

whatever it was—more meaningful. It was only rarely that the father told him how a trick was performed, waiting—so the son believed—until the time was ripe for him to receive a full enlightenment:

'But there was one thing—one of the things he did tell me and I don't think it was meant to be any kind of secret. Yet the other men appeared not to know. I remember a horse laying down near Redgrave Church. That was with a wagon of corn, and it was supposed to be going to Mellis station; but suddenly it went down in the middle of the road. I'd never seen it before, nor had they. It wouldn't get up. And Father said: "I can get it up if you can stop it when it do get up." (The man who was in charge of the horse was an ex-cavalry man in the 1914–18 War, and he knew a bit about horses but not enough to be a real horseman.) Anyway, Father went to the horse and stood over him and whispered in its ear. And that horse got up and started to *run*, with a full load of corn! And the chap told us when he got back that he pulled him up at the station which was three and a half miles away. It's a wonder that didn't kill that horse. But afterwards my father said to me:

"You know what I done, don't you?"

"No. I thought you talked to it."

"Which I did, but that was only for the men's benefit."

'He'd got little pockets in his waistcoat; and each one had got a little tin with something different in it. And this one, the one he used on this occasion, had got the shot out of a 4–10 cartridge. He poured it into the horse's ear, and when it shook its ear with the little lead pellets in it, they must have sounded like thunder. And that—you could just see it going round the bend of the road with a load of corn. But when it shook the last one out, and the noise stopped, it simply pulled up. I couldn't have been more than thirteen at the time; and though my father didn't tell me to keep it a secret, I never told anyone—not till after farm horses had finished.

'Talking about this sort of thing, some of the information handed down has already got rather vague—as I told you—but there are some things I know for certain. For instance, I knew Dad put the shot in the horse's ear. He told me he did, and he showed me some of the shot afterwards. But had he not have simply said that, I would have had to tell you he whispered to the horse, because I would have seen only what all the other men saw, not ever knowing the truth. And so many of these stories, I'm sure, there was a little more attached to it than we'll ever know.'

This was a drastic practice and, as J. S. Rarey pointed out, it could easily kill a horse. But it was fairly common among country horsemen (see the drawing below); and Charles Gardner, a native of Diss, gave me an example of its use with a similar appliance:

'My father had another horse that he bought at Garboldisham. This man who sold him the horse said to him: "You'll never use it. You'll never use it!" "I'll see," he said. He brought it home and of course put it in the stable. And I think my sister has got the ring: it's a ring

Appliance to fit lead into a horse's ear

about as big as that copper ring with a piece of wax thread and a bead tied to it. He went to the horse and put the ring over its ear, and dropped the bead inside. He talked to the horse, and just before he went to bed he took the ring off—for about a quarter of an hour. He then got up three or four times during the night: pulled it out, put it back; pulled it out, put it back—till the morning. And in the morning he put the harness on and put the horse into the cart and drove it. I said to him:

"I thought that man said you wouldn't be able to use it."

"Ah," he said, "he didn't use the right methods!"

Later, during the First World War, when he was in a cavalry regiment in Egypt, he astounded his Colonel by subduing an untractable horse which the Colonel boasted only he could ride. He used the same method. The countryman did not, however, reveal how he had done it.

The second trick is of the kind that was practised by the gypsies and the less reputable horse-dealers where only one moral precept— if it can be called that—was invoked: *Let the buyer beware*:

'Another thing Father did to me. I was a long way from being twelve or thirteen (by the time I left school there was only one horse left on the farm, and I left school at fifteen) so this was purely a very early preparation. But he told me over the years lots of things I could— or rather he could do to a horse to make it ill, temporarily—limp for instance. On a Sunday afternoon when he felt in the mood, he'd take one of the horses and do whatever he liked to it, and then see how many tricks I could spot. My favourite one, the one I could always get right was tying a horse's hair round the hock to make it limp. Pull the hair out of his tail, and put it round his hock, and if you tied it at the right spot, right at the joint, it could feel the hair cutting into the joint and that would hurt. It would limp on that foot. And he reckoned those old gypsy horse-dealers, if you took a good horse to them, one would talk to you and distract you, and the other would make the horse or pony limp that you were trying to sell them. It would knock the price down twenty quid, say; and the minute you'd gone they'd take the hair off, and there was nothing wrong with the horse. I saw my father play this trick, but the horse wasn't his and he never made anything out of it; and it puzzled me why he did it.'

The third example is more of an exhibition of skill in horsemanship rather than a trick:

'This again involved an ordinary fork used on the farm. The fork was again stuck in the muck but in the horse-yard where the ground was level. Father pushed the fork into the muck, put the trace-chains of the two horses together, just put the hooks into one another and a piece of string from the hooks to the handle of the fork. Then gradually he took the horses out in opposite directions till they tightened the chains up. And without pulling the fork over in either direction he got the horses to lay with their chests in the muck—flat out in both directions. And yet the fork had never got any tension on from either side. Whenever I tried it, no matter how hard I tried to get even forces (and I knew the horses fairly well) it never worked: one horse always tended to pull a little more than the other. His horses always pulled even: I never learned why. The horses' front legs were straight and they gradually went down on to their chests.

'The only thing I might mention here is that he was very particular about his chains. Hooks must be facing inwards and covered with (probably) sacking, to make sure that if a chain broke, the hook never tore the horse's stomach open. It took a long job of preparation if we were pulling a threshing drum out. I have seen him hook six horses, one behind the other, pulling a drum and elevator out of a muddy stackyard. And that took often three-quarters of an hour walking round and turning the hooks outward, and making sure that all the links were in good order. I saw a man get the sack—Father normally went to the closest horse to the drum and tightened the chains up on that one by easing the horse forward; and then he worked from that one round to the next examining all the trappings and tightening the chains up on that one, and gradually work to the front before the horses were allowed to move. Well, this particular man, who had been a horseman and not a very good one, the minute my father finished with the last horse he examined, this man he shouted, "Go on!", and of course they all started to pull. And Mr Bedwell sacked him on the spot. He supposed he was a good horseman, but he was the only one who did consider that. He was one of the horsemen that ruled with the cane. He was a horse-breaker: he'd ruin good horses. He didn't like the way my father handled horses—he was too gentle— and he hated to see a horse do something as if it was asked and not as it was told. I consider, and I think my father did, that his own horses did what they did because they wanted to do it; because they wanted to please rather than they were afraid not to do it. I had to go through this procedure every time I got my horse and tried this trick [with equal pulling on the fork] and practised with them so that I could get it right. And that was the only thing: he used to stay and watch, when the horses were prepared to see the chains covered and that sort of thing. Then he'd leave me to it. He watched but he was distant and yet friendly. I always considered that me and my father got on more as a horseman and a workman rather than father and son. He would swear at me and correct me just like one of the men. But as for this pulling on the fork, I never got to do it as he could do it. The horses went before I was old enough to do it properly.'

I suggested earlier that it is profitable to concentrate on the horse, which was in the centre of the arable farming here before the advent of the tractor, for the reason that around the horse and the horseman accrued the richest and most extensive lore of the prior culture in East Anglia. The horse was the mainspring of the farming, the traditional work that had been carried on relatively unchanged for centuries and in which inheres that tough though adaptable continuity that is so remarkable in the rural history of an homogeneous region such as this. It is possible, as has been shown, to come across material in customs, usages, vocabulary and attitudes, where the observer has the impression that a number of centuries have been telescoped together to illuminate the background of a word, anecdote or custom that has appeared in his field of sight. Often the historian ignores this kind of material as being too marginal to deserve his attention: it is bracketed as folklore and excluded from the historical pale. Mervyn Cater recounts two examples. The listener or the reader is not asked to *believe*, at the intellectual level, in what is recorded: they are brought to his notice to illustrate the continuity in usages and attitudes of mind already referred to:

'I wouldn't like to say that there is not such a thing as black magic but I know of a coincidence, or something that happened regularly. No one has been able to explain it to me (it's nothing to do with horses, by the way). But it's a strange kind of thing that happened in this part of the country, the kind of story you get in Suffolk and Norfolk. There was this old girl at Blo Norton. Her son was the biggest poacher—he was a devil: he'd rob your house in the middle of the day, and let you see him! But the police could never catch him. If they went to the house and saw him move into the door, they'd turn out the family, look everywhere and he was not to be found. But his mother would be sitting there with this black cat in her arms: she'd always got this black cat when he weren't there. The police would search the house and he was never there. And you never saw that cat when he was there! Now this will surprise you, I know; but my mother has pointed that out time after time. She said:

"You go along that Blo Norton road and you'll never see the black cat unless Alby [we'll call him that, though that wasn't his proper name] if Alby had disappeared out of sight the black cat was there. You never saw the two together."

'People in the village said she was a witch. But this is . . . you can make of it what you like, can't you?'

The next story is probably of little value as a sidelight on the history of farm workers' dress in East Anglia, but it does give a very valuable insight into the relations between farmers and farm workers before the big modern changes in farming:

'According to my father the waistcoat started in Suffolk, the sleeved waistcoat as we know it. According to his grandfather the waistcoat started in Suffolk because the farmers made the men work with their jackets off all the winter. But the women noticed that the white inner sleeves of the jacket, if turned inside out, looked as if they'd got shirt-sleeves and a jersey or pull-over on. So the men turned the jacket inside out so that the white inner lining of the sleeves was showing. And from the farmer's house it looked that the men hadn't got their jackets on. And they developed the waistcoat with the sleeve of a different material. My father told us he remembered the days when the men used to turn their jackets over after they got to work; and then at dinner-time turn 'em round in case the boss turned up. So he didn't know any different. And Father reckoned that that was when the waistcoat started in this area. The farmers wanted the men to work without their coats on because they reckoned they'd have to work harder to keep warm. They've done that to me in my time! I've been told to take my coat off—I'm now forty years of age [April 1976] I've been told in snow, that was snow, to take my coat off. But that was at the point when there were too many jobs about, and I told the farmer what he could do; and he went on hoom. But he was an old farmer, and he still kept his attitude: he could tell you what to do!'

From the above it may be inferred that the relation of the farm worker to the farmer was an entirely subservient one under the old community. It was virtually so during the long farming depressions, for example, before 1914 and the period between the two wars, and in areas where the men's union was weak: here farm workers had to be almost supplicants for jobs, particularly after the gathering of the corn-harvest. Yet the East Anglian farm worker had many ways of keeping his dignity; and the better he became at his job the more secure and the less dependent he was. This applied in particular to the head horseman and the shepherd. These were the aristocrats of the farm. In fact, a farmer—unless he was very firm—could find his shepherd running his farm for him: if, for instance, a farmer had a flock of 500 ewes that was essential to making his farm pay, he had to handle his shepherd with kid-gloves. And when the shepherd would demand that a certain field should be sown with such-and-such a crop 'for *my* sheep', the farmer invariably had to accede. Again, at the lambing season it was no use the farmer asking his shepherd how many lambs he had got: he just would not get an answer. But most East Anglian farmers of the old school were wise enough to refrain from asking their shepherd such a question.

The head horseman was just as independent as the shepherd, and few farmers would interfere with him as long as he did his job efficiently. Walter Cater's relationship with his employer is described clearly by his son; and it typifies the relationship between a farmer and a first-class craftsman, and defines it—perhaps a little over-dramatically. It was tacitly assumed that each—farmer and workman —should have a sharply defined status, not necessarily defined by the laws of ownership. As one head horseman told his employer who declared he could 'do what he liked with his horses because he owned them';

'That you can't! While the horses are in my charge they are *my* horses, and I don't want anybody interfering!'

Mervyn Cater: 'But this was the thing: my father, being a horseman—that kind of horseman I should say, not necessarily just a horseman—he had to be head man in every respect. And the men and the horses reacted to him in the same way. So did the boss. I've seen him knock the boss down in one particular case! The boss would come over when there was a load of corn come in, seed corn or something like that: he *would* stand in the narrow doorway of the barn and count the bags that were being carried past him. Well, to carry a comb of corn through a narrow doorway with the boss, an oldish man leaning on a stick in there! Well, he picked the worst spot in the barn to stand. That was a huge barn and he had to stand in that there doorway. Father said: "That's time we moved him!" So, of course, he took the next comb of corn and he just kept walking; and he knocked the poor man down. And he got up and started to mutter about that was unnecessary. And Father said:

"Look here! I and the men can look after ourselves. We are at work and you are doing nothing. If you can't find a better spot to stand. . . !"

'He treated the boss as if he was one of the workmen *while they were at work*. But before he started in the morning, when the boss walked into the stables to give orders for the day that was the only time he was the boss. Once he had told my father what he wanted

130

done that was up to father to see that it was done, and done correctly. But he didn't want him keep walking up to him; for instance, if he'd had picked up one of his plough-spanners or even looked at the plough, Father would have hit him. No one touched that plough. But this never happened: the farmer was too experienced for that. That was the same kind of thing:

"I know my job: you tell me what you want done and I'll do it!" '

In the process of describing his apprenticeship as a farm horseman Mervyn Cater has etched, incidentally, a firm-lined portrait of his father. Judging from my own knowledge of head horsemen in various parts of East Anglia, the picture is also a very accurate one. Head horsemen were acutely aware of the special nature of their skills, as Mervyn Cater suggests, having inherited it to a large extent from their ancestors who had followed the same craft over generations. Usually family pride came into it: these men were perfectionists with the highest standards in all aspects of their craft, in the field or in the stable; and it was a point of honour with them never to fall short of their own self-set standard. If they did so they felt they were lessening or cheapening themselves. And when others who were in their charge failed to reach this standard they reacted as though they had been offered an insult to their own person. They were positive, on occasion to the point of arrogance; ruthless and hard in many respects, yet kind; and although they were often forced to adopt what can only be described as cruel methods in taming a vicious horse that had been spoiled by mishandling, their general attitude to the horses under their charge was one of extreme concern. To describe it as humane would perhaps be to miss the main point in their relation with their horses. They did in fact *identify* with them in some strange way: by a curious empathy they were *one* with them exactly as Walter Cater was for the brief periods when he used to play with his colts; and, as many wives and children of old farm horsemen have told me over the years, they thought at least as much of the horses under their care as they did of their wives and children. Mervyn Cater confirms this in describing his father's relation to Pansy—The Big One—the mare the children had grown up with: when she was put down he shed tears just as though he was losing one of his own children. But his son's account of a particular incident shows the other side: the hardness in him that designed a quite unsentimental, not to say Spartan schooling, for his son.

'I don't think he ever treated me quite as a son. He always considered I was a bit like his horses: I needed correcting as regularly as
a horse. He threw clods at me; and sometimes I could hear him shouting two fields away. I started ploughing one morning: one of the few
things I was allowed to do was to plough back into the furrows, just
turn the furrows back so that the harrows would level down. It was
one of the jobs I was allowed to do because it didn't really matter too
much whether there was a good job done or not. I remember very
well one morning—very well: it must have been early March, bitter
cold. He saw one of my horses nodding as it walked; and he could
see the further horse: that meant that the chains of the left-hand
horse were longer than on the right. And when he did eventually get
there he found I was a link out: he'd seen it from the side of a twenty-
acre field, and I hadn't seen it. The fuss he made over that, as if the
whole world was going to come to an end. But when he got home that
night, and I think it was after he had cooled down, he explained that
the front horse was doing nothing: that the horse that was tied short
was doing all the work. I was making one horse do all the work while
the other was just walking beside him. But at that time I was so concerned about getting the plough in the right place I never took time
enough to see to the horses. That was one lesson I didn't forget in a
hurry. You could hear him shouting; and the rotten part of it was,
was the fact that the other men could hear him shouting at me. That
was the part that hurt me. He knew that hurt me; and that is why
he had a little talk that night, later on, to put things right between
us.'

After the thrombosis in his legs Walter Cater did not return to his
horses. The black corner cupboard where he kept his notebook, his
oils and the rest of his horse material became a symbol of the end of
the old horse regime on the farm where he had been in charge. His
son said:

'All the things he had in that black cupboard when he retired—
within a week they were gone. The cupboard had gone as well. My
father got rid of them. He had some brasses too. They were struck
by the blacksmith at Occold who made the brasses for the estate in
this area. And he struck or cast one purely for that estate; and they
were the only ones ever cast. There were eight of them, and he gave
one to my father. That was a sea-horse—you know the figure with a
curly tail. They would be worth a good bit of money because only

eight were cast. My father had one and he sold it. I know why: he was ill months and months, and his legs were blown up and blue with thrombosis; and he was very badly off. His copper kettles—all the furrow-drawing prizes he'd won—disappeared within about three months. He sold everything, oils as well.'

# 12

# The Depth of the Lore

In order not to hinder the flow of the narration in the last two chapters comment has been purposely withheld or limited. It would be as well at this stage to fill in the gaps while the material is still fresh in the reader's mind.

It should be stated, first of all, that many horse-experts during the nineteenth century—and indeed at the present time—have scorned the idea that the horse's sense of smell could be used to any advantage in the training or control of a horse, and they have dismissed the effectiveness of drawing oils or jading substances out of hand. Many, too, of the younger people who have tried out these oils in recent years have been disappointed with the results. This is understandable for the reason that the oils as used by the older farm horsemen sixty and seventy years ago are no longer obtainable. Many of these oils as already stated were imported and as the demand (chiefly from farm horsemen) fell off these oils have been no longer available on the market. It appears that they are still nominally available at chemist shops but often what is sold as the original oil is only a substitute and quite ineffective for its use as a drawing or calling oil. The experience of the blacksmith, Hector Moore, already given shows the practical difference between an authentic drawing oil and a substitute. About that time the smith showed me a large bottle of the substitute oil he had recently bought from a chemist. It had none of the volatility of the true oil and I had to take the cork out of the bottle before I could detect any smell at all. This was in sharp contrast to my experience with a small bottle of the same oil that had been given me by an old, retired farm horseman. I had it in a drawer in my desk for a few days before passing it on to the smith, Hector Moore, who could use it, and for months afterwards I could smell this oil unmistakably every time I opened this particular drawer in my desk.

J. S. Rarey, the American horse-trainer, was one of the outspoken critics of the importance given to the horse's sense of smell.

*Or you may soak a
peice of tow or list in
the oil of charon oil
of vidgin and tincture
of myrrh and put in
the tube it has two holes
one at Each End to suck
it out +
the home made
tube for useing dry
Opium
or
tobaco and
Laudanum for
stilling horses*

*Or wild Colts may use
Rhodium and oil of Spike in tobacco
from 15 to 30 drops*

Opium device on bit (Rarey)[1]

He was first drawn into the controversy by being accused of getting his spectacular results through the use of secret oils, most particularly the results he got in rehabilitating horses that had already been spoiled by cruel mishandling. Rarey maintained that of the horse's senses—seeing, hearing, smelling and feeling—feeling, the sense of touch, was the most critical; and it was most instrumental in soothing a nervous horse. He said: 'I believe that it is much more for the purpose of feeling that the horse makes use of his nose—as we would our hands. It is the only organ by which he can touch or feel anything with much susceptibility.'[2] He maintained that it was the handling of the horse, the stroking, fondling and talking or *whispering* that soothed the horse and not the scent itself. 'How long do you suppose a horse would have to stand and smell a bottle of oil before

[1] Opium or laudanum was easily available in East Anglia at the time the *Notebook* was compiled (1893). See *Fenland Opium Eating in the Nineteenth Century* by Virginia Berridge, *The British Journal of Addiction*, 72, Longman, 1977.

[2] *The Art of Taming Horses*, p. 45.

he would learn to bend the knee and make a bow at your bidding?'
Rarey asked with rather heavy irony.

But the country horsemen I have come in contact with would not
expect any such spectacular manœuvre to follow from a use of the
oils. Their purpose was to engage the curiosity or to titillate the interest of a nervous horse with a sweet-smelling scent merely to make
initial contact with him. Having done this it was up to them to use
other devices in their armoury to bring the horse to accept their control.[3] Compared with those other means the importance of the oils—
the drawing oils especially—is minimal; but this is not to say that a
knowledge of them is useless. I have collected many examples from
the countryside where an appreciation of the acuteness of a horse's
sense of smell has been useful. Here is an example from the Big House.
The squire had been up in Scotland shooting; and he had brought
back a good supply of venison with him. In the event the supply of
meat was too ample, and the household was tired of it before it was
all consumed. The remnant was buried in the park not far from the
drive to the main gate, and the episode of the venison was apparently
forgotten. But for weeks afterwards the coachman experienced great
difficulty in getting his horses past the spot where the venison was
buried.

The importance of the personal odour of the horse handler was
also recognized by the older East Anglian horsemen, and they often
capitalized on this by keeping some of their drawing or attracting
'tit-bits' about their person before giving them to the horse. A frequent injunction in horsemen's notebooks was: 'Sweat the cakes under
your armpits', that is, before giving them to the horse. Again, modern
horse-trainers have learned to take precautions not to confuse a young
horse during his training: 'We don't take a bath after we begin work
on halter-breaking on foals; or working with unbroken horses. The
less change a horse has to accept in his environment—and that includes scent—the better.'[4]

Concerning this question of the importance of scent or bodily odour,
it is worth noting that a member of the Society of the Horseman's
Word in Scotland is said, by virtue of his expertise as a horseman,

[3] See for example the drawing on p. 135: wadding soaked in laudanum
and fixed to a horse's bit to quieten him.
[4] Jeff Edwards, The Wild Horse Research Farm, California, *Cruiser Courier*,
April 1977.

to have an equal ability to handle a woman. Perhaps he used the same technique as the Balinese male in courting a woman: he could more easily win over his dance partner by wiping her brow with a handkerchief he kept beneath his arm. But in the Scottish Society after the horse has been attracted by the scent the sequence is clearly laid down: that is, 'the five points of feeling' in the horse (still part of the secret lore of the Society) were then exploited. They were referred to by a member of the Society: 'Well, of course that is again one of the secrets. But I can say this much: a horse has five points of feeling, and the theory is that if it is an unruly beast, difficult to master, you attack (attack is not the right word but it's as near as I can get) you attack the horse through these points of feeling, one by one; or if you are clever enough, all at once. And if you master them one by one or all at once, then you are master of that horse; and he will eventually follow you like a doggy.'

But the most striking aspect of the material contributed by Mervyn Cater is his account of his father's carefully cultivated *identity* with his horses: he lived with them, played with them and almost gave his whole life to them. But this was nothing unusual, as I have observed, with farm horsemen of the old school in Suffolk: they lived for their horses and they could well be excused disputing with the farmer and telling him that while they were under their care they were not his horses but theirs. I have also gained some information concerning this conscious building up of an identity with the horse from a member of the Society of the Horseman's Word. And it seems to me that this is the most remarkable quality that distinguishes the old regime of the horse on the farms in Britain, and not the more spectacular calling and jading of the horses and the dramatic, exhibitionist tricks through which certain horsemen paraded their skills and built up their reputations.

Norman Halkett (born 1910), a farmer's son from Aberdeenshire, has described this as he saw it a half-century ago on the farms of north-east Scotland, and later when he became a member of the Society. When the Society was fully active, with horses working on all the farms, this bond between horse and man was ritualized and regularly reinforced in the meetings of the Society. Moreover it appears that the secret *word* that was given to an entrant at his initiation into the Society had no magic pretensions at all but was a symbol of this identity between the horse and the horseman. ('But the greatest mastery over the horse is obtained by none of these things but through the power of the *word* itself, that is the applied psychology of the word, which if you can make it work, will do far more than attacking the horse through the five points of feeling.') It was also something more than a symbol: it was an ideal to which the horseman would be persuaded to aspire to if he wished to have complete and permanent control over his horses, a control that was gained not by fear or discipline but by a mutual trust. This, too, was enshrined in the oath taken at entry to the Society: 'There was the taking of a very definite oath, an oath which holds the horse just as sacred as your fellow horsemen. This is important because to my mind it is the basis of this enormous bond that has always existed between the farm servant and the horse.' The Scottish ploughman, so it appears, had at his finger-tips all the skills, the herbs, the drawing oils and so on that were possessed by his East Anglian counterpart. But he had something more in his possession of the secret behind the *word*: 'It is a kind of marriage in which every time you think the horse will react. It is something almost psychic. It does not depend—wholly, anyway—on a practical handling of the horse. As I've said it is psychological.'

The inculcation of this attitude in the mind of the initiate was the chief purpose of the initiation ceremony of the Society of the Horseman's Word. In this it is exactly similar to the puberty initiation ceremonies of the primitive[5] where the young boys are inducted into the clan, and where the relation of the initiate and his fellows to one another and to the totem animal, representing the clan in depth, was defined and ritualized. As for instance in the Scottish Society, the horse was as much a 'brother', a member of the group, as the horsemen; and their relationship with him was ideally no different from their relationship with one another. And if a horseman was seen to be treating his horse in any way that did not consort with this ideal relationship, the wrath of the other members would fall upon him.

This kind of relationship is undoubtedly a totemic one, and it is likely that we are here concerned with a pattern of behaviour that goes back to man's first involvement with animals. Totemism, it is admitted, is a very tricky term to handle, especially since we are told[6] that there are at least forty-one different theories about the term's meaning. It

---

[5] Mircea Eliade, *Rites and Symbols of Initiation*, Harper Torchbooks, New York, 1965, *passim*.

[6] Claude Levi Strauss, *Totemism*, Merlin Press, London, 1963, p. 33.

would be as well, therefore, to make a tentative definition for the sake of the present discussion. Totemism was essentially the religion of tribal society: each clan of the tribe identified itself with a natural object called its totem, and members of the clan looked upon themselves as being at one with the totem species—usually an animal or a plant. This is what, in plain terms, kept the clan alive; gave them sustenance. And their religious ceremonies were performed in order to ensure that the numbers of the totem animal or plant would never fail but would, instead, increase. It has been suggested that totemism arose out of the primitive horde for the better sharing of the food supply in its environment. At first, one group would appropriate one animal or plant for its sustenance; another group another, and so on. From this mechanical division where groups or clans formed disparate parts of the whole—the tribe—there was a progression in course of time to a stage where the tribe gradually became more integrated by a further development: each clan would henceforth be responsible for its own totem—chiefly the celebration of the increase rites—but instead of consuming the totem as before, it would conserve it for the use of the other clans, and the eating of the clan totem was *taboo* to its own members: it was sanctified, only to be eaten ceremonially on special ritual occasions. Thus following this theory the whole totemic complex was engendered by early man's dire economic need; but as he refined his techniques for getting a living from his environment, passing out of the more primitive modes of food production, the totemic system lost its economic basis, and was changed into a magico-religious system that became an analogue for the structure of society in which the system had developed. What remained was the feeling of kinship within the clan, the practice of exogamy,[7] and as stated, a ritual eating of a little of the totem by the clan chief or 'priest'—a 'getting of the totem inside him' the better to perform the necessary ceremonies.

The relevant point here is that the clan animal was an equal member of the clan along with the human beings; and it is suggested that it is this feeling that had persisted in country communities which, until the last seventy or eighty years, were in many respects not all that much removed from their primitive prototypes. The horse here is equal brother to his keeper: this was given ritual significance, and it

[7] This, too, probably had its origin in a practical stimulus: the need to circulate the food supply.

is this feeling that comes out of a study of traditional farm horsemen, and it is this that is given prominence in the ceremonies of the Society of the Horseman's Word and symbolic representation in the Society's secret word.

It may, however, be objected that it is attempting to stretch credulity too far to ask the reader to believe that what has obtained among farm horsemen here in twentieth-century Britain has its roots in a past as remote as the time when primitive tribes had a full totem organization. At first glance it may seem incredible; but we can point to two 'totemic' survivals which will possibly make an objector pause before he dismisses the suggestion as frivolous. First, the taboo on the eating of horse-flesh is, as far as we know, as absolute today as it must have been in pre-Roman times when there was a dominant horse-cult in these islands. And we have recently[8] had a strong confirmation of the fixity of this taboo when there was an outcry about the serving of horse-flesh in the form of steaks at certain transport cafés in East Anglia. It was even stated that heavy horses, the Shires, were the victims. This rumour was dismissed by a Shire Horse official as 'a load of rubbish'. Again, without impugning the validity of their religious symbolism, it can be pointed out that the ceremonies both of the Mass and the Communion are in direct line with the totemic original.

Primitive origins are frequently traceable in many horse matters. The expertise of many claimants to complete control over a horse is said to come from primitive sources. James (Dan) Sullivan, the prototype of the horse-whisper, got his secret by chance:[9] 'Sullivan's own account of the secret was that he originally acquired it from a wearied soldier who had not money to pay for a pint of porter he had drunk. The landlord was retaining part of his kit as a pledge when Sullivan, who sat in the bar, vowed he would never see a hungry man want, and gave the soldier so good a luncheon that in his gratitude he drew him aside at parting and revealed what he believed to be an Indian charm.' In recent years Barbara Woodhouse has written about her method of breaking wild horses on a lonely cattle ranch in Argentina,[10] and she says that she first heard of the technique from an old Guaranee Indian. He told her that they do not break their horses in the Western

---

[8] BBC, *Look East*, 14 April 1977.
[9] *The Art of Taming Horses*, J. S. Rarey, p. 9.
[10] *Talking to Animals*, Faber and Faber, 1954.

manner: 'they catch them with a lasso and then stand near them, with their hands behind their backs, and blow gently down their nostrils. The horse understands this as "How do you do?" in its own language and returns the greeting by approaching the human being and sniffing up his nose. From that moment the horse has no further fear, and breaking is simply a matter of showing the horse what you want.'

It would be a good place to interpolate Jennie Caldwell's experience here: 'I've never come across a really difficult horse, not a really bad one. Some are a bit awkward but they come all right in the end. Talk to them nicely. I keep talking to them. Some people believe I'm daft, I think! Breathing down the nostrils. I've done that. I found that with a filly when we were trying to load her up in the van. She was going cranky. I tried that—breathing into the nostrils, and she came up—as good as gold. Several times I've done it. Some will respond though, and some not. It doesn't seem to work with every horse. We had a foal that used to nip me a lot—when its mother was there, quite often. I breathed down its nostrils and it never tried to bite me after that. Good as gold since.'

Another method comes from the North American Plains Indians who would tame an unbroken but mature horse to endure a rider on its back—within an hour. This was by means of the so-called Indian Blanket Act. The main principle used is the one exploited by Walter Cater: 'In first getting to know a colt stand still, remain passive, and let the colt come to you.' Here is a description of the Blanket Act.[11] 'The Indian's horse would first be driven into a small corral, but a corral not so small as to infringe upon the animal's flight distance—the distance between a horse and a threatening object at which point the horse feels he must flee or fight. The coralled horse's attention was held with a soft undulating robe, blanket or mackinaw. Being careful not to excite the horse or to overstep the "flight distance" boundary, the Indian operator kept the horse's attention fixed on the blanket. Such a technique allowed a horse to examine at his leisure and with the senses of sight, sound, smell and touch the "frightening" blanket and operator.

'The Indian technique did not excite muscular tension associated with physical resistance, and the horse soon advances to the performer and stands quietly, totally without emotional expression of any kind, excepting possibly an unusual feeling of attachment for the

[11] *The Cruiser Courier*, December 1976, Vol. 2 No. 4, pp. 2–3.

performer', explains Dr George Dawson, an eye-witness to the results of the Indian Blanket Act.

Dr Dawson also recorded that both the horse and the Indian Medicine Man 'were blanketed in brilliant scarlet, giving the appearance or thought that they were blanketed together, more or less "a unity of all life".' This last phrase is of intense interest in that it duplicates the key symbolism that is so important in the Scottish Horseman's Society.

Jack Leeder (born 1901) of Knapton, North Walsham, Norfolk was a farm horseman for most of his working life; and he is a witness to the bond that grew up between the horse and his handler who spent most of his day working with and tending him:

'Rushing about in cars and the speed of modern living, and we are no happier than we were years ago. It would take a week to get somewhere: today we take an hour; and we are no happier and no more forward; and I think that's the same with nearly everything at work. I used to get up in the morning, five o'clock to feed my horses. I'd whistle and they'd come; and I'd put the halter on them and they came; they'd go down to the farm. Now when you went across that field (I'm not a very good sort of bloke at all: I don't mean that at all!), but if you couldn't believe there was a Higher Power than you when you used to see the trees bursting into bloom, your horses neighing to you when you came to them, the feeling you had between you! I had a blind horse, and we had a bond between us: you talked to him; you loved him; he loved me, I'm sure he did. He relied on me —which way to turn and everything. It was a marvellous thing when he went away: he went away for horse-meat to Belgium! I wouldn't have minded if they'd shot him on the place and had went off then. He was blind and I could see him being hit on the head: of course, he didn't know where to go. They didn't realize that horse had to work for them and had earned them pounds of money! That was altogether wrong. If I'd ha' known—well, I cried when he went; and I wouldn't be ashamed to say so. My wife used to tell me that I thought more about my horses than I did about her. I didn't really. But there's something people miss: I can't explain what it is. It was a bond. It wasn't any trouble for me to feed them and groom them. I'd give any amount of time to them. I think if people could get back some of those ways with the horse to the countryside, with the trees bursting out and the butterflies and the cattle we'd be much happier.'

The subtlety of the link between a horse and his handler and the
the deep level at which communication is established is brought out
by the following two incidents. A friend, Frederick Foster, a Yorkshire-
man who latterly lived in Ipswich, told me of an experience he had
when he was a young man. After leaving the Army at the end of the
First World War he was unsettled and went to Canada to work on a
farm. On his first day there the foreman told him to go out into the
nearby paddock and bring the horse that was there into the stables.
He went out to get the horse and noticed that two or three of the
men in the yard were eyeing him with interest, but he paid little regard; and he brought the horse in without any trouble. But after he
had stabled him one of the men came up and said to him:

'That horse is a killer. He put a man down a few days ago!'

It is unlikely that the horse would have come in to the stable so
willingly if the handler had been warned of his temperament *before*
he went out to get him.

The second incident was related by Ron Wood, the stud groom at
Hollesley Bay Colony:

'There is one thing I'd like to tell you: we are always hearing this
tale of telepathy between horseman and horse. My predecessor, Mr
Andrews—we were talking one day about this, and he gave me an instance that happened with him. He had a young [unbroken] horse in
the stable alongside a horse that was working, doing a day's work.
Now a young chap who hadn't been in the stable long—he didn't
know one horse from another—he harnessed this young horse that
had never had anything on it but a head-collar. Mr Andrews noticed
this horse going along the lane, this two-year-old horse that had never
been harnessed before: it was going along quite happily with the lad.
So he thought quietly to himself: "I don't know what to do about
this." So he got on his bicycle and cycled past the lad and the horse
and said to him:

"When you get to the end will you turn your horse round and go
back to the stud?"

'Which the lad did. He led that horse round and put it in the stable.
The point of this story is that it must have a bearing on this telepathy—between the nervousness of the handler and the horse. This
horse was quite at ease because this lad thought in all respects that
it was his horse, the one he had been working with all day. I thought
this brought the point of the argument out very well.'

An exhaustive examination and recording of such 'extra-sensory' experiences and of the irrational practices discussed in the last two chapters is justified in my view for more than one reason. First, a lot of sound practical horse-lore is bound up with them; second, they illustrate how prevalent these practices were in the old country communities that have been displaced in this century. Most of them were centred in the horse because the horse—at least during the last three or four centuries and right up to the first quarter of this—was the chief motive power in the cultivation of the land as well as in transport and communications. Third, they also illustrate that although the practitioners of horse magic were few and far between they had a disproportionate effect on the corpus of beliefs in their community: they were given credence by a large number of their contemporaries simply out of the inexplicable success of their practices, and it is not surprising that they were referred to as witches. This comes out in the two previous chapters where Walter Cater's practices were so mysterious and effective that many, even of his fellow-workers on the same farm, had the suspicion that he was using black magic: as his son, Mervyn observed many of them, not knowing the way these feats were performed and their solidly rational basis for them, took them for witchcraft.

The following account, given me by a Suffolk horseman who was born in 1893 and died a few years ago, shows how near some of their practices in fact were to what is commonly known as witchcraft. He lived in a village where many of the cottages are semi-detached. They were known locally as 'double dwellers', and the two families shared a common chimney structure:

'When my wife was alive she couldn't get on with the people who lived next door. They used to worry her. So one night I told her:

"Don't you worry, gel; I'll see to 'em."

'I took a few hairs out of the nape of my neck and put 'em in a saucepan with some chemical—*aqua fortis*. Then I sealed the window and the doors; and I told her to sit quiet and not to be afraid. And as it got near midnight I put the saucepan on the fire, and we both waited quite still. Presently the saucepan began to boil: suddenly there was a loud roaring and shouting in the chimney. And that was the end of it!

"What happened?"

"Well, the beggars next door, they were gone in six months!"

The old horseman believed very firmly that having gone through this ritual he was instrumental in causing his neighbours to move. That they would probably have moved in any event was ruled out by the tenacity of his belief in a traditional practice that was more appropriate to the sixteenth and seventeenth centuries than the twentieth.

To illustrate the widespread nature of the belief among farm workers, who were not within the inner ring, that these men were practising witchcraft, here are further instances from a different part of the region: Walter Hurst, a Hengrave (west Suffolk) farm worker did not himself believe in the frog's or toad's bone complex, but he was of the opinion that those who practised it believed in nothing but the Devil: 'They could make their horses do anything. They could leave their horses so that they couldn't move. And it wouldn't do for anyone to go near their horses.' His friend George Jolly, a farm worker from the same village, told me:

'I knew a man who could do what he liked with horses. He used to live down near here. He'd come up the road with his wagon this old boy would and leave his wagon outside his house with two young horses. The thrashing tackle was going by one morning and they stopped when they saw this wagon with the two young horses. One of the men went to his door and called out: "Ted, you'll have to come out and look to your horses. We won't go by until you come out!" He said:

"You goo togither," he say, "they'll be all right."

'Of course they went by, and he carried on with his breakfast. And they were right young horses, and as they came by on the road they didn't turn a hair. Whether he had a toad or not I don't know. He never even came to the door to see how they were going by.

'And there was this man from Wickhambrook. His name was Keel. He could knock on the barn door and the door would fly open. Just the same with the fowls. When he wanted a fowl he'd go at night, and he'd have a stick. He'd put this stick in the *slip*, the little hole in the side where the fowls came out in the morning, he put his stick through and just tickle the hen's feet and they'd light on his stick one by one, and he'd take 'em out and put 'em in the crates he had—without opening the barn door. People used to think he'd been through this frog's bone thing. I don't know whether he had or whether he hadn't. He was a rare owd bo'. He could do anything. Chickens, horses— whatever you want. But whether he had any toad-skills I don't know.'

There was also a widespread fear and suspicion of the special skills of the old horsemen, and a belief that whoever dabbled in them would become unhinged. Jack Leeder spoke of this:

'I mentioned about trying to get one of these toads' bones years ago. But I was advised by an older man not to have anything to do with it because he said he knew one or two men and they had finished up in the madhouse. That's what he said. I don't know if there's any truth in it or not. My father's grandfather, he was supposed to have them: he worked with Lord Hastings. I know he'd do anything with a horse—lay it down and so on. He was supposed to have the bone; but he went wrong. But I would have liked to have known how to get the toad. It's a running toad, and you put it in an ant-hill and so on, and when you are getting it—this bone that goes upstream—the Devil is there with you. I would have liked to have tested it. But there are a good many people believe it. The older generation did believe it. But I cannot vouch for it.'

Roger Clark and his wife, Cheryl, gave me additional material about the toad's bone, and the practice of jading a horse:

'I've heard a very interesting piece about the frog's or toad's bone business. This was from another chap who'd been a horseman and his variation of the thing was this: you went through this business of the running stream and this, that and the other; but when you got the bone, you then boiled it and you got the power from a wild rose. The briar—that was as thick as your finger, and you cut that off and you dipped one end in the water or whatever you were boiling the frog's bone in. That was supposed to do the job. Why I don't know: I've never heard that before but I thought it was worth recording.

'The nearest I've got to the secret of the frog's bone—I believe— was what I got from a gamekeeper. A horseman at Boxford Hall where he was an apprentice gamekeeper used to ask for a stoat and a rabbit together; where a stoat had killed a rabbit—if he could shoot the two together. Apparently he wanted the liver from both of them.'

Cheryl Clarke, Roger's wife, confirmed this reaction of a horse that is implied here: 'This is a fact! Can you remember a horse I took up this lane and it suddenly stopped? It was absolutely terrified, and I got off it. And there was a stoat killing a rabbit and I could not get that horse by. I'm sure that there is some substance in connection with the stoat and the rabbit, perhaps just as it's being killed, that is so offensive to a horse's sense of smell you can't get him past it.'

A similar incident happened to Charles Rookyard, an old Helmingham horseman: like the horseman mentioned above he had a special interest in the stoat's encounter with the rabbit. He was ploughing a field with a pair of horses when they suddenly stopped for no apparent reason. Being an experienced horseman he made no attempt to urge them forward but looked round to discover what had frightened them:

'My surprise was there was a rabbit about forty yards away. This rabbit started shrieking which upset my horses. So I got them into another stetch and watched. There was a stoat after the rabbit. The rabbit was mesmerized by the scent of the stoat. And it went round until it got right to the wind: as soon as it got into the wind that approached the rabbit and collared it behind the ears—and that was finished. Well, for my horse I had a bit of the rabbit and I had a bit of the inside of the stoat. I cut that up and dried it; made it into powder and mixed it with other chemicals. And with this I could leave my horses, and I could go home into the farmyard and they'd still be standing there nice and comfortable when I came back. I'd also stick a stick up and walk to the top of the field; and I didn't want to turn round to see if my horses were all right. They still stood there. And I'd also get my entire horse on the road or any other place, and just give him of this chemical. I'd hold my stick up and walk forty yards backwards. Time I held the stick up he daren't move; but as soon as I put my stick on the road he knew what that meant: he would come forward and put his nose on my shoulder.'

Roger Clark uses cord to master a difficult horse:

'I've got access to an American book that shows methods of breaking colts that have never been handled; and using the method in there I'll lay a £100 I could get any horse to follow me right round the yard after twenty minutes. That's using no oils! That's just a little bit of cord. I believe half these horse-tamers knew this trick. I've done it dozens of times on horses bad to shoe or to clip. I'm not saying that it will work every time. There's always a variation of these methods. Now Captain Hayes—the horse authority—he wrote a very good book on horse-breaking, and a lot of these methods are in there. Now his methods were very quick and effective and I'm sure that a lot of it was with cords.'

It is worth recording that many old farm horsemen have also told me that they used cords with some of their horses. One particular horseman revealed that he was careful to choose or make a cord that had the same colour as the horse's coat so that it was invisible except under very close inspection. Undoubtedly many used a hair plucked out of the horse's own tail as did Walter Cater when he made the horse limp (p. 126).

Roger Clark said that he had tried oils and he had tried cords and he would prefer cords every time: 'It makes an impression on a horse. If you know where to put a cord on a horse you can get him to follow you round the yard; and this is how the circus people did it: this business of a horse pushing you from behind. That's how that was done. And the best part about it is it doesn't make a horse *head-shy*: it makes him more friendly towards you because he knows he can't get away from you. As long as a horse will recognize that you are the boss he will be happy.

'I've puzzled it out a lot: when you weigh it up you take a piece of cord in your inside pocket—nobody can see that—and if you've got something you can just get up to the horse; and you can put this cord on the horse. Then you've got him: you can sit in the manger and let him get on with it. This would probably answer for the fact that no commotion was ever heard in the stable—or very little. You don't get any commotion. I've shod very bad horses when I'm by myself, and I've gone for that every time. But I'm not saying—well, there's no method when you can say you're a hundred per cent sure it can work every time. But if you've got a variation of it there isn't many jobs you can't get round with it. We break in a lot of colts here: we do several. We have all sorts; and ten to one the ones we get are those that other people have managed to mess about.'

Additional proof that many of the old horsemen actively believed in witchcraft—up to the period of the First World War, and in some instances long after it—came from a Suffolk harness-maker, Leonard Aldous. He was born at Debenham in 1900 and I recorded him in 1964. He told me then about the use of the witch- or *hag-stone*[12]: I have collected further examples of its use from horsemen after this occasion. Although many men followed the old custom of hanging a holed flint above the horse's back when he was stabled at night, they had no real knowledge of the rationale of its supposed power. They kept up the custom out of inertia, following it and believing it as a vague but reassuring gesture that would enable them to keep on the

[12] See *P.U.P.*, Chapter 18.

right side of Fortune; and what they were doing more or less consciously was to invest in an old talisman simply as an insurance against bad luck descending on their stables. But a minority of horsemen undoubtedly believed that hanging a holed flint on a wire above the back of the stabled horse would prevent the hag or the witch mounting to ride him.

The hag-stone was also used in the cowhouse or *shippen*. Rachel Young, who is a tutor with the University of Cambridge Board of Extra Mural Studies, remembers seeing one during the last war. She was in the Women's Land Army and was working on a farm in the parish of Gonerby, near Grantham in Lincolnshire. She and the farmer were responsible for milking thirty cows by hand every morning and afternoon. One morning the farmer noticed that the hag-stone which always rested on the window-sill of the shippen was not in its usual place. He became very anxious and insisted that it must be found before they could begin the milking.

'There was a very queer atmosphere altogether about that occasion,' Rachel Young recalled. 'It was four o'clock in the morning and the only light we had—because of the black-out regulations—was a candle in a bucket. He kept saying "It must be found!" Eventually we found the stone under the bedding straw in one of the stalls, and we were able to start milking. The farmer didn't tell me why all this was necessary; but an old man who worked on the farm said afterwards: "The milk wouldn't have *come down* unless the stone was where it should be." '

As we have seen with the horse there is a strong reaction between the behaviour of an animal and the subjective state of its handler. We can therefore assume (with regard to the fifteen cows the farmer himself was responsible for) that the milk would indeed have not come down had the stone been missing. The farmer believed implicitly in its peculiar property, and his anxiety that it was not in its usual place plus the tension that this induced would have finally communicated itself to the animals. They would then have withheld their milk—a well-known phenomenon where cows have been disturbed at milking time.

Harold Smart (1889–1973), another horseman from the Hargrave area of Suffolk, recalled that in addition to the toad's bone another ingredient was used in the ritual to ensure that a man 'had the power'. This was the spores of the bracken—*fernseed*. This was traditionally supposed to have magical properties: it was linked with thunder and lightning; and in some parts of Britain pulling up a fern was believed to bring on a storm. It was also said to endow its possessor with invisibility. Referring to the preceding generation of horsemen, he told me:

'They used to go down anywhere where there was bracken growing, down to a brook or a bit of disused land or anything. There's some in this village. There's what is called an old *planten* [plantation], near a sort of a river. They used to say they'd go down there and gather it: they had to go at twelve o'clock at night and gather this bracken seed. They used to make out that thunder and lightning and rain came down. Well, they used to get this bracken seed and they brought that home. Then they'd find a toad, one of these *water toads* and put it in an ant-hill, make a hole and bury it till the ants ate the flesh—which they will—and they used to get these bones and then go to a stream in the middle of the night and pick out the bone that would go upstream; and that's the bone they carried.'

A fourth reason for treating these old country beliefs, however irrational or fantastical, with the seriousness they deserve, relates to the potential enlightenment they hold for the historian. In my own experience, after living in different villages in East Anglia for over forty years and having extensive contact with the generation of country people who came to maturity before the First World War, I have become convinced that peasant attitudes and beliefs did not change for centuries; and it is only in the younger generations that they have changed appreciably within this present century. The oldest generation I came into contact with and recorded—the people born about 1880—had lived in a different era. Their attitudes and beliefs had been acquired before the break-up of the traditional rural communities: they were *historical* attitudes as compared with their contemporaries' in the towns. My contact with this particular generation—not only in East Anglia but in Wales, Scotland and Ireland, most especially Ireland, and through working in the field and assessing attitudes and beliefs indirectly while searching for material on other topics, has given me the absolute conviction that as far as folk beliefs and even religion are concerned, earlier centuries—the seventeenth century, for instance—did not end in 1700 but continued in most rural areas of Britain and Ireland up to the first quarter of the present century and the opening up of the old communities in the critical years following 1914. Yet it is worth repeating here that the historical longevity of peasant beliefs, attitudes and customs has been remarked upon and demonstrated as long as seventy years ago when John Cuthbert Lawson[13] went to Greece with the purpose of finding out whether or not the beliefs of the people of classical Greece were at all reflected in those of the contemporary peasant communities. His researches convinced him that ancient beliefs and customs had lasted in vigorous and almost identical form right up to the twentieth century. Nearer to our time there is strong evidence that the seventeenth century, in respect of religious beliefs, is still with us, at least to the degree that the phrase Walter Scott used in *Old Mortality* to describe the seventeenth-century troubles in Scotland—the *killing time*—can still be used about the present, not dissimilar conflict in Northern Ireland.

On this showing it would seem unscholarly for historians here in Britain to ignore researching the attitudes and beliefs of the survivors of the old communities if their concern has any relation to religion or folk beliefs. It would, too, seem naïve for them to take the documentary evidence of seventeenth-century witch trials, for instance, at their face value without an examination of similar practices that were traditional in country communities and which have survived up to recent times.

[13] *Modern Greek Folklore and Ancient Greek Religion*, Cambridge, 1910 (recently reissued in USA as a paperback).

# *13*

# Nineteenth-Century Horse-Tamers

During the period of the late 'Fifties while trying to get a full picture of the farm horse in Suffolk and the farming and the men associated with him, I came across the names of many of the well-known horse-trainers or tamers—either through the memories of the old horse-men themselves or through the notebooks they had compiled for their own use. Two men were outstanding and most often mentioned: James (or Dan) Sullivan, the original *Whisperer*, and James Samuel Rarey. Rarey was first brought to my notice by a sketch in a Suffolk horse-man's notebook,[1] and he was also referred to by Herman Biddell, the compiler of Volume One of the *Suffolk Horse Stud Book* (pp. 653–4). Rarey took in hand a vicious horse, Barthropp's *Hero 88* (that had recently killed his handler), and tamed him on the stage before a London audience.

Rarey was the best-known and probably the most skilled of the numerous horse-tamers of the last century. He was a young American farmer from Ohio, and his early training involved the 'breaking in' of horses of five or six years old, horses that had run wild until that mature age. At first he used the old English rough-rider method which meant getting on a horse's back and riding him until he was subdued. In the course of his work Rarey was said to have broken nearly every bone in his body. Understandably, he was not satisfied with this tech-nique and sought a new one. He got to know the methods of wander-ing horsemen and circus trainers, and read every book he could come by about the training of horses. He claimed that by this research and study he had arrived at the principles of horse management that had made him famous.

The main principle he used was identical with that of the primitives: gentling rather than breaking the animal, treating him as an equal and identifying with him as much as possible. It was a principle that

---

[1] *P.U.P.*, p. 250; see also p. 154 here.

had been established as early as the time of Xenophon, who wrote: 'Horses are taught not by Harshness but by Gentleness.'

A contemporary wrote:[2] 'The value of Mr Rarey's system consists in the fact that it may be taught to, and successfully practised by, a ploughboy of thirteen or fourteen for use on all except extremely vicious and powerful horses. It requires patience—it requires the habit of dealing with horses as well as coolness; but the real work is rather a matter of skill than strength. Not only have boys of five or six stone become successful horse-tamers, but ladies of high rank have in the course of ten minutes perfectly subdued and reduced to death-like calmness fiery blood-horses.'

An example of Rarey's technique is his way of driving a colt from a pasture:[3] 'Go to the pasture and walk round the whole herd quietly, and at such a distance as not to cause them to scare and run. Then approach very slowly, if they stick up their heads and seem to be frightened, stand still until they become quiet, so as not to make them run before you are close enough to drive them in the direction you want them to go. And when you begin to drive, do not flourish your arms or halloo, but gently follow them off, leaving the direction open that you wish them to take. Thus taking advantage of their ignorance, you will be able to get them into the pound as easily as the hunter drives the quails into his net.'

Or his directions for stabling a colt without trouble: 'The next step will be, to get the horse into a stable or shed. This should be done as quietly as possible so as not to excite any suspicion in the horse of danger befalling him. The best way to do this is to lead an already broken horse into the stable first, and hitch [tie] him; then quietly walk round the colt and let him go in of his own accord.' Go slow, that is: *Haste makes waste.*

As already implied above, this method of gentling will not work with a vicious horse, a horse that has a high spirit that someone has tried to *break* unsuccessfully instead of attempting to win him over by quieter means. To meet the problem of the vicious horse, Rarey devised or adapted a method of laying a horse down, throwing him by tying up one of his forelegs, and gagging him if necessary. Rarey

[2] *The Art of Taming Horses*, by J. S. Rarey. A New Edition with great additions and illustrations, by the Hunting Correspondent of the *Illustrated London News*, G. Routledge, London, 1858, p. 12.

[3] *ibid.*, p. 40.

claimed that this method soon makes the horse feel that the handler is his superior, and yet at the same time neither excites his terror or his hatred. The horse was left to struggle until he realized that he could not get up except by leave of his handler. It was a drastic form of treatment but it was necessary for a horse that had been spoiled or made vicious by wrong usage. The horse had to be de-sensitized or de-conditioned and by Rarey's method it was done in such a way that would convince the horse that the man was on his side, was his friend and not, as he had previously experienced, his enemy.

Rarey's method of tying a horse before casting him

The instructions for tying up the horse are not complicated but the manner in which it was done was all-important. The instructions[4] begin with: 'Take up one forefoot and bend his knee till his hoof is bottom upwards and nearly touching his body; then slip a loop over his knee and up until it comes above the pastern-joint, to keep it up, being careful to draw the loop together between the hoof and the pastern-joint with a second strap of some kind to prevent the loop from slipping down and coming off. This will leave the horse standing on three legs; you can now handle him as you wish; for it is utterly impossible for him to kick in this position. There is something in the operation of taking up one foot that conquers a horse quicker and better than anything else you can do to him. . . .' And so on for the rest of the instructions until the horse gives up after he is thrown and lies completely passive.

[4] *ibid.*, pp. 68 ff.

But the distinctive element in Rarey's approach, even in this patently forceful method, is emphasized throughout. The horse is not thrown out of vindictiveness but out of necessity, and even while he is engaged in throwing the horse the handler is already starting to win him over. Like every other operation involving the horse it was done gently and accompanied by soothing words: 'Come along. Come along, old fellow!' but with a complete absence of chatter. It is an ironic comment on nineteenth-century horsemanship that Rarey's technique of throwing a vicious horse got more publicity than the philosophy that underlay his general approach to horse training. But this is perhaps understandable, as the casting of the horse was dramatic and, moreover, could be learned by rote and was easier to absorb than the nuances of Rarey's advocacy of an entirely new attitude to the training of a young horse. Again, forceful methods were more in the spirit of the age during the last century. Authority spoke and those who were commanded must obey without question or demur. And exactly the same technique was used both in subduing spirited, young children and in training colts: Be completely in command; and if either child or colt shows resistance mercilessly break its spirit.

But what brought Rarey, an American, to Britain? In the course of his work in the United States, travelling about and teaching the horse-training method he had devised, Rarey met a New Englander called Goodenough, 'a sort of Barnum', who realized that there was money to be made out of Rarey and his technique. He formed a partnership with him and persuaded him to show his skills in Canada. There he came to the notice of General Sir William Eyre, commander of the armed forces. General Eyre was impressed, and—probably at Goodenough's request—gave Rarey letters of introduction to the Horse Guards in Britain, and to several people close to Queen Victoria. The burden of his recommendation was: 'the system [Rarey's] was new to him, and valuable for military purposes.'

Rarey and Goodenough arrived in England in 1858, and shortly after landing Rarey gave proof of his skills by taming a black or iron-grey horse that had been returned by Sir Matthew White Ridley to a horse-dealer as unridable because of his viciousness. Rarey was then introduced to Tattersall of Hyde Park Corner, a firm that even at this date was nearly a century old and had established a world-wide reputation for fair dealing. Tattersall investigated Rarey's system and pronounced that it would be of immense benefit to horses and horsemen in general, and that it would do away with a great deal of the severity and cruelty then practised on the best-bred and most high-spirited animals through the ignorance of those whose business it was to break in colts and handle horses.

By subduing the black horse Rarey had made good his claim to tame the most vicious animal brought to him; and he got entry, with Tattersall's backing, into the highest 'horse circles' in the country. But a difficulty arose about the question of how he was to be paid. His methods were so simple that once taught to another person it could afterwards easily become common knowledge and would put him out of business. Tattersall generously agreed, after consulting with Rarey's patrons, to open a list at their Hyde Park Corner headquarters for subscribers to a course of training in horse handling, to be conducted by Rarey at a cost of ten guineas to each subscriber, 'each signing an agreement—under a penalty of £500—not to teach or divulge Mr Rarey's method and Messrs Tattersall undertaking to hold the subscriptions in trust until Mr Rarey had performed his part of the agreement'. Just after the list was opened Rarey left for Paris and there tamed a vicious coaching stallion called Stafford. On his return he found that the subscription list had mustered only 320 names, much fewer than expected. But he started his course on 20 March 1858 in the private riding school of the Duke of Wellington. The first meeting was a private lesson to a select party of noblemen and gentlemen including Lord Palmerston and Admiral Rous of the Jockey Club. Their favourable report began to fill out the list of subscribers, many of whom were more stimulated out of curiosity and a desire not to miss a fashionable occasion than out of any compulsion to become horse-tamers.

But then came Rarey's greatest triumph so far: he subdued the notorious stallion Cruiser, the property of Lord Dorchester. Cruiser was favourite for the Derby in Wild Dayrell's year (1855), but broke down in training. He had the reputation for being the most vicious stallion in Britain: 'He could do more fighting in less time than any horse in the world.' His groom was once ordered to take him from one stable to another with the injunction that he was not to put him in an inn-stable or anything like that on the way: if he did he would never get the horse out. The groom, however, developed a distressing thirst on their journey and put up the horse in a country inn-stable while he went in for a drink. The outcome was that the roof of the building had to be pulled off before they could get the horse out. Lord Dorchester described the occasion when Rarey tamed this stallion:

'Greywell, April 7, 1858

Mr Rarey, when here, first subjugated a two-year old filly, perfectly unbroken. This he accomplished under half an hour, riding on her, opening an umbrella, beating a drum upon her, etc. He then took Cruiser in hand, and in three hours Mr Rarey and myself mounted him. He had not been ridden for nearly three years, and was so vicious that it was impossible even to dress him, and it was necessary to keep him muzzled constantly. The following morning Mr Rarey led him behind an open carriage, on his road to London. This horse was returned to me by Rawcliffe and Stud Company on account of his vice, it being considered as much as a man's life was worth to attend to him.

Dorchester.'

After his conquest of Cruiser the subscription list filled rapidly, and Rarey was obliged to move to a school in Kinnerton Street (Knightsbridge). Cruiser was brought here as evidence of Rarey's skill, and the crowd that gathered in the narrow street outside was made up of distinguished horsemen and a fashionable mob, including ladies of highest rank, offering ten-guinea subscriptions just to get into the school.

Originally it was agreed that at least 500 names should be on the subscription list before Rarey's lessons began. After the above episode the London subscription list alone passed 1,100 names. Added to this were the fees Rarey and his partner received in the provinces, in Dublin and in Paris. It was estimated that the enterprise realized upwards of £20,000 when the secrecy agreement with Rarey's subscribers was extinguished and he republished here in Britain a pamphlet (already issued in the USA) describing his method. In this Rarey had outlined his system, though it is to be doubted whether the bare instructions given there would enable an absolute novice to get very far in the art of horse-taming.

The above-mentioned book, *The Art of Taming Horses*, was issued in 1858, the year of Rarey's initial triumphs in Britain. It includes Rarey's pamphlet, edited and with additional notes and essays by the writer. Among these he gives a 'personal sketch' of the famous horse-tamer: [5]

'Mr Rarey is about thirty years of age, of middle height and well-proportioned figure, wiry and active rather than muscular—his complexion is almost effeminately fair, with more colour than is usually found in those of his countrymen who live in the cities of the sea-coast. And his fair hair, large grey eyes, which only light up and flash fire when he has an awkward customer to tackle, give him altogether the appearance of a Saxon Englishman. His walk is remarkably light and springy, yet regular, as he turns round his horse; something between the set-up of a soldier and the light step of a sportsman. Altogether his appearance and manners are eminently gentlemanly. Although a self-educated and not a book-educated man, his conversation, when he cares to talk (for he is rather reserved) always displays a good deal of thoughtful originality, relieved by flashes of playful humour.'

The writer went on to claim that Rarey, following the dissemination of his humane method of horse-handling, would rank among the great social reformers of the nineteenth century. Alas, this did not happen; and it would be interesting to speculate why Rarey's name remains comparatively unknown today, even among horse-lovers. Was it that he was attempting, with his advocacy of *festina lente*, or plain patience, to go right against the tide at a time when the horse was one of commerce's most important sources of power, when time was costly and a competitive urgency tended to drive out any considerations except those directly related to getting ahead and making a business pay? It certainly did not appear to have made—if we may judge by the observations on page 102—much impression on the training of Army horses in spite of the potential of Rarey's technique in this field being recognized even before he came to Britain.

Yet Rarey's immediate success must have been apparent, and news of it quickly crossed the Atlantic. For in the following spring a news item in an American periodical[6] announced that yet another American horse-tamer was packing his gear in Kentucky before making his way to what no doubt appeared to be a profitable field:

[5] p. 24.
[6] *Spirit of the Times*, 23 April 1859, Vol. XXIX, No. 11, p. 126. By courtesy of Freddie Steve Harris, Texas, and of *Cruiser Courier* (Sharon E. Creiger, editor).

*'Look Out, England!*

Denton Offutt, the original horse-tamer of the United States, who claims to have taught Rarey only twenty-six of the thirty-one great principles included under the head of his art, last week—per steam-ship—left for Southampton. It is his purpose to teach the art of tam-ing vicious animals to the nobility and gentry of Albion, and he claims that he can do all that was ever accomplished by Rarey, and something more. Offutt is an original in his way, and goes into the philosophy of things, not confining himself, like the curry-comb, to the surface of the horse but working his way under the skin and into the muscles and bones and developing what he is pleased to term "the magnetique and galvanick powers, as connected with the navis [nervous] sistem". We ask for our old friend a *horsepitable* reception—no other kind will suit him: he will be found a Daniel come to judgment, and what-ever he may say to the contrary, all that he don't practically know about horses "needn't be learnt".'

It has not been possible to discover what happened to 'Doctor' Offutt after he landed here: it is likely that he became swamped among the numerous 'professors' and 'doctors' that proliferated after Rarey's successes. Yet not all of them came from abroad: there was a notable home-product practising here before Rarey's arrival. He was a North-umberland man called James Telfer.[7] He had been giving demonstra-tions of horse-taming, it appears, before Rarey's rocketing to fame; and when an engraving of Rarey taming a horse appeared in the *Illustrated London News* in January 1858, Telfer's friends urged him to challenge Rarey's claim to using an unique system. This sort of dispute was to set the pattern for many years to come when individual horse-tamers accused their rivals of plagiarism or copying, like so many prickly, disputing book-authors. It is one of the reasons why each practitioner put his pupils under oath not to divulge his secrets, as Rarey did. Something like this still obtains today in an American system, the Beery, where trainees are told: 'trust you read the ideas over yourself and keep them strictly your personal property.'

It is likely, however, that many of these horse-tamers took their ideas from a common traditional source, then built on them and left their own impression on the original ideas, just as Rarey did. For instance, when a Wiltshire farmer first saw Rarey cast a horse he ex-

[7] *Cruiser Courier*, February 1977.

claimed: 'Why! I knew how to throw a horse in that way years ago; but I did not know the use of it—and was always in too great a hurry!' Perhaps here was the secret of Rarey's dominance: some aspects of his system were patently common knowledge among horse-tamers and were responsible for the charge of plagiarism; but it was the philosophy behind the system, the constant attitude of patience, respect for the animal, of hurrying slowly, that distinguished Rarey and enabled him to brush off the charges that he had no claim at all to originality. But the charges came, thick and fast. Telfer was a much older man than Rarey; and one of Telfer's pupils, a man named Fred Taylor, became active on Telfer's behalf. Taylor had spent his youth in Her Majesty's 8 Royal Irish Hussars, and later he became a reporter for *The Review*, *The Field*, Charles Dickens's *Household Words*, *Sporting Life* and so on. Taylor's main line of attack was that Rarey was more popular than Telfer because of his youth, while Telfer was on the wrong side of fifty. Moreover, Telfer was 'an honest, hardworking fellow', a 'true Briton' who had never been 'out of the smoke of his own chimney'. He maintained that Telfer's native talent was directed towards those whose everyday work was with horses, while Rarey's appeal was directed to 'young drawing-room ladies, or antiquated dowagers, and the majority of young men in peg-tops[8] and white kids besieging the doors of Mr Rarey's sanctuary'. Telfer was, he claimed, the genuine article and refused to teach 'old maids!'

To settle disputes like this Rarey, backed by his powerful supporters, put up a thousand guineas challenge on 23 April 1858: this sum would be given to any man who could prove that he knew Rarey's system. Several challengers appeared, including a man called Cooke of Astley's circus. All had to confess failure. This pattern of intense rivalry and virulent recriminations was repeated a few years later. Professor Sample, another American horse-tamer, arrived in this country (c. 1885) to practise his art; but he found that his method of horse-taming was already being practised here by an Australian named Osburn. Osburn had reached England six months before the Professor, having first got to know his method while the Professor was touring in Australia. Sample blew up and forced Osburn to work for him and to introduce him to those notable contacts he had already made in the horse-world. Osburn changed his name to Galvayne with

[8] A kind of trousers very wide at the top and narrowing towards the bottom.

its inevitable cognomen of 'Professor'; and along with his brother-in-law and Sample formed a company to exploit what Rarey had proved to be a rich province. Galvayne's company, incidentally, was written off by a contemporary as a 'motley crew'.

But Galvayne attained public notice, especially after an audience with Queen Victoria. He marketed everything he could make money on, from a 'Galvayne Gripe Drench' to 'Galvayne's Snaffle and Bridle'. He also wrote books, the best-known of which is *Horse Dentition*.[9] In this book he claimed to enable the reader to tell exactly the age of a horse up to thirty years by an examination of his teeth. Galvayne, whose name is often prefixed by the epithet *Groovy*,[10] 'is credited—rightly or wrongly—with discovering the groove which appears at a horse's upper incisors at the age of ten, is half-way down the incisor at age fifteen, reaches the bottom at age twenty, has disappeared from the upper half of the tooth at twenty-five and has disappeared completely at age thirty'.

The Beery system of horsemanship was first brought to my notice many years ago by an old horseman, Harry Denny, who worked at Manor Farm, Witnesham, Suffolk. He was born in 1895 at Wetheringsett, not very far from Witnesham. He served throughout the First World War, and shortly after he was demobilized he came across a Canadian who taught him much of the Beery system which he was practising. The Jesse Beery School of Horsemanship is still flourishing at Pleasant Hill, Ohio, USA or was until recently; and one of its special items of horse-gear is the Beery double-action riding bit. A catalogue of the equipment necessary to use the Beery system shows clearly that his method is substantially similar to Rarey's, at least in its approach to a difficult or vicious horse. The horse is brought under control using some of the following: knee-pads, foot-straps, double safety rope, combination halter and bridle, back band and crupper attachment, shaft carriers and belly band, breeching and hip straps, four-in-one Beery bit, breaking bridle, and guy line and throwing strap! The teaching of horse training and the imparting of a professor's secrets appears to be as highly commercialized now as it was in Rarey's and Goodenough's days. A note in the Beery system's pamphlet *Money-Making Secrets in Horse Training* (For Beery Students only) shows this clearly:

[9] Sydney Galvayne. Thomas Murray, Glasgow, Third Edition (not dated).
[10] *Cruiser Courier*, 'From the Horse's Mouth', Sharon E. Cregier, 1976.

'Above all, the suggestions which I give about prices to charge should be kept secret. I give you this little book with my compliments, hoping you will not merely appreciate it but that you will write me later, telling how much money you have made as a result of my suggestions.'

In recent months I learned the existence of another American horse-tamer who came to Britain about the same time as Sample and Galvayne. He was Professor Henry Miller, and I came to know of him through a remarkable series of coincidences. During the course of our stay in Peking I met Mrs Yvonne Preston who was there as foreign correspondent for an Australian newspaper, *The Sidney Herald*. Yvonne Preston had been brought up in Ipswich, Suffolk; and during our discussion of the town that we both knew very well she mentioned that she had been born in Britannia Road, on the Rushmere Heath side of Ipswich. Her parents, Mr and Mrs Stanley Miller, still lived in Suffolk in a village which is about an hour's car-ride from where I am living now. I promised to telephone her parents when I got back home to give them their daughter's greetings. When I returned, however, among my correspondence was a letter from A. E. Bixby, an ex-Ipswich man, who is passionately interested in horses. He wrote to tell me of an Ipswich colt-breaker whose practice it was to cure a jibbing horse in a very individual way: when the horse stopped and refused to go any farther, he made no move to urge it forward. He waited till the horse decided to move of itself. But as soon as the horse stirred the handler held him there and would not let him move an inch. This, he claimed, was a certain cure for jibbing or balking. The colt breaker's name was Henry Miller and he lived in Britannia Road, Ipswich. To assume that these two pieces of information, gathered in a random way from such diverse sources, were in any way connected seemed to me at the time to be very rash indeed. I decided, nevertheless, to telephone Stanley Miller, Yvonne Preston's father. And so it proved: he was the son of the Ipswich colt-breaker, Professor Henry Miller, and the lady I had met in China was his grand-daughter. Shortly afterwards I went down to Finningham where Mr and Mrs Stanley Miller now live, and during my visit he told me about his father, Henry Miller (born *c.* 1870: died 1939).

'As far as I can tell he was born in America and he came to this country in a cattle boat—at a very young age, I should imagine. He was very reticent about his young life. But we had several letters from

# BATTLE

## BETWEEN

# Man and Stallion!

### DRILL HALL, MERTHYR.

## 1 WEEK LONGER!

POSITIVELY CLOSING SATURDAY NEXT, AUG. 18TH.

## TO-NIGHT, Aug. 17,

### PROFESSOR HENRY

# MILLER,

### King of all Horse Educators!

A Single Man with an Indomitable Will against Brute Strength.

On this occasion the PROFESSOR will meet the

## Vicious Stallion!

### The Notorious Biter & Kicker.

The Owner has great fear of his doing serious damage, and is anxious for the night to come when he will be conquered. He kicks, he strikes, he is dangerous, they are obliged to blindfold him, he is so vicious.

## This Night Only, the Man-Eating Horse
### A VICIOUS AND DANGEROUS BITER.

They are compelled to approach him through a trap door or the side of his stall. He is pronounced by his owner to be a Vicious Man-Eating Brute. An event to be recorded in the history of Merthyr.

## 6 WILD, VICIOUS, AND NERVOUS HORSES 6
### FOR THIS GRAND NIGHT.

Every Horse handled on this occasion will be specially selected to form the

### Grandest Programme ever Presented.

Read the manner in which these Vicious Brutes Kill their Grooms.

When he entered the box stall to feed the Stallion, it turned upon him, and seizing his arm, with its teeth, raised the Groom from his feet and gave him a vicious shaking. The human sufferer's cries summoned help, and with bale sticks endeavoured to beat the infuriated Stallion. At every blow the animal reared, carrying his Groom high in the air. Finally the brute loosened its hold, and the

## DYING MAN

Fell to the ground. The Stallion's teeth had penetrated deep into his elbow joint, his shoulder was dislocated, and his head badly cut.

## THE MAN IS NOW DEAD

And the family mourn the loss of an honest, true, and loving husband and father.

I GLORY IN MEETING THESE

## Destroyers of the Human Race!

And I will meet them, MAN v. STALLIONS, and convince all that I have justly earned the title, KING OF ALL HORSE EDUCATORS, and before the Public, on Friday Night, August 17th, at the DRILL HALL, I will subdue these

# Murderers!

Broadsheet of
'Professor' Miller's performance
at Merthyr Tudful

his relations in America. He lived in New York, and the address they wrote from was 356 Clinton Avenue, New York. They were big music people. There's a story concerning this: when he was about to be married, the parson asked him what his name was. He said:

"I don't rightly know: it's either Müller or Miller."

"I don't think it's Müller," the parson said; "I've never heard of the name."

'But that was his real name: our real name is Müller. He had quite some bit of money at different times from his American relations. He wasn't the man to speak of himself or his young life: he went the opposite way to what his father wished because they were all in the music business. But he used to tell us that he was the first man that drove a four-in-hand over Brooklyn Bridge. Although I've never been able to verify this. He learned his skills with horses in America. I was over in America last year [1975] and I wanted to go round the area where his relations lived but I didn't have the time. I found out where Clinton Road was in New York but I couldn't find Clinton Avenue. I haven't heard from his relations for years now.'

Before he reached the town of Ipswich, where he eventually married and settled down, Henry Miller—as his son Stanley believes—must have been a member of a circus and travelled the halls up and down the country in his own right. In support of this he produced the broadsheet shown on page 163. To me this is not only a revealing document in itself but another link, too, in the strange chain of coincidences that brought me to Henry Miller's son, Stanley, as Merthyr Tudful is only a few miles from my home and is a town I know well. It was one of the first big iron- and steel-making centres during the Industrial Revolution; and when it was in its hey-day it had a mixed and lively population giving great support to the theatre and the music-hall. Later, however, when the local supplies of iron-ore gave out and the ore had to be imported, the steel industry moved down to the coast, to Cardiff and Newport, and the town of Merthyr decayed. The broadsheet is, as Stanley Miller suggested:

'Unusual! Out of this world. *Professor Henry Miller, Horse Educator!* He used to tell me that he performed in places like this all over the country.'

The broadsheet reminds me of the remark of an acquaintance after I had lent him a Suffolk farm horseman's notebook (it was compiled in 1893, about the same time as Henry Miller was touring the country): 'Reading that makes me right glad I wasn't a horse in those days.' Stanley Miller continued:

'After he had toured as a circus performer, training horses and so on, he came to Ipswich. He first took lodgings at The Brickmakers' Arms: Mrs Crickmore used to keep the public house at that time. He lodged there for quite a while; then he apparently got to know my mother whose father kept The California Arms (the pub is not there now). I've heard my mother say they never walked out together. She was usually in the public house with her parents, and I suppose all their courting was done in the public house anyway. When my mother's parents died my father took over the business; and he was there for some years. In the meantime he had become a colt-breaker and broke in horses from there. There was a colourful side to his character: I suppose keeping a public house he got to drinking occasionally. Anyway, they moved out of The California Arms. I don't know the real reason. Two of my brothers and my sister were born at The California Arms. I was the only one who was born [1909] at Britannia Road where we moved. There, of course, he broke in horses. I remember one time we had about ten horses at Britannia Road, and we also had a lot at Crabbe Street. We used to have stables in a big house there, as well. I was a boy, of course, and we had to clean those out at that time o' day, before we went to school. They were mostly carriage horses, no heavy horses at all. He carried on that for several years. To my knowledge he was supposed to be able to break in horses that nobody else could break in. There was another colt-breaker at the old Red Lion on Major's Corner: his name was Fisher. He used to break in horses, but my father used to get most of the unbreakable ones, you might say. He was the dominant party: they would submit in the end if he wanted to break them. That would be broken. There wasn't no case of half-breaking then: they were broken in the end.

'When we were children we used to have a lot of work to do, cleaning the harness and one thing and another every Saturday; and also assisting him in breaking the horse. He was a very heavy drinker at times. I've known the time when we've been to see a gentleman to show him his horse—how it was progressing—at The Marsh Tavern on the market; and I've seen the man hand over twenty or thirty pounds, part payment of the breaking in of the horse. And my father would have nothing left of the money after he'd got home. I don't remember the time when he never had horses. Then the war broke out, and he went—the First World War. He was a sergeant in the Army Veterinary Corps. He came back from the war, and there wasn't a lot of work after that, not in the breaking of horses: they were then on the way out, and motor transport was coming in. He did work at one period after the war in building the old tin sheds at St Helen's Hospital. After that he got back into breaking horses again; but they were never on the same scale as they were before the war. He was very fortunate in having the experience when he did.

'He couldn't read nor write: he could write his name but that was all. He was about five feet nine inches—no, he wasn't tall. He was a thick set man, very strong. He could pull a horse over while it was moving. You've seen them in these cowboy films—well, he could pull them over in a cart, just as easy. He had several bad accidents: he was driving a fractious horse down Tavern Street, Ipswich and it went through a plate-glass window.

'When I was a lad at school we were asked to write an essay on *My Father*. When it was completed I was brought in front of the class, the teacher pointing out to me that something I'd written concerning my father was untrue. I wrote about his breaking horses, and about a photo we had in the front room,[11] depicting that he was *The Greatest Horse-tamer since the Days of Rarey*. It was his photograph and the words were round the top of it. The teacher at that time said it was absolutely untrue because there wasn't such a person as Rarey. She said: "It must be Raleigh!" "No," I said, "it's definitely Rarey because it's on the photograph in our house." But she wouldn't have it. She was determined it was Raleigh; and I was made to look very silly in front of the class. I always remembered that—until a few years after—just after my sixty-seventh birthday—I was able to prove I was right by a book I had got.

'My father was a very aggressive man at times. In our young days what he said was gospel. His drinking habits were very bad, yet he would give it up for a couple or three months; wouldn't have any, and then he'd start again. His business, I suppose, was the cause of a lot of it. We had a very poor home life. I suppose it was general at that time o' day. When he was drunk he had the funniest ideas: he would come home sometimes about eleven o'clock—drunk; and me and my brothers would be abed. He would get us up. He'd say:

[11] See Plate 19.

"We'll take the horse up the Heath."

'To break a horse in we had to put it in the cart. You couldn't do this in the street here: it would do a lot of damage. So we had to pull the cart up to the golf-links at Rushmere—at eleven o' clock at night, the horse as well. And he'd put it in the cart and break it in; and after that you could put the horse in the cart outside the house. That's the type of thing he used to do; and it was very riling, it used to be, when we were young. We didn't know how he was going to be when he came home. At different times, though, he would be a real gent. I remember one time when I was lad, he came home about nine o'clock. He said:

"You come with me with a crate and you can have all the pigeons in the loft in The Globe Inn in St George's Street!"

'This was after the trolley buses started to run—they hadn't been running long. Anyway, I went down with him, and we got the pigeons out of the loft, and we put them in this chickens' crate. And coming home we brought them back in this trackless trolley. Well, you can imagine the commotion it caused among the passengers to get a whole crate of pigeons cooing and going ahead. He was—he could be kind; but when he was drunk he was terrible.

'He was a past-master at his job; and he never failed to cure a horse of bad temper and so on. He had, somehow or other, an uncanny knack with horses. I remember my eldest brother—he had to fetch a pony one day. A Shetland he was: he had to go and fetch it from the owner who wanted it broken in. My brother and me went to collect it, and the owner said:

"You can't get into the stable for it: it will bite you!"

"How do you feed it then?"

"Well, I throw the hay in from the other side."

'Anyway, my brother went after this pony and he bit him twice on the chest. Drew blood. Well, we managed to get it and get it home. My father asked what the trouble was, and my brother told him it had bitten him twice on the chest. "I don't know," he said. "I don't like this, but we'll have to break him in." What he done to it I don't know; but in about a week we could go into the stable. He wasn't any more trouble. It was quite a nice pony in the end.'

Later, Stanley Miller told me that he thought his father cured the pony by hitting it on the forehead, between the ears, every time it came to him: he knocked it out with a twitch stick. This was an old remedy once used by a French horse-breaker[12] 'whose remedy lay in a loaded whip freely applied between the ears when any symptom of vice was displayed'.

'He knew a horse from A to Z: he never used a veterinary surgeon. He treated the animals himself. He used herbs, all different kind of things. He had a horse oil which people used to come and ask to buy from him. He made it up himself from different things. It was very strong, too: if one of us had a cold we'd have a sniff of it.

'After the horses went out he went to work in the funeral department of the Ipswich Co-operative Society. He worked there until his death. He married again, married a second time. It wasn't a very happy marriage, and he went back to live with my second brother. He was taken ill one evening, and my brother asked me to go over and see him because he was living on the other side of the road, just opposite us. He was very ill: he was dying. The doctor said he never knew a man to walk round to his surgery, as he did the day previous, with a heart-beat of twenty-seven. He collapsed on the road apparently as he was going to the doctor (we didn't know that at the time); and when he got there it was so serious the doctor brought him home.'

Henry Miller was probably the last of a long line of American horse-trainers who came to Britain in the nineteenth century. J. S. Rarey gained the greatest prominence over here; but some Americans believe that other practitioners—Dennis Magner, Montagu Stevens, Professor Sample—were equally as skilled as Rarey if not more so. The difference they believe was due to Rarey's becoming under Goodenough's management a more successful showman. The Americans, however, give the palm to an Irishman, Captain M. Horace Hayes, as the greatest exponent of them all. Hayes was a well-educated man, a qualified veterinarian who was in the Indian Army for a decade. He developed much of his technique of handling horses from studying the methods of the American professionals, and he developed them while touring in India, South Africa and Australia. He also studied the art of dressage and high school riding in France and Germany. His books are still among the best on horse training; and they illustrate his wide experience and the depth of his understanding of the way a horse thinks and reacts.

It is an interesting question why it is that so many horse experts had either their origin or their formative experience in North America.

[12] *The Art of Taming Horses*, p. 14.

The answer seems to be that, in the 'frontier' stage of the early and mid-nineteenth century, stock-raising conditions gave rise to the development of more unruly horses than anywhere else in the world. Great numbers of horses ran wild, and often they were mature animals before an attempt was made to break them in. When they were rounded up and tamed by the rough 'whip and spur' methods, usually by men who themselves were 'as strong as a horse but as stupid as forty', the animals soon acquired the temperament of dangerous outlaws. 'Any man who could handle them successfully usually found horses, regarded as "man-eaters" in other parts of the world, comparatively simple to "tame". American experts surpassed the rest of the world as horse-breakers because they had abundance of material on which to experiment.'[13]

The Americans had also got to know, and were able to improve upon, the methods the mustang-riding Plains Indians had developed for handling wild horses. But they were not above dressing up their hard-won knowledge and experience with a rather blatant showmanship: this is illustrated by Henry Miller's broadsheet (p. 163). Experience taught them that only by using this kind of ballyhoo would it be possible to attract a sizeable audience. They knew that the number of people who attended a performance really to learn how the expert handled a vicious horse was negligible. Like the fashionable people who attended Rarey's demonstration they wanted most of all to see a dramatic display of skill and courage mastering brute strength and violence.

In England, however, as in America skilled demonstrations of horse-training methods ceased: as soon as the internal combustion engine effectively eroded the dominance of the horse, the highly professional trainers passed into limbo, exactly as did the majority of their no less skilled but humbler brethren on the farms and the roads. And Henry Miller's experience in Suffolk illustrates how drastic and complete was their descent from the bright lights of public acclaim.

[13] John Richard Young, *The Schooling of the Western Horse*, University of Oklahoma, Norman, 1954, p. 9.

# 14

## Collecting the Lore

Because the farm horse was an important focus of rural life, especially in a predominantly arable area such as East Anglia the anecdotes and reminiscences of those people who were connected with him have given us a rich archive of the tradition: they have made a valuable contribution to the social history of the East Anglian countryside during the first half of this century, the late nineteenth century and, by extension, to the social history of much earlier periods.

My own recognition of the value of this tradition and my particular method of attempting to record it grew out of my early experience in the Suffolk village of Blaxhall where there was so much historical material in a relatively undisturbed context. It appeared to me at the time that there was no need to debate how this material should be classified: it was urgent to salvage as much as I could before it would be lost; for many of the old generation that had the tradition in its fullest form were at the very end of their lives. At first I made no effort to structure the results of my collecting except very loosely, with the conventional disciplines—history, English language, folklore, sociology —at the back of my mind. But even at the time of doing this I suspected that the orthodox disciplines, each with its more or less rigid boundaries, had very little relevance to the actual field where I was collecting. If I had been pressed to define what I was doing I would have said that I was concerned with *folk life* which implies a holistic approach to a defined field of study. For all the material was part of a working or organic whole and the inter-relation of its various aspects was infinitely more apparent than would have emerged from any exercise in an individual discipline. As I gained experience it became clear that to approach my informants with a rigid, pre-formed concept of what I wanted or what I should expect to find (which would be inevitable if I worked within one discipline) would be to constrict my ultimate findings.

170

Using the indirect approach I found that oftentimes valuable information not recorded in written form came up while I was attempting to steer the conversation to something else. Later I began consciously to use this oblique approach, adopting an apparently passive role of listening to an informant and asking only an occasional question. Here the collector sits, so to speak, patiently like a fisherman waiting for whatever the river or the tide may bring—at least in the initial interviews. When he has caught something that is worth taking home, then is the time for the questioning and the close investigation. The oblique approach is justified although it takes more time and seems to the observer to be without purpose. But a chance remark will occasionally lead to a rich reward that is worth days of apparent drifting. It was such a side remark that first set me on the track of the migrant workers who yearly left East Anglia for the maltings of Burton-on-Trent, a search that came just in time to salvage historical material that was poorly documented and survived chiefly in the minds of men who had themselves gone to Burton half a century earlier. This was a decade ago, and most of these old maltsters have now gone on their final migration.

It was in this way, too, that I came across the 'magic' side of the lore about the farm horse. It was through going for the whole complex— the history of the farm horse and his work on the farms, and the life and routine of the horsemen—that I came across mention of this unusual side of the history of the farm horse. I did not know it existed, and I suspect that I would not have got very far in my questioning had it not followed on naturally from my research into the whole background. I found, more by luck than judgement, that a shot-gun aim was very much more effective than trying to pick off a particular topic with a quick-firing rifle of questions. It is certain that in such a delicate topic as this, where few horsemen were ready to open up, there was a great deal to be said for the kind of approach recommended in the old country aphorism: *If you want to buy a pig, talk about the weather.* This is the artistic rather than the positivist method: not going to a situation with a preconceived idea of what you expect to find, but going with a full, uncommitted awareness, trying to discover whether there is any structure inherent in the material itself: it is like the primitive sculptor or wood-carver who looks for the shape that is imprisoned in the block of stone or the piece of timber, considering that it is his task merely to release this inherent shape from its prison rather than to impose his own, perhaps unsympathetic or alien concept upon it.

The 'listening' rather than the 'questioning approach' also has one outstanding advantage: the direct question, by its very directness and specific emphasis, often defeats itself. It can cause a wary informant to tighten up in some circumstances: with a co-operative one, on the other hand, it has the danger of inducing him to tell you not exactly what he thinks or knows, but what he believes to be the answer you are seeking. This, I suspect, is the greatest weakness in the questionnaire or survey type of inquiry.

The anecdote is a good example of the kind of approach I have come to use, a way of obtaining an unconscious statement or comment revealing an attitude that would not be evoked in such pure form by more direct questioning. To illustrate this it would be best to give a definite example which incidentally demonstrates the centrality of all material about the farm horse in the social history or sociology of the old village community. It is an account given me a year ago (1976) by Charles Gardner (born 1902) of Diss. He told me about his grandfather who was born, and spent the first part of his life, in Suffolk:

'My family came from Uggeshall in Suffolk, and my grandfather, William Gardner, was born there in 1847. He had to help his father in the woods until he was eleven years old, then he started an apprenticeship to a blacksmith. He was paid three ha'pence a week. He had to work from six in the morning till six at night except Saturdays: that was six to five. Out of this three ha'pence he used to give his mother a penny and the other ha'penny he used to spend; he used it to go to night school—two nights a week with this ha'penny so that he learned to read and write. This was about 1855–7. He was apprentice for four years; and when he had served his apprenticeship his wages were then ninepence a week. Then on a Sunday—he needed money so he used to go scaring birds (crows), or keeping pigs and cattle on the common; and in those days he earned a penny because he worked on a Sunday.

'Anyhow, he stayed there until he was about twenty when he got married. Prior to that, after he had served his apprenticeship, he used to go to Flixton Hall. One week in the month he used to spend at Flixton Hall shoeing the hunters and the carriage horses. He used to go there and stay at the Hall for one week. He was such an excellent smith. When he was about to marry he said to his boss at Uggeshall:

"I think I shall have to move from here. I can learn more, do more work. . . ."

"Well," the blacksmith said, "I can't afford to pay you any more."

"I'm going to get married."

"Well, the best thing to do is to look for another job."

'He looked for another job; and the people at Flixton Hall would have engaged him but they hadn't got sufficient work for him to do all the time. So he saw in the local paper that there was a job advertised at Creeting near Claydon. He went there; saw the man, and he asked:

"How did you get here?"

"I walked."

"From Uggeshall?"

"Yes."

"And how are you going back?"

"I shall walk."

'And he did walk. Anyhow he got the job, and his money was quite an increase on what he'd been having. So he was quite happy, and he moved into a little cottage with what odds and ends of furniture he could afford to buy. He carried on there for quite a while, and he had a family. But one day he said to his boss:

"Well, I think I'd like to work for myself."

"Well, if you don't start now working for yourself, you never will."

"I've heard where there's a blacksmith shop to let, and tomorrow I'll go and see if the place is all right for me to hire, and if there's a house with it."

So he walked from Creeting to the village of Billingford, and he was looking round the blacksmith shop when Mr Flowerdew, who was the owner and farmer of Billingford Hall—he walked into the blacksmith shop.

"Young man," he said, "what are you doing here?"

"I'm looking for a blacksmith shop to hire; and I've come from Creeting to . . ."

"Well, if you come from Creeting, you get back to Creeting. We don't want you here!"

'So he said: "Oh. You are the biggest farmer in the village; I was coming to see you, to see if I could have some work."

"You won't get no work off me," he said, "the best thing for you to do is to get home."

173

"No," he said, "I'm glad I've seen you: you made me determined to have this blacksmith shop."

"Oh, are you? Well, you don't want to hire that. Mr Woodcock of Scole have all my work on contract. You won't have nothing from me."

"Nevertheless, I shall come here."

'Then he walked from Billingford to Diss to Mr Whiting who the property belonged to, and he hired it and agreed on the date that he should move in; and he walked back that night to Creeting; and didn't get back very early. Next morning he saw his boss, and his boss said:

"How did you get on?"

"I liked the blacksmith shop and I liked the little cottage; and I could have it for a fair rent. So I've made up my mind and I'm going to hire it."

"Very good. When do you want to go?"

'So he told him the date he wanted to leave, and he arranged for a local farmer to bring his odds and ends of furniture to Billingford. When he loaded up the furniture to come away, his boss said to him:

"There's two large bundles of rasps [rasps they clean the horses' feet with]. Now," he said, "you make a lot of chopping hooks out of these rasps. So when you get to Billingford you can start to make chopping hooks to sell to the villagers. That will help to give you a little start in your life." '

Mention of William Gardner's rasps brings out an aspect of the anecdote that I have frequently noticed. A story is embellished by a wealth of detail that at first sight appears to be carrying little weight and contributing little forward momentum to the story. Yet these details are the essential mark of a well-told tale, giving background and colour to its hard framework; and occasionally, too, as here, giving a striking glimpse of the similarity of the rural pattern at different times and in different parts of the region, emphasizing by doing so the holistic quality of the culture. 'Everything tied in', as an informant once told me: very little was wasted; and there was a recognized secondary use for many objects—tools, for instance—that had served their purpose and outlived their use in the field they were originally designed for. Nearly thirty years ago an old Blaxhall resident gave me a farrier's rasp that had been refashioned into a hook: I still have it. The man who made the hook, George Messenger, was born in 1877: he told me he had beaten it out in the blacksmith's shop at Snape

Maltings (the site of the present Concert Hall) when he was a young man. He said that the farrier's rasp was made of the finest steel, and was prized for making hooks because of the fine edge the steel gave. An accident of size and shape has made George Messenger's hook (see Plate 22) not dissimilar in design to a Roman reaping hook or sickle (*falx messoria*) though its irregularly pitted blade suggests that it once had a smooth edge and was not serrated like a true sickle.

'So,' Charles Gardner continued, 'my grandfather moved to Billing-ford and he settled in and opened up the blacksmith shop. He made these chopping hooks of course; and after a short while he found that the gypsies were taking their horses to him to be shod; and he had quite a busy time shoeing gypsy horses. He always said: "I really owe a lot of thanks to the gypsies for helping me in my start." Anyhow, he got a few horses from Besthorpe Hall, and one or two of the little farms; and he jogged along until the time came when Mr Flowerdew came into Diss on a market day, and he saw my grandfather. He'd come into Diss to pay a bill at Aldrich's the ironmongers. He said:

"You haven't got time to be in Diss. You want to be home looking after your business."

"Well," Grandfather said, "I don't get any business from you, so I don't have to thank you."

'Anyhow, Grandfather had been down to John Aldrich's at the bottom of the hill and he'd bought himself a grin'stone for sharpening tools. And he said to Aldrich:

"Now, can I pay half this month and half the next?"

'So they said: "Who are you?"

'He told them who he was and where he'd come from, and they told him: "Come back in an hour's time and we'll see."

'He went back and they said, Yes, he could have it, and their horse and trolley was going round there at a certain date and would deliver it. So Grandfather said: "Thank you very much", and he got home. And who should walk into the blacksmith shop but this Mr Flower-dew:

"You're a determined man to stay here, aren't you?"

"Yes, I am; and I'm going to make it my home."

"And you've been to Diss today and bought yourself a grin'stone?"

"Yes, How did you know?"

"Well, if it hadn't been for me, you wouldn't have had it, because they asked me your character. And I could have given you a bad one

175

or I could have given you a good one. But I told them they didn't
want to worry, I would pay for the grin'stone. So I paid for it. So,"
he said, "you now owe me the money."

"Well, of all the nerve! To think they would come and ask you!
But I don't want the grin'stone. They can take it back. I won't have
it!"

"Oh yes you will. You'll have it. And don't you send it back either."

'Well, my grandfather erected it; and of an evening he would be
very busy sharpening up chopping hooks and one thing and another.
He went on making different things—sets of harrows he used to re-
lay. But he still didn't have any work from this Mr Flowerdew. Although Mr Flowerdew used to come down occasionally and see him:
sometimes they would have a row and sometimes they were quite
friendly. Anyhow, my grandfather he still carried on. Then one day
Mr Flowerdew he went out and bought a horse, a rather special horse;
and when he wanted it shod he sent it to the blacksmith shop at Scole,
Mr Woodcock's. And he couldn't shoe it. So he sent it to Hoxne: they
couldn't shoe it. Thorpe Abbots: they couldn't shoe it. He went to
Broome: they couldn't shoe it. So he said to the man who led the
horse, Sam Burch:

"Take it and try that man at Billingford," he said.

'So they brought the horse down, and Grandfather said:

"Well, we won't have it in the trav'us; we'll have it outside."

'Over the trav'us door, on the top, he had a hooked ring; and he
tied the horse to this ring. So he walked round it and he patted it, and
he said to Sam Burch:

"Do you like beer?"

"Oh yes," he said, "I like beer."

"Well," he said, "you go in the pub and have a pint of beer. You
don't want to be in any hurry. I shall see what I can do with this
horse."

'When Sam Burch came out of the pub he said:

"Oh, my word!" he said, "you got two shoes on the back feet.
However did you do it?"

"Oh," he said, that's easy, bo'," he said. "Have you drunk your
beer?"

"Yes, I've drunk my beer."

"Well, you'd better go back and have another one."

'He sent him back to the pub; he sat there for a while, and when he came back he'd got the front shoes on. Rasped the feet all up, and blacked them with black; made them look spick and span.

"Here you are, my man," he said. "You can take that home."

'So Sam Burch took the horse home, and Mr Flowerdew looked at it.

"Oh my word!" he said, "what a tradesman! How did he do it?"

'So Sam said: "I don't know."

"You don't know!"

"No," he said, "if I'd ha' stopped he wouldn't have shod it. He sent me into the pub to have a drink, and when I came out he had the two back shoes on. I went back into the pub; came out and it was finished, and I brought it home."

"You left the horse in his care?"

"Why, yes."

"Well, you are sacked!"

'And he sacked him on the spot. And Sam Burch went to see my grandfather next day and he said:

"I got the sack over that horse."

"Why?"

"He wanted to know how you did it?"

"Well, if you'd ha' stood here I wouldn't have done it. I should have sent it back. As you went into the pub I wanted to prove to your master I could do it. But I didn't want you to see how I done it."

'The next time the horse came back to my grandfather to be shod, "No," he said to Mr Flowerdew. "I'm not shoeing that horse. You take your bad horses where you take your good ones."

"Oh, that's like that is it?"

"Yes, that is. And another thing you haven't paid me for shoeing the horse the last time."

"Oh," he said, "you think I can't pay you?"

"I don't think anything of the kind, but you haven't paid me."

"Well, I'll pay you."

"I want double for shoeing that horse because it's a bad one."

"I'm not going to pay you double."

"If you don't pay double I shall take those shoes off and no one else will ever put them on."

"Well," he said, "I want you to take them off; but those shoes are so good I want you to put them back on again."

"Would you pay me double?"

'So Mr Flowerdew he did pay him double; and my grandfather said:
"Now take the horse away. I won't shoe it unless I have some of your good ones."

"Now look! If I give you all the horses to shoe off Billingford Hall Farm, will you shoe this horse?"

"Yes," my grandfather said. "You go and give that in writing to my wife in the house. She can read."

'And he tied the horse up; took the shoes off and put them back on again. Mr Flowerdew said: "That's easy. Is that all you done?"

"Yes,' and he said to Mr Flowerdew: "Now you pick hold of the hair on the heel of the horse and lift the foot up."

'Of course, Mr Flowerdew he put his hand out and took hold of the hair; and the horse nearly went berserk. And this is what the other blacksmiths had done: they'd got hold of the horse's hair and the horse couldn't bear it to be touched. Well, my grandfather he used to put the claw of his hammer under the hoof, and he picked it up. And when he'd got it up he put his hand under the hoof, laid it on his left knee and cleaned it—and that's how he shod it. He said:

"I didn't pull or touch a hair on the horse's leg to have any effect. I knew what was wrong with that when it came to me. I've had one or two before, but perhaps not so bad."

'Anyhow, he got all the horses from Billingford Hall; and about a month later he got the horses from Hoxne farms, and some time later he got all the horses from Redgrave farms. They were all going there. From Redgrave they used to start at six in the morning; and there used to be a string of horses, tied head to tail, going from Redgrave to Billingford. And he used to do the lot in one day: it was too far to go backwards and forwards with one or two. The Hoxne farms, they always went in fours, and the Billingford farms, too, always went in fours.

'Billy, his eldest son, my uncle, he left school and as soon as he left he went as apprentice to my grandfather. He taught him and he was quite a good man; but he died of cancer at the age of fifty-seven; and the blacksmith shop really got messed away. It gradually fell by the wayside. Then Mr Hall, he had it open about one day a week. Then he closed it up about thirty years ago. And of course no one reopened and the old blacksmith shop fell away.

'My grandfather died in 1935 at the age of eighty-eight. But there's something I didn't tell you. Some time after he retired (he worked until he was seventy-five or seventy-six: he shod his own pony a month before he died) he said to my father:

"Are you going to Ipswich market next Tuesday?"

'He said, Yes: he drove a horse and cart in those days.

"Well, I'll go as far as Claydon with you, and I would like to get off and walk through a footpath into a lane and into Creeting, to have a look at the old blacksmith shop. I haven't seen it for sixty year."

'So my father took him, and he got off the cart and off he went. And when he got into this lane he was about a hundred yards off the village. There was a stile there and an old man beside it. And Grandfather went and spoke to him, and got talking about one or two things; and my grandfather said:

"It was sixty years ago since I left this place, I used to work for the blacksmith."

"Well, if you worked for the blacksmith," this old man said, "that was me!"

'And the old man said that he had talked about my grandfather many times and he said:

"I've always said you were the best blacksmith I ever had."

"You must be over a hundred!"

"Yes, I am; and this should call for a little celebration."

'So they went up to the village pub and had a few drinks. And grandfather caught a bus up to Ipswich market where my father was, and they drove home. He said:

"This has been in my mind for a long, long time. I must have chosen this day to have gone and met this man. This has really made my life. I've just about completed it now."

'As I said, he shod his own pony a month before he died; and I don't think he should have died when he did. He just gave up: he'd lived long enough. In the latter part of his life he lived with my father and mother. He was a nice old chap really.

'Another thing he used to do was the post round. He did the post round for nigh on thirty years; and his wife had the post office. It's still in the family. I have a cousin who runs it now. She's seventy.'

On the surface this is a tale, remembered and recounted out of family piety, of a grandson telling us about the conflict of his grandfather with a powerful farmer and of the ultimate success of the smith who from his position in the village appeared to be the weaker man. But to anyone who is interested in the power structure and the social relations in the rural villages of East Anglia before the break-up of the traditional communities the story is revealing, not so much for what is said but for what is not said. At the time of the story's action there were two types of village in this region: the *close* (or closed) village and the *open* village. In the close village the squire or lord of the manor usually owned all the land and all the property in his parish. He had to a large degree absolute power within the parish, and the only checks on it were public opinion and his own conscience. Most squires appeared to have treated their dependants with humanity as most of them considered that their wealth and position implied social obligations which they usually carried out conscientiously—according to their lights. But they could prevent anyone they did not approve of from coming into the village, and they easily could show those who did not behave themselves the way out. Only when they became afraid that there was a direct challenge to their class interests did they act cruelly: in those circumstances even the most humane squire was quite capable of using the steel fist.

It is clear from Charles Gardner's account that Billingford was an open village at that time for the story demonstrates the chief characteristic of an open community: at least some of the property was owned not by a powerful landowner but (typically) by small tradesmen who often lived in the nearby town. Here the smithy was owned by a man from Diss. Therefore the farmer did not have the ultimate sanction that the squire in the close village had: he could not turn the smith out of his smithy; and therefore he was bluffing when he tried to frighten him off. The smith knew that if only he could acquire sufficient custom without the farmer's help, he could—if not ignore him—be proof against his hostility. But it seems to me that the most telling aspect of the story is that the narrator made no overt comment on the farmer's pretensions to arbitrary power. It was not that he was not aware of it, but that it conformed so nearly to the general pattern of social relations in this region—a pattern that lasted well into this century—that it was so *usual* as to be hardly worthy of comment. After living for a long period in various parts of East Anglia I believe that this is the truly significant part of the story for a historian. And for him to ignore the anecdote as a potential historical source or to play it down for not having relevant, verifiable 'factual' information, for its not being what it was never intended to be, argues an indifferent view of the historian's function.

# 15

# Horsemen's Anecdotes

The following tale comes from the *Saints* district of Suffolk, a remote and sparsely populated area south of Bungay. It was told to me while I was trying to find out why it was that the oral tradition had very little to say about hiring fairs and the practice of young men living in the farm houses while employed on the farms. There were, however, hiring fairs in East Anglia during the early nineteenth century; and there was a hiring fair at Harleston, a town quite near the *Saints*, as late as the mid-century. But by the 1890s, as reported by A. Wilson Fox,[1] while the hiring system of engagement still prevailed in the north of England, 'In Suffolk and Norfolk the engagement of ordinary labourers is in practice a daily one.' Why did the hiring system and 'living in' cease so early in East Anglia? One explanation has been put forward: the earlier development of farming towards purely commercial enterprises and the consequent 'gentrification' of the farmers resulted in their wives wishing to shed rather than to add to their housekeeping responsibilities. Whatever the reason, the practice of living in appears to have lasted longer in the *Saints* than it did farther south in the country. Jack Page (1895–1974), born in the *Saints*, had lived there for most of his life, and he told me in 1970:

'My father used to live in at a farm in St Andrew's. There was a head [horse] man, second man, and third man lived in there—and a boy. They used to have their tea about eight o'clock at night; and they knew every day what they were going to have for their meals, every day of the week they knew what they were going to have: the same old rations week after week. The housekeeper looked after them for this owd chap; and she was a bit of tight 'un, so they said; and they weren't allowed to go in after their tea till eight o'clock at night. And to keep warm in the winter-time they used to—one got on a horse's back, and one on another, and another—and so on. And they used to

[1] Assistant Commissioner, *Royal Commission on Labour*, Vol. 1, Part III, 1893, pp. 6 and 8.

lay there to keep themselves warm until it was time for them to turn the horses out into the yard at night; and then they'd go in after tea. Then, of course, they never had eggs and different things and that like, at that time o' day. So they decided one was to gather up some eggs. They got one of these long worsted stockings they used to wear years ago to put the eggs in; and they gathered these up and went into breakfast one morning. They picked the morning when the owd lady was going to wash. And they watched her and hung the stocking into the copper; and kept the lid tight. Then they said: one get some pepper and salt; one get some butter; and the other one get some bread. Well, when they came out and got this out of the copper they went into the stable where they were going to eat these here eggs. But when they got 'em out—they'd been a-cooking for half an hour—they were as hard as shot! They couldn't eat them. So they got done that way. Dear, oh dear!

'My father was born in 1845, and nearly all of the young men used to live in the farms—a rum lot did—at that time. And they did when I was growing up: when I was a boy and went to school a lot used to live in in the farm house, they did. All Saints here, Newson here— I remember three being there: one man was Leveret, one was Jimmy Hunt, and one was Charlie Pigeon. Charlie Pigeon is still about there now, and the chap Leveret is at Denton. They always had a good bed [in the house] to lay on. Of course, they lived better that time o' day —better than the time I'm talking about my father. I'd heard my father talk about that owd *household cheese*. Well, I wonder what they were. He said you might *hull* 'em or bowl 'em, from here to Hanover they'd never fall to pieces! They used to laugh over that. What sort this household cheese was I don't know: they used to toast 'em agin the fire and get a piece of pork to put on top of one and eat it like that. Dear, oh dear!

'The owd boy [his father] used to tell me all manner of tales while we sat agin the fire at night. 'Course, he was in a farm there, the Grove Farm at St Margaret's. He was there twenty year with owd Flaxman. When they lived in they made a bargain for so much money to live in. That was what they called board and lodgings, wasn't it? Board and lodgings, and so much money at the end of the year. Some of them made a bargain for the year; and another would make a bargain for the month—a month's notice either way. So he could leave with a month's notice; and if the master want to get rid of him he could give him a month's notice and he'd have to go. But by the year, you'd got to be there a year: take all comers say, good, bad and indifferent!

'The owd chap told me a story about a young chap [who was living in] and had to cut chaff every day, this here boy did. Of course, that was a real owd-fashioned go that was: they used to do that every day—cut some chaff by the owd hand machine [turning a wheel that was fitted with two knives which cut the hay as it was fed into it]. This boy had bread and cheese for his dinner, and he was in the barn a-turning this owd wheel, and he was a-singing:

*Bread'n cheese, work at ease:*
*Bread'n cheese, work at ease.*

'So the owd farmer stood outside the barn, and he was listening. It didn't suit him, and he went round and told his wife:

"Missus," he said, "you'll have to get something for that boy's dinner different tomorrow. He's in that barn singing *Bread'n cheese, work at ease.*"

'Well, the next day for his dinner the boy had pork and potato pie. 'Course, he had his dinner that day, and the owd farmer say:

"You'll have to go and cut some more chaff."

'The usual thing, and the owd man followed him again to the barn door, and stood there after he'd got a start. And he was getting on a little better:

*Pork and tater pie, work accordinglie;*
*Pork and tater pie, work accordinglie.*

'That was a little different, so the farmer went and told his wife again:

"Missus," he say, "you'll have to get something different tomorrow. He got a little better tune today."

'So he had beef and pudding the next day (beef dumplings we always call it but it was beef and pudding). And after he had his dinner he went and cut the chaff. And the owd man he went round to the barn a-listening. The boy had gone in the barn and he was getting on: he'd got a better stroke on him and he was a-getting on: *Chip chop,*

*Beef'n pudden, work like a good 'un:*
*Beef'n pudden, work like a good 'un.*

'So the owd gel solved the problem at the last, didn't she? What?'

Jack Page's contribution is a good example of the worth of the anecdote in bringing to the surface authentic peripheral material that helps to fill in the social history of a region. It also confirms the truism that if you record a man talking about his work, a subject he knows intimately and in great detail, you can rarely fault him. It also re-affirms the classical—if, on the surface, sentimental—pre-condition for the effective handing down of tradition, the father telling his young son his stories and experiences while they both sat before the fire on a winter's night.

The first piece of indirect historical information in the account is the mention of *household cheese*. This is undoubtedly the much maligned Suffolk *bang*, a very hard, skim-milk cheese which was part of the accepted fare of those workers who lived in the farm house. And the accuracy of Jack Page's transmission of his father's account is attested by the evidence of an old farmer from north Suffolk—recorded over twenty years ago.[2] He described the cheese and the manner of its preparation by the workers before they went out in the morning with the same detail as is given here. This reference to Suffolk bang also shows the historical continuity that is such a striking feature of any research that uses oral evidence in an attempt to reconstruct the recently displaced communities in the countryside. One is fre-quently coming across beliefs, customs, work processes, and everyday practices that can be established from written or printed evidence to have persisted for centuries. In this instance there is a full des-cription of Suffolk *bang* in Robert Bloomfield's eighteenth-century poem, *The Farmer's Boy* (Spring):

> *Unrivall'd stands thy country Cheese, O Giles!*
> *Whose very name engenders smiles;*
> *Whose fame abroad by every tongue is spoke,*
> *The well-known butt of many a flinty joke,*
> *That pass like current coin the nation through;*
> *And, ah! experience proves the satire true.*

One of the current jokes was that 'Hunger will break through stone walls and anything but a Suffolk cheese.' And Bloomfield himself wrote in the same poem:

[2] *A.F.C.H.*, p. 70.

*And strangers tell of 'three-times skimmed sky-blue'*
*To cheese converted, what can be its boast?*
*What, but the common virtues of a post!*
*If drought o'ertake it faster than the knife,*
*Most fair it bids for stubborn length of life,*
*And, like the oaken shelf whereon 'tis laid,*
*Mocks the weak efforts of the bending blade;*
*Or in the hog-trough rests in perfect spite,*
*Too big to swallow, and too hard to bite.*

Jack Page said of the cheese that you could *hull* it from here to Hanover and it would still be intact: the use of the name Hanover here is a reminder of how often you hear this word in the East Anglian dialect. If one can judge from the frequency with which they are referred to in the dialect, mostly unconsciously, the Georges must have made—at least initially—a great impression on East Anglians. It is possible that the manner of the arrival of the first George at the seaport of Harwich fixed their accession indelibly in the minds of country people here, especially when you consider that East Anglians are rather fond of flinty jokes. Apparently, the landfall was not very well planned. Parson Woodforde[3] wrote in his diary for 17 June 1777:

'It [a phrase] took rise from George I landing at Harwich for the first time of his coming to England. Harwich then was nothing but hurry and confusion.'

The Parson was referring to a dialect phrase that is still heard in East Anglia: *All up at Harwich* (or *Harridge*), meaning all in a confusion; and the related expression, *Gone to Harwich* implies that someone is hell-bent for rack and ruin. One of the East Anglian dialectologists, Robert Forby, in his *The Vocabulary of East Anglia* disagrees with the above derivation of the expression and prefers to point to its origin in the old verb *to harry*, from the French *harier*. But the frequency of the local references in the dialect to Hanover and Harwich argues for the old Parson's derivation.

But to return to Jack Page's story: this type of tale, told in north Suffolk dialect, unfortunately does not reveal its full flavour here on paper. It is necessary to hear the original tape recording to capture its humour and its special quality—a certain texture or an **extra** dimension it loses by being transcribed. The loss would be even

[3] *Diary of a Country Parson.*

185

greater if an attempt had been made to 'tidy it up', removing some
of the speaker's repetitions and provincialisms. Attempts to render
into standard English tales told originally in the dialect bring to mind
the treatment modern composers give to the folk song. Like the traditional tale or anecdote the folk song is *sui generis*; and as Douglas
Kennedy has said:[4] 'The *realizing* of a folk song usually gives it a
highly intricate and sophisticated musical setting; but in abstracting
the essence of its music the composer turns the folk song into something else. It's not the real thing.'

That is the main reason why tales—the whole of the oral tradition,
for that matter—deserve to be transcribed verbatim with all the
roughness of texture. Polishing them up involves an abstraction of
much of the feeling of the actual event, and by removing the local
colour, often held to be irrelevant, the tale is deprived of its most
vital ingredient.

Often an anecdote will reveal, indirectly, an authentic historical
background: this is especially so where it concerns the use of common land of long standing. It was told to me by George Jolly of Hargrave, Suffolk:

'We used to have at the farm where I worked an owd roan cow, a
poll cow. The farmer used to turn his cows out on Depden Green.
He used to pay a man to *keep* them; and at one time I used to go
on, seven days a week. And this particular cow I used to have to look
after. I would take her on to the Green, and she'd sit down on her
behind, just like a dog; and all the other cows would be a-standing
there: sometimes, of course, they'd be a-laying down. I went there one
day and there she was sitting down, and I said to her: "Come along,
owd dear, we've got to go home, and I want to milk you!" And I put
my arm around her neck and the owd gel stuck up her ears." And I
said:

"Come on! It's all very well, but I want to git you home to
milk."

'She moved back and fore on her haunches grunting like this here:
Ugh, Ugh! "Come on," I says, "Git up." Afterwards she would get up.
And do you know, I didn't find out till long afterwards, that I was
being snapped with my arm round the owd cow's neck! She was just
like an owd woman; and she'd do this grunting and moving back and

[4] Personal communication. See *Folksongs of Britain and Ireland* by Peter
Kennedy (editor), Cassell and Co.

fro—more, when she was in calf. She was a good milker, though; and I was sorry when the owd cow went.

"Well, one day I turned her down Hargrave Green, and there was an owd lady living in the end house. I left the cow on the Green, and she got off and went into [the front of] this house where the farmer used to let his men have the corner of his field for a garden; and there were a nice lot of cabbages in there. One morning, the owd gel came; knocked on the farmer's door:

"Mornin', Mum," that's how he used to talk, "Mornin', Mum."

"Mornin', Mr F."

"What is it now?"

"Do you know, one of your owd cows has got into my garden after my cabbages!"

"Go on," he say to me, "go and get the owd cow off. It's in Mrs M's garden."

'Of course, I went, and she stood against the door with a stick (I couldn't help laughing). She took the end of the stick and she said: "Hunt the damn thing off!" Just like that. (I couldn't help laughing.) For the owd cow stood there looking at the woman, and she put her tongue out, and her old tongue was as long as my forearm; and she wrapped it round one of her biggest cabbages, and she *clew* it up.

"Don't stand there damn well laughing," she say, "Look at it!" she say.

"You are standing there letting the damn thing eat all the cabbages. That's nawthen to laugh at!"

'Well, I got the cow off. And whenever I were passing her gate that owd cow would know. She could see the owd lady come down the yard with her stick. This owd cow, she'd then stand against the gate as though she wanted to do her business. Then the owd woman would say:

"Shooh! Don't let the damn thing stop here! You know what's she's a-going to do!"

'That cow would stop there. Would she create! She say:

"I know you'll come back and clean the mess up what she make!"

'I couldn't help laughing, and the owd woman would swear: I daren't repeat that. The owd cow knew; I'm sure she did it purposely. She knew what the owd gel was coming to the gate for. And I used to lead the cow on: I didn't used to blunder after it. I used to let it because I knew very well what it was a-going to do.'

The setting of this story could well be mediaeval; and some of the dialect words that stem from the fourteenth and fifteenth century confirm this. *Keeping* cattle (or pigs, etc.) is a technical phrase used since early times for looking after animals and seeing that they do not stray from an unfenced pasture or stubble. It was the job of the person— usually a young boy or girl—who had been specifically allotted the task. *Clew* is the Middle English strong perfect: standard English, clawed. This old form is fairly common in East Anglian dialect: *mew* for mowed, *snew* for snowed, *shew* for showed, etc. The prefix *a* before the verb, as in *a-going*, is also a Middle English survival.

# 16

# Tales of a Horsewoman

Here is another group of reminiscences from south Cambridgeshire. They, too, concern a near relation, and they are valuable for more than one reason: they are chiefly anecdotes and are told in a lively style, giving us an amount of marginal but authentic detail about a rural village at the beginning of this century. They communicate the feeling of village life, the atmosphere that was dominant only two or three generations ago; and we get from them something that the facts of conventional history very rarely supply but which comes out—if at all—in autobiographies or reminiscences similar to the following.

Mrs Ida Sadler (born 1902) is the widow of George Sadler (1905–66) of Whittlesford, a well-known farmer and breeder of Shire horses.[1] She is the daughter of the former blacksmith at Whittlesford, Albert Merry (1875–1962). Her father was a man of many skills: he had been apprenticed to his father, Sidney Merry, who ran the smithy and the public house adjoining it. Albert Merry took over the smithy and the public house; in addition he kept a herd of cows; and his daughters—the *Merry Maids*—delivered milk round the villages. He also had a livery business:

'We had landaus, gigs, traps, vans, vans of all sorts, broughams—if only I had them now! We had ponies, donkeys, heavies, cobs of all descriptions for running about. I should think we had six or seven horses. We also had this dairy business, and I used to deliver milk and make butter. Alongside the blacksmith shop there used to be this pent-house; *pent'us* we called it. There were actually two, one either of the blacksmith shop. They were where they shod the horses. There were two forges in the blacksmith shop: the brewers who built the house for my grandfather to come there also built the blacksmith shop; and it was considered to be a very modern thing, with two forges. There was a lot of carts re-tyred for one thing and a lot of ironwork to be done in implements, and a lot of shoeing. They used to come there

[1] See *F.A.V., passim.*

from all around. And Phillips, their name was, the brewers at Royston —Royston Crow[2] they called the place—they built the blacksmith shop and my grandfather had this business in the pub next door which was called The Three Horseshoes.[3] The old pub that was there before was a very old thatched building alongside the road. It was supposed to be the worse for wear and they pulled it down. That was called The Gentle Shepherd. They pulled that down. I've heard my father say that his father—Phillips said to him: "Well, Merry, Phillips will build you a better place, Merry; build you a good shop here: two forges, two pent'uses either side of the blacksmith shop."

'In this sort of weather [the very dry summer of 1976] the carts would be coming in because the tyres were coming off. And the farmers would be standing their wagons in the ponds to make the wheels swell.[4] Behind the blacksmith shop there was a brick-built furnace. It was an oblong-shaped building with a strong iron door at the narrow end, and a chimney in the centre. And all the burnable rubbish we could ever find we used to put in there in preparation for a tyring day. After my father had prepared this iron bar for the wheel it would go into the furnace to be thoroughly heated. Alongside this furnace there'd be a very thick iron platform, circular, with a hole in the middle. The wheel was clamped to this when they put on the red-hot tyre. We'd love this day—cans and pails of water to cool the tyre down as it threatened to set fire to the wood. Loved the tyring day. But we didn't like it when a horse was in the *stocks*.[5] The leg was lifted up—the foot which had to have the shoe on—and the horse couldn't move: it was fixed. There was a lot of shouting going on; running with red-hot shoes and so on. We called it the *brake* or *stocks*. A big wooden roller on one side with a wide, thick leather band which could be wound up from the other side so the horse could rest its belly on this strap, if it collapsed or anything. The people brought that kind of horse to my father because it was the only one around here for miles.

[2] After a bird once considered as a separate species of crow, *corvus cornix*, the Gray, Hooded or Royston-crow (Lloyds *Encyclopaedic Dictionary*, 1895).

[3] The sign, appropriately, of the Master Farriers.

[4] cf. Constable's *Hay Wain*. See also *Kilvert's Diary:* 'The horses were driven into a pond in order to drink and cool their heels and tighten the tyres of the omnibus wheels. (What a beautiful accidental couplet)' Penguin Books, 1977, p. 68.

[5] A wooden frame used when shoeing a fractious bullock or horse. It was called a trave in Suffolk, and the equivalent name for the pent'us was trav'us.

'The blacksmith shop was a popular place to go to talk, especially on Whittlesford *Feast* (that was on 11 June, my husband's birthday). All the old characters, the gypsies came. And Mother was a very hospitable woman. She used to make hot-pots for the Feast; and put something good in their beer. And there was what we called the Long Shed at the back of the blacksmith's. It almost joined the village store, near the old Guild Hall. They used to dance in the Long Shed, and the music was a man with a concertina. I can picture the tap-room in the pub with hams hanging up on the beam.'

Mrs Sadler's fullest memories, however, are about her accident-prone father, Albert Merry:

'He was always having accidents—talk about a cat with nine lives! Many of the accidents involved horses, of course. He had a heavy horse fall on him once: the horse couldn't stand properly. Horses were always running away with him (we had some strange horses, poor things, sent from the Army. They were shell-shocked in France, no more use for that work; and we had them here. But they never got over the shock of the war, and you never knew what they were going to do.) I know one horse ran away coming home to Whittlesford. When a horse is coming home he is anxious to get there quickly and he'll go into a gallop if you let him. And this horse got into a gallop, and my father was in one of those tall things with iron bars over the top. They used them for carrying stock in those days to Cambridge market.[6] Well, this horse was keen to get home; got into a gallop; turned the thing over; and my father was trapped inside. He was taken to a house on the Shelford corner there, The Prince of Wales corner. There was such a big bump on his head. He got over that: he didn't seem to be the worse for that!

'He was nearly drowned; he was also struck by lightning—all the accidents that could possibly happen to anybody happened to him. He was nearly drowned in a place called Earith where there are a lot of dykes. I could tell you the story! He was a blacksmith there for a man called Thoday (you probably know the name Thoday round that way: there may be some of them still alive). He'd been to Somersham, a village quite near, with a friend to a Christmas party of sorts where there was a *draw*, among other things. They'd gone on bicycles, and

[6] A bullock cart, a low hung vehicle used for transporting bullocks. It had a cranked axle and bars across the top to prevent the animals from trying to get out.

coming home—my father didn't drink a lot but he didn't realize how deep the dyke was; and coming home he got into this dyke. He had an awful job to get out of it; and if hadn't been for his friend he would never have got out of the dyke. I know when he got home—you see, there was this *lucky draw* for a duck among other things. And when my father got into the house, my mother was in bed (I was only a young baby), and she called out to him: "Is that you, Albert? Have you got the duck?" "No," he said, "but I got a bleeding ducking!"

'He got struck by lightning up at the farm at Whittlesford. There had been a lot of heavy rain, and the guttering that went round the cowshed was blocked and all the water was running anywhere instead of into the tank. He climbed up onto the tank—an iron tank where the pipe was coming down into it; and the lightning struck. But he was wearing Wellington boots; and that saved his life. I remember there was a terrific clap and vivid lightning. Soon after he came into the house; sat down and started taking his boots off. And when he got his boots off he said he felt as if he had been knocked across the shins with an iron bar. There were two red marks right across the front of his legs.

'Another accident (I'm going back to the old village blacksmith shop). We were leaving the blacksmith shop to go into the farm; and he was dismantling some old buildings—he had cows there as well. He had built the place himself and he was trying to dismantle it. And he'd got a pile of corrugated iron standing somehow: it must have been against a rafter that gave way. He fell off this rafter and caught his chin on the top of the corrugated iron. He cut a terrible gash, the shape of the corrugated iron, underneath there. I wasn't home at the time, but they took him round to the doctor again in his pony-and-buggy. And the doctor—Doctor Edwards at Sawston—said:

"Merry! Grip the arms of this chair!"

'And he stitched him up sitting on that chair. Then he said:

"Now you go home to bed: I'll come and see you tomorrow."

'And after a day or two—it shook him up a bit—the doctor came; and he got a mirror from the dressing-table and said:

"Don't you think I made a good job of you, Merry?"

'But you could always see this wiggly, wavy line where the stitching had been. The doctor told him: "You're a lucky man!" The jugular vein —or some vein—it just missed it. I recall the picture: he had a towel wrapped round his neck to stop the bleeding. I know I was at Shelford at the time. I had to go driving about—driving people about who wanted to go to places; no buses; before the days of the buses. I used to take Mr Maynard, an agricultural engineer and his daughters: he used to like them to go to this private school at Shelford—Great Shelford. And I was coming home; and we had a maid-of-all-work at the pub. She came up to me—and you talk about breaking the news! She just outed with it. She ran up to me and she said: "Your father cut his throat!" I nearly collapsed. I thought he'd committed suicide. Imagine that: someone running up to you with news like that. I thought I'd never get over that, you know. She'd been upset about it, I suppose, and that was the only way she could convey it to me.

'Then there was the time he got into the pigsty. Oh yes, he shouldn't have done that. He shouldn't have done that! He went into a pigsty where there was a sow with a litter of new pigs; and he was picking these up, moving them about and making them squeal. And the sow went for him. Sows are big things you know, heavy things. She got him up against the wall; and sows have got feet with claws, and she threw herself onto him and broke his ribs. He said that was the most painful thing he'd ever had—his broken ribs.

'But—to cap it all—he was nearly killed by a bull; and if it hadn't been for my husband with a two-tine fork—he stuck it into his neck —he'd have been a dead man. He tried to drive this bull down to water, and this bull didn't want to go (you can take a horse to the water but—it's the same with a bull!). My father was wearing a long overcoat; and the bull turned on him and got his foot on this overcoat so Father couldn't get away from him. That was terrible! He was black and blue! The doctor said he'd never seen a man so discoloured in all his life. But he got over that; got over all sorts of things my father did. The bull knelt on him; got his horns under him and kneaded him about. My father couldn't get away from him. But it didn't last for all that long because my husband was there in the barn and ran to his assistance with a two-tine fork.'

The encounter with the bull made a great impression on George Sadler who came to the rescue; and he left a written account of it. As he said, it was an episode he would never forget. He wrote it down in his ledger which he used as a kind of diary-cum-commonplace book; and by the vigour of his writing he has brought the encounter vividly to life:

'My father-in-law was a silly old man in some ways. As you have

193

been told, he kept a herd of cows, and also a bull. This Bull was a bit furious at times. He lived in a good loose-box, and was let out to water twice a day. This day, Merry—my father-in-law—had got him out; and the Bull was not keen on going to drink. The water-trough was about twelve yards from the barn door where I had just appeared; and between the door and the water-trough was a single post. I could see that the old Bull was not going to be forced to drink, and he protested by coming after my father-in-law who made for the post. I shouted:

"He will knock you arse over head!"

'But Merry left that post to run into the barn near me. Now that Bull weighed nearly a ton, but he leapt off the ground like a bird; hit Merry in the back and knelt down and got his horn between Merry's legs. He then tried to toss him in the air. But the Bull was kneeling on Merry's overcoat; and that saved him! It ripped the coat right up. I got a two-tine fork and shoved it into the Bull's neck and shouted. The Bull withdrew a bit, and I said to Merry:

"Get to that pigsty!"

'He managed to get almost there while I was fighting a rear-guard and desperate battle with the Bull. Merry collapsed on a heap of mud, and the Bull tried his damnedest to get him. But Merry crawled and got into the pigsty; and I almost fell on top of him and slammed the door. I said to my in-law:

"You silly old bugger! We could both have been killed!"

'But Merry had about six weeks laid up over it. A neighbour of ours heard me shouting, came and looked over the fence, and cleared off! I had a pair of slacks on, tied round the waist with a necktie (I always do this). Well, that tie broke and my trousers kept coming down; and that added to the trouble. I shall never forget that! Of course, the Bull would have killed him had I not been there.'

George Sadler was a remarkable man. He was a breeder of Shire horses, and his whole life was devoted to the heavy horse. I first met him at the Cambridgeshire Agricultural Show at Newton in the middle 'Sixties. He was independent, direct and outspoken, hating sham and sentimentality, as I soon gathered from his conversation. Without preamble he said:

'You know, these writers about farming and the countryside haven't got it right. No more they haven't! I think I'll have to have a go myself.' I agreed with him and said it would be a good idea. But unfortunately he was killed a couple of years later in a road accident in his home village of Whittlesford. Had he lived he would undoubtedly have produced a lively and authentic testament of his life and of the farming that he knew so well. The following piece which he wrote a year or so before he died has the same vigour and the same concrete images that were so noticeable in his conversation:

### 'Plough Monday

'The Monday nearest to the 14 January is called Plough Monday. I I can well remember Plough Monday as a plough boy 40 years ago. The horsemen and their mates would go around a village cracking their whips, or in many cases whipping a stick on the boards or door-step to make a row like a cracking whip. Some would pull a single plough around the village. They would go to their employers and the pubs and the houses where they would get a few coppers. Then they would go to the pub and spend it on a few gallons of beer. I heard of one case where the squire would not give anything. In fact, he said he would put his hunting crop across their shoulders. So when it quietened down they went back with the single plough and ploughed across his lawn. Nothing was said; but the squire knew his good men had done it.

'The custom was for the horse-keepers to meet about 6 p.m. Well, they had no real whips: they could not afford to buy whips. And they did not need whips for their lovely horses: they had more sense and discipline than half the human beings. During the afternoon of the occasion the horsemen would get his racking up done and then make his whip for the night. He would take a *top-thong*[7] out of a pair of wooden hames and tie it very tight on his stick; and that was his whip. I had better explain what a top-thong was, and still is! I have measured one today in my treasure trove: it is made of leather, about half an inch thick and two feet six inches in length. There is also the *chest-thong* which went in the bottom of the hames; and it was a work of art to put that one in in the proper way. Now I have told you that, I will get on with the whip-cracking. Of course no one can crack a whip made with a top-thong—and that thong, remember! had got to be back in those hames by 6 a.m. next morn. So they also had another good stick with which to hit the doorstep or some old wooden building to make a noise similar to the crack of a whip. Us boys had two

[7] Or top-lash which ties the hames or sales together at the top of the collar. The chest-thong secures them at the bottom.

pieces of boards to clap and they made some effect. The Lord, the leader of the band, would say: "We are the poor plough boys." That's before we got our few coppers; and "Thank you," afterwards.

'I remember going to one farmer called Baker. And old Brick Morley was just giving the old man's shit-house socks with his stick. Out come the farmer smoking his pipe. They laughed about that because they reckon he had been asleep in there. Yes, they would spend a lot of time in those litttle shacks in those days.

'The village done, and then to the pub to reckon up and spend the night's takings on beer. Ginger beer for us boys at a penny a bottle. There might have been a dozen of us, and a few locals in the pub. During the evening, one by one they would stand up indicating a song. The Landlord would say: "Order, please! the singer is on his feet!" And then you would hear the The Old Rustic Bridge, I Will Take You Home Again, Kathleen, The Gypsy's Warning, or Don't Send My Boy to Prison—all sung in the old country style with some lines left out and some mistakes. But what did it matter!

'I can still see the upright figure of one of the singers: ruddy, weatherbeaten face, with his cap off, his fore-top to one side as he had no parting in his hair; and as upright a guardsman, hob-nailed boots, sleeved waistcoat, red handkerchief tied in two knots and through his braces. That man has brought a tear many a time to my eye. He was a good man, hard—and his life was hard.'

I am including this last section of Mrs Sadler's memories chiefly for the phrase *Over Will's Mother*[8] which she uses. This phrase is not uncommon in East Anglia, and I have recorded it in Essex, Suffolk and Norfolk as well as in Cambridgeshire. But no one knows who Will's mother was: her identity remains a mystery. She may have been anything from a fairy to some old, memorable village matron whose name, through her son, became a legend.

'Well, before that new house was built there was an old cottage— Chantry Cottage. There's also an old tithe barn that still stands there, where they put the corn in to pay for the parson's stipend. Now the old cottage in those days had diamond-shaped panes in the lead; but that was before our time. It had been renovated by the time we lived

---

[8] Used, in my experience, in this way: It's raining over Will's Mother [in the distance]. It's a-leaning over like Will's Mother [about a badly constructed corn- or hay-stack].

there. I was looking out of that window there in the kitchen, and there's a farm road going straight up—to the field: it rises. And Bill Wardley (that's his name; he's dead now) he was leaving off work (I can't remember whether it was at lunch-time or five o'clock tea-time). But there was a beautiful rainbow. It seemed to come across from Whittlesford Station right over the fields and ended on that roadway. All the colours! It looked so wide, and all those beautiful colours you have in a rainbow. And Bill Wardley, he looked as if he *must* come through it. I saw him coming, and I sat and watched. And I saw Bill Wardley come right through the colours of that rainbow! I'd never seen it before, and I don't suppose I shall ever see it again. I could hardly believe it. I was all alone, and as he came by I said:

"Did you know you came through that rainbow?" He didn't know and I said,

"Did you notice anything? Did you feel anything? There must be a pot o' gold somewhere up there, so I've heard."

'That's all there is to it! But I saw him coming through a rainbow, a perfect rainbow.

'I've seen another thing while coming down that same road. I've got a cutting about it from the paper.[9] It happened on Good Friday in 1929; and the next morning I expected everybody to be talking about it. George and I saw it; and it was on that selfsame road. The sun was setting over *Will's Mother*, as they used to say, the sun was setting over Will's Mother. It was a gorgeous sunset, beautiful, rosy-coloured. Then after it had all cleared we both saw it: there was a cruciform shape, a cross left in the sky. It was of this rosy hue and the sky was a creamy bluish at the back; and it was a perfect cruciform shape. Shortly afterwards George went to Suffolk where his mother was living—at Gazeley in those days; and she'd seen it. And as I said there was some mention of it in the newspaper. Nobody round here saw it. But we were on a bit of high ground on that same road. I still go back to see if I can see it again. Every Good Friday. It was on a Good Friday in 1929. It made it seem very impressive to me. We happened to be on high ground facing west.'

[9] The *Daily Express*. Reported as being seen also at Burnham Overy, Kings Lynn, south-east London and on the south coast at 6.40 p.m. in the western sky.

# 17

# For Continuity

Looking back on the couple of years I have spent in compiling this book it seems to me that to whatever extent the heavy horse is used in his proper work in the future he has already re-established himself in the consciousness of hundreds of thousands of people who had almost forgotten his existence; and there is now no danger at all of his becoming a dying breed. Although most people were aware of how important the heavy horse had once been as the power that gave society its muscle, it was in the countryside that he was most regarded. Here he was a kind of social leaven; for apart from his indispensability—which the countryman took for granted—he was the ordinary man's *thoroughbred*, a familiar lodestone of his deepest interest and a symbol of his relationship with Nature and his daily living. This I take to be at least a partial explanation of the surprising fascination the farm horse has for the displaced countrymen who have lived in the town and cities for a couple of generations. They appear to respond to a sight of the horse with a satisfaction they would be hard put to explain and, indeed, appear to be hardly aware of. It is this kind of response that causes thousands of people to move out—as has already been remarked—each week-end just to have a sight of heavy horses working against a traditional background.

The resurgence of interest in the farm horse, however occasioned, also illustrates how difficult we find it to escape from the past. Like Nature itself, you can frighten it off with a pitch-fork but it always returns. The tremendous technological advances made in our time gave farmers and governments the confidence and the apparent licence to jettison the past to a large degree and to start afresh, making a big break with a former way of life—to make a new and profitable beginning. At this date we are less confident than we were, even thirty years ago, that our new beginning will result in a practical and long-lasting pattern of living; and this is not entirely due to our failure to recognize that the past, even the distant past, will always be with us and is, indeed, co-extensive with the present. It is partly owing to a faulty metaphor of time that we do not see the historical continuity that is implicit in any concept of the present, however different *our* particular present may seem.

At this point the specific charge is likely to be that the giving of undue weight to the past looks something like an excuse for indulging in pure nostalgia. Nostalgia, however, is a word whose pejorative use is usually uppermost even when it refers to a *healthy sickness*, the ache or the longing to win back from the past something that is worth possessing. The word was in great use in recent years as a very useful whip to urge on laggards who were not moving fast enough to the envisaged technological Utopia; but it has lost much of its sting as an argument now that the new land begins to look very much like a Dystopia and not the promised better place. The past refuses to be dismissed, and it would be the worst form of disaster to reject what is good in it alongside the bad, to burn not only the straw but the corn as well. The old country communities, for example, had a tremendous fund of good—practical good—in their healthy respect for the soil and their environment: they also had an underlying moral good of an integrated, caring community. Unfortunately, recognition of this has tended to be obscured in recent years by the shadow of an undoubted, ruthless class exploitation.

The value of the past has come home to me more than ever in the writing of this book through my being made more than ever aware of the health of the oral tradition and its usefulness in many of its aspects to present-day society. More particularly I have become convinced of its importance to the historian both as a repository of fresh sources and for the new understanding it can offer him of the nature of his discipline. The most important lesson I have learned here is that one cannot collect the tradition or any oral evidence in isolation. It is essential, after researching in the books and documents, to go to the community itself and to record anything that is related to its historical roots. To isolate one aspect and to exclude almost everything else is to condemn one's researches to an uncritical and ultimately boring, partiality. If, for example, one is researching the history of folk customs and beliefs in a rural area it would be wrong to attempt to collect them directly. By their very nature they are tied to the community's traditional way of life, and it brings greater rewards to study first of all the material culture, the work, the home life of the people, their dwellings, their furniture and their work implements to which most of the customs and beliefs are tied. This type of research requires, too, as an essential, a working knowledge of the dialect of the area. But here again it would be unhistorical to attempt a study of the dialect on its own, and also unpractical—as unpractical as it is to gather directly intimate personal beliefs. You can go round asking people about their personal beliefs—and many do—but this it seems to me is as ultimately productive as going round asking: 'Do you know any folklore? or any good dialect words?' The only practical approach is the holistic one, recognizing that you are studying a community where everything once 'tied in', and that it would be best to start with the bed-rock, the traditional work, whether it is arable or pastoral farming, mining or fishing, quarrying and so on. Out of this full context it is then possible to select and examine more surely the specialist information you are concerned with. It is only by examining every aspect of a community that a full enlightenment can be gained. We already have many examples of what results when such an approach to a historic community is neglected. To take one sector: too many sociologists are prone to research in rural areas without first having a firm grounding in the area's history; and their findings are much less convincing for this reason.

A failure to grant the importance of a much wider approach to rural history has similarly led many critics to undervalue oral tradition. Certain of them have taken an isolated historical event and have examined it after its filtering down through two or three generations in the tradition. From their findings they have concluded that oral tradition is unreliable and cannot be used with any confidence as a historical source. But in making this objection what is their criterion? They imply that there is in existence a perfect, watertight historical source, and if only it is transmitted word for word 'as it happened' we have the historical truth. Of course, oral tradition of an isolated event is distorted, even though it may preserve the framework of the event reported. But we do not necessarily have to bring the time factor into it to show the inevitability of 'distortion', or that the belief in an immaculate historical truth is altogether a wrong presumption. It is well known that half a dozen witnesses of a contemporary event will not agree completely in their account of what happened, and often their disagreements are not only about marginal details. Whoever is trying to find out what is the truth about an event—whether he is a judge, member of a jury, historian, sociologist or scientist—after considering all the evidence has to decide for himself what actually happened. He can only do this by bringing his common sense to bear on the event, which is only another way of saying that he must draw on his experience of living among men in a certain environment over a considerable period of time; that is, he puts the event in the widest possible context to help him to interpret it.

The oral tradition has obvious limitations in reporting the isolated event. It is not much use, for example, asking the average country dweller of the date of a past happening. That is not the way he thinks. He will recognize a year not by the abstract symbol but in the concrete setting of his life: 'That was the year of the big blizzard,' or 'It was in that year we had our biggest corn harvest.' Where the tradition excels is in this wider context of a community. Allied to the material culture it can be a powerful enlightener, as it has been in agricultural history where tools and processes that had been in continuous use for centuries were still used by men living in our time. This continuity was only made possible by the long survival of a tradition of subsistence farming and of its linked hand-tool economy. It has been shown that oral tradition, as transmitted by a dialect speaker, can be of valuable help in translating and interpreting fourteenth-century farm manuscripts. And it is my experience that where oral tradition is tied to and monitored by the material culture—chiefly the continuing work by which men get their living from soil or sea—it is unimpugnable. I am bold enough, therefore, to think that this has been demonstrated here in what we can call the penumbra of the material culture—the beliefs, customs and attitudes that are so closely linked with it.

Mention was made earlier of the use of a faulty metaphor in looking at the past; and I believe that the failure of many conventional historians to admit oral evidence into the canon of their techniques is due to the mechanical way they tend to regard the past. The implicit metaphor of historical chronology is symbolized by the time-chart. This is no longer as popular as it used to be a comparatively short time ago but its subjective image is still with us. This is that time builds up more or less uniformly on a wide front in clean-lined layers. We tend to think of the fifteenth, sixteenth, seventeenth centuries, and so on, with a bold line in our understanding, separating one century from another. We give to a century (after all, only an arbitrary division of time) a validity that it does not really possess. But this is not to deny that it is a necessary convenience, as is any unit of time: we have to stay the flux, immobilize it temporarily, dividing it off and thereby creating a provisional isolate. But if we take the metaphor—the figurative convenience—for the reality, what we are doing is to create a false isolate that effectively masks the fluid nature of historical time. The vertical metaphor which is welded into the historian's consciousness, although a convenient one in some respects, is apt when used in certain circumstances (notably in connection with the countryside) to betray us into some wrong thinking. In estimating the value and the use of oral tradition as a historical source a horizontal metaphor is a much more convincing trope: time flowing like a flood on an uneven front, leaving behind long inlets and sometimes islands of former cultures that can be visited and studied by those who have already been carried along much farther by the flood, much farther into the future. Put in another way, the *present* for a historian writing in the fastness and seclusion of a university is a very different *present* from that of a country-dweller whose attitudes, the whole pool of his living, are much farther upstream. The countryman who lives in the midlands of Ireland, the highlands of Scotland or Wales, and the remoter parts of England is living in a truly *historic present* and is in a very real sense a potential source document for a perceptive historian.

It may be thought unnecessary at this stage to labour in defence of using oral evidence in history, but the following quotation illustrates the die-hard, positivist position some historians still hold:

'I have been inspired by the principle of the great French historian, Fustel de Coulanges who wrote: "History is not an art, it is a pure science. It does not consist in telling a pleasant story or in professional philosophizing. Like all science it consists in stating the facts, in analysing them, in drawing them together, and in bringing out their connections. The historian's only skill should consist in deducing from the documents all that is in them and in adding nothing they do not contain. The best historian is he who remains closest to the texts, who interprets them most fairly, who writes and even thinks at their direction." '[1]

Many modern historians would consider this definition extremely naïve for the reason that it begs two of the questions that are their

[1] Quoted in *The History of Impressionism* by John Rewald, London, 1973.

main concern: the nature of the *fact* and the validity of the *text*. Because a fact is printed or written on paper or parchment does that of itself make it a historical fact? And do written or printed texts provide the only sources that can be used by a historian? It is at least of some comfort to reflect that we have progressed a little way from this position of historical fundamentalism, and that both these questions can now be regarded as purely rhetorical.

To end on a personal note: my first interest in the Suffolk Punch was over thirty years ago, and I have recurred time and again to the heavy horse in my writings. Would it not have been more and more convenient from the reader's standpoint to have had the whole of the matter relating to the horse in one volume? Undoubtedly this would have been better than having the material in its present scattered form. But having in mind the method by which this material was obtained this would not have been possible, for this reason: unlike the conventional researcher who goes to the documents or the books and finds them usually in the approved places, who knows roughly the size of his task, the man who is working in what we can call, for the sake of discussion, the field of social anthropology is constrained to recognize his documents and books almost solely to be ordinary men and women. In the first place they are not physically available on request, they cannot be produced at will; and even when found their relevance is not conveniently marked on a spine or a title-page. He has to discover all this for himself, and it can sometimes be a long and laborious process. For my own part, in collecting and collating the traditional horse-lore I have borrowed my lights not so much from the written or printed word but almost entirely from people who were involved with the horse, who did the work with him and were steeped both in the work itself and the rural and social environment that formed the horse's familiar habitat.

From the start of my search I knew only vaguely the extent and depth of my subject. Indeed, the subject itself was obscure, for most of it was secret or at least half secret. It was so because much of the content of the lore I was after gave the possessor direct economic advantage and was therefore kept very close. Again, a large part of it was often identified with witchcraft and was regarded, understandably, in an ambivalent light: it was treated as curious or at best innocuous and on the other hand it was looked upon with great suspicion and was a completely taboo subject if not to the horseman himself almost certainly to his wife who usually took the view that it was a topic that we should not be discussing. An example will illustrate what I mean: I was recording an old horseman on magnetic tape. I knew him very well and had recorded him many times before. I had called on him early one afternoon and I set up the apparatus in the living-room while his wife went into the kitchen to wash up the crockery used in the midday meal. When she had finished she came back into the living-room. By this time the horseman had got onto the subject of his secret involvement with one of the rituals used by him and his older colleagues to gain, as they thought, power over horses. As soon as she heard what we were about, the wife remarked tartly: 'You're not on about that again!' Taking my lead from the horseman who ignored the comment I kept the machine running, whereupon the wife went to the hearth and noisily proceeded to 'mend' the fire. Whether it was intentional or not, this action effectively ruined the recording.

The gatherer of lights such as these is more exposed to the accidents of daily life than is the orthodox researcher; and much of his material has to be collected obliquely, through waiting with an open and expectant mind rather than through too active a searching. For as I have said, I have found that too earnest an enquiry often had a negative effect. It was by trying to find my way through the larger environment of the rural past, especially the history of the farm, that I came across valuable insights into a body of traditional lore that was documented only in the minds of men. But to hoard up this material for long years while I was collecting it was alien to my temperament and to my expectations, I therefore published it—spoke about it publicly—as I discovered it. And I am glad I did so, because by making what I had found widely known I brought others into the discussion; and their contributions in the form of letters and personal contact added immeasurably to my understanding of what I was doing.

In the process, as I have already confessed, I discovered my own limitations as a collector of the tradition in that I underestimated its toughness and durability. But coming back to it—although not through any premeditated intention—at a time that coincided with a public renewal of interest in the heavy horse, I had hopes that I would be making a worthwhile supplement to the record I had already made.

# Appendix One

*Bullocks on the East Anglian Ploughs*

While collecting information over a period since the last war about the old horse-farming, I have recorded—in the margin, as it were—oral references to the earlier cultivation of the land by bullocks. At no time did I go out purposely to find such references, and had I done so I would probably have found many more in various parts of East Anglia. But the examples I recorded confirm the inertia that is built into old farming processes, enabling methods of cultivation, for instance, that have lasted for thousands of years to persist into modern times.

My first reference came from Robert Savage of Blaxhall in Suffolk. He told me of the use of bullocks on the Ogilvie estate near Thorpeness. This was later confirmed by William Ward of Aldeburgh.[1] He had seen bullocks ploughing and a bullock drawing a tumbril on this estate. A farmer called Robert Makens of Ringshall near Stowmarket[2] used bullocks in the 'Twenties; and within the past few years I found a photograph of a farmer or farm worker ploughing with bullocks at North Elham, Norfolk.[3] At Blundeston in Suffolk I recently talked to Herbert James (born 1884), an old horseman who worked for most of his life in that area:

'An old man what worked with me—he was over eighty year old—in his young days he used to plough with bullocks on a farm called Hobland Hall Farm. Many of the farms used to plough with bullocks he told me, but that was afore my time. And when they were done with the bullocks they fattened them up and they went to the butcher's. They didn't used to wear a collar like the horses do: they had a sort of beam across the chest.'

The following information comes from Samuel Ellwood of Brooke. He was born in 1891 at St James in the *Saints* district just south of Bungay. His father was a horseman and moved into Norfolk when he was

[1] *F.M.M.*, p. 56.
[2] *H.I.F.*, p. 52.
[3] *W.B.W.A.*, facing p. 65.

very young. Later his father became head horseman or *team-man* as they were called in Norfolk:

'Now when we lived at Tunstead [near Wroxham, Norfolk] they used to plough with bullocks there. I was a lad, and there was a farm not far off us. There were two chaps, two brothers, kept four bullocks; and they used to take two of these owd bullocks out—two owd long-horns —and they used to break 'em in to use 'em. That was in my time. They had collars, no yoke; put the collars on and strap 'em up top. They ploughed with 'em; and when they ploughed round the field, they'd go right steady; and if there were old roots anywhere they wouldn't break nothing. That were nice a-seeing on 'em. And I've seen a bullock and a horse a-ploughing and a-harrowing. Yeh, I see a bullock and a horse. That's true that is! And when they fed these bullocks—when they had their breakfast they used to lay down; and they'd take 'em home and put 'em out in the yard and feed 'em just the same as these other bullocks with these owd skeps. Another time I happened to look and there was a horse and a bullock there in another field a-hoeing. I tell my brother about it. But it were a funny job to break 'em in. They broke them in like a horse, but you couldn't get their necks like a horse. And they would stick their horns into the ground and into the hedge. They would! They had these big old long horns. But they used to break 'em in; and that's funny, the bullocks knew: they knew *cuppy* and *wheesh*[4] just like a horse. They'd break them in. Some people think I'm *running on;*[5] but that's a long time ago. They wouldn't think I'm eighty-two. They don't think that. They think: well we don't know nawthen about that.'

It is worth noting that the earliest references to the use of the horse in the ploughs of East Anglia comes from Suffolk where there was a plough-team of eight horses in the 1190s; and also in the twelfth century, mixed teams of bullocks and horses on the Abbey estate at Bury St Edmunds.

Roger Clark gave me an additional example of a mixed team and, incidentally, an interesting confirmation of the pioneering work of Suffolk agricultural implement firms at the beginning of last century:

'An old man I used to knock about with at home—he'd be well into his nineties now if he were still alive—his father had a brother in Staffordshire. Every year in the spring his father used to take a horse

[4] Left and right.
[5] joking (Lloyd's *Encyclopaedic Dictionary*, 1895).

and a new Smythe [Peasenhall] drill from Suffolk down into Stafford-shire. He'd drill all the seed up there on contract. Then he'd sell the drill and come home to Suffolk. On one particular farm up there he worked the horse with either a bull or a bullock beside him. That's how he did the drilling.'

Yet in spite of the frequency of the references to the use of bullocks in the plough it could well be argued that bullocks or oxen working into the twentieth century on British farms were a curiosity even if not a rarity; and that this was not altogether due to the inertia or con-servatism of the country mind but to the continuing presence of a kind of *nostalgie de boeuf*, a clinging to the past by self-conscious con-noisseurs. This appears to be true, at least on the surface, as far as Suffolk is concerned if we accept Robert Bloomfield's (an accurate observer) statement in his poem 'The Farmer's Boy'. The relevant couplet refers to Suffolk farming in the late eighteenth century:

> *No wheels support the diving pointed share;*
> *No groaning ox is doom'd to labour there.*

It would be difficult, however, to be definitive about the reasons for the late survival of the ox in farming; yet the question may well prompt us to wonder whether the use of the horse in farming today is not similar, and that the horse has or will have no more real contribution to offer the farming of the future than the ox has made over the past century and a half since it was effectively displaced by the horse. But the position now, it will surely be agreed, is very different: if the horse returns to the farm in appreciable numbers it will be out of necessity; it will be because he will become once more an essential agent of traction or even cultivation, and not as an arbitrary alterna-tive chosen by some individual praisers of past time.

*Further Rumination on Traditional Farming*

The following are pieces of information about the traditional farming in this region. I collected them in the course of getting material for the present book and I believe they should be included here. The first is from a conversation I had with Albert Hupton, a retired farmer who is my near neighbour. He was born in 1889 and he recalls ploughing with Suffolk horses when he was a lad:

'I went to plough when I was fourteen year old, on some of the heaviest land ever I knew—except perhaps where Seething aerodrome now stands (some of that is blue clay up there). With ten-furrow[6] work the horse never had to tread on the land, nor the wheels. The *stetch* is roughly the same width as the drill. That's the furrow and on the other side that's the furrow. The horses walked up there—a horse in each furrow. The shafts of the drill were offset to the right-hand side of the drill, and one horse walked in that furrow. The other horse was attached to the drill with a whipple-tree and he walked in the other furrow. On a Smythe drill there were three horses: there was an extra trace-horse walking in the right-hand furrow in front of the shaft horse. They didn't put a foot on the land if they could help it: they knew it would damage the land, especially in a wet time. Different from today! I reckon they should have a couple of horses on every farm, because a horse can do the work where they can't go with a tractor. They *should* have some horses because a horse can sometimes do what a tractor can't do, the same as a tractor can do things a horse can't do. Some of the old farmers realized at the time that they shouldn't have let all the horses go. So will the young ones before they're finished—get a few more years this way! We won't always have oil, the farmers won't. Therefore I don't know what is going to happen.

'I think the horse will come back in years to come. Not in my lifetime but in years to come. They'll have to come back. I remember when they were going out I had horses until I finished farming in 1964: if I wanted a tractor I hired someone to do the job for me. I remember meat was short just after the last war; and I went to a horse-sale where there were a lot of horse-slaughterers' men bidding for the horses. There was one standing against me, bidding for the horse I was bidding for. I made up my mind that whatever I paid for that horse I'd outbid him; and I did!

'It broke my heart when I had to give up my last horse. There was a clay-pigeon shoot on, not many fields away from mine. That was on a Saturday afternoon when the horse went. They come and got him about two o'clock. And instead of me going to that pigeon shoot to have a go, I didn't take no gun. I just walked across the field; and somebody say: "Aren't you going to have a shot, Albert?" I said: "No, my horse has gone today. I don't feel like shooting." 'Course, you get used to a horse, just like a dog. It's one of the family nearly: they know everything you say to them.'

[6] *H.I.F.*, Chapter 2.

Albert Hupton recalled a little scene that had been sharply etched on his memory for nearly eighty years:

'Years ago there where Captain Kerrison had the farm—he was my captain in the Yeomanry—there was an old man, an old horseman, a good old man, a good ploughman and a good worker. He had another chap with him as mate. And I was in the yard one morning, and the stars were shining—six o'clock, dark, when they were turning out at six. The old man, he was on his horse, riding sideways, and he shouted:

"Look at 'em, boy. Look at 'em! Look at the stars!" he say.

'He was then a-laughing, waving his arm above his head and pointing to the stars, going to plough the land in starlight. Six o'clock in the morning he was going up to a thirty-five-acre field, right 'joining me:

"Look at 'em, boy. Look at 'em a-shining, look at the stars!"

'That poor old fellow; and he'd likely to be still a-ploughing till late into the afternoon. Six to six were the hours then.'

Jack Leeder of Knapton, north Norfolk, also recalled the time when he first went to plough:

'But when I started ploughing with horses you had to find a lot of it out for yourself. I first used horses on the plough after harvest. We used to what we called *riffle*—that's lightly turn the top soil over. And the boy always started with one horse. He didn't have two: he didn't have a very deep furrow, you see: just turn the top soil over. When I went home at night some of the men used to alter the plough. And when I went next morning that would be—well, you had what we called *drawing chains* on the plough. If you tightened one side it *pulled* it. They used to alter this chain or the *skimmer* on the plough, and I used to be in such a muddle. I said. "I don't know what's the matter with my plough!" "Well," they said, "you find out. That's the way you'll know more!" And you had to find out yourself. They just wouldn't show you.'

But his work-mates were more considerate in teaching him some aspects of his craft such as sharpening and *hanging* a scythe:

'They showed me that. Now sharpening the scythe with a rub: it's a gift. You can easily put it on and take it off. You get an edge and then take it off. To do it properly it's laying your rub on the back of the scythe, you may say so, that thick part that comes just away from the edge, till you get it nearly sharp; and then you get it to the edge. There's a bulb part on the rub: well, that wants to be about there about half-way, not on the edge. So you're thinning it down; you gradually get that to the edge. That's what all amateurs do: instead of putting an edge on it they take it off!

'Hanging a scythe now. That's a skilled job, and if your scythe wasn't hung properly you'd make hard work of your mowing. To hang it you'd have a piece of string, and you'd go from the neck of the scythe or the grass-nail, and the string would reach down to the point. Then you'd bring the string down to the stick—to the bottom of the stick. And if you were too far, if the string went beyond this, they used to say your scythe is *out*—out too far. You couldn't mow like that. When you started the men would do this for you. Later in my time I used to hang the boys' scythes when they came on the farm. That skill has gone now.'

Finally, in a discussion with Roger Clark the use of the *whip-line* in ploughing came up. This is rarely seen in Norfolk and Suffolk but is still in use in the Cambridgeshire Fens. I first came across it in Downham Market on the edge of the Fen country, where Dennis Sneezum, the ironmonger, used to stock whip-lines to supply farmers and horsemen. He gave me one of the last in his old stock. It is a piece of rope skilfully twisted to form a loop, and it has an overall length of thirty inches. The rope which is about an inch in thickness at the top reduces almost to a point. (This reducing—according to a naval historian—is one of the most difficult exercises in rope-making.) The loop is fixed on to the left-hand stilt or handle of the plough, and to its tapered end the ploughman tied a thin cord that went along the horse's flank: the other end was tied to the horse's bridle. By touching the whip-line with his fingers as he still gripped the stilt he could signal to the horse, the cord moving lightly against his flank. Most Fen ploughmen used only one rein with their pair of horses: hence the use of the whip-line. Roger Clark commented:

'When Bob Claridge comes down here from the Fens he can't make out why we use two lines [reins] to drive the horses because they always plough on one line up there, even with the team-horses that they use to show—with a four-horse team. They always use one line. In ploughing they fix a looped rope with a tapering end over the left-hand stilt of the plough. It's called a *whip-line*. A piece of cord is tied from the tapered end of the whip-line and goes along the horse's flank to the dutfin [bridle]. I asked Bob how they broke these horses in. Apparently when they break the colts in up there they have this whip-line through this ring on the side of the dutfin, and they have another line on this side. Now when they go round to the left they call the horse round; when they go round to the right they shake the cord, give it a slight jerk, and they keep him round with the other line. And apparently with a plough-pair it's always the land horse is the line horse, and the furrow horse is either tied with a holder to the other horse's hames or with a stick from his mouth to the bottom of the other horse's collar. Then they have what they call a *false line* which is on the off-side of the dutfin; it goes over the horse's back to the other horse's trace; and it's just adjusted so that it keeps—if he goes forward that keeps him straight. That's how they do it; and if they've got three horses that's the middle horse is the line horse, and it pushes the other ones round.'

This one-rein method of ploughing is used in Holland, and this would perhaps help to explain its apparently exclusive use in the Fen country which the Dutchman helped to drain in the seventeenth century.

# Appendix Two

## The Horses

Barely a twelvemonth after
The seven days war that put the world to sleep,
Late in the evening the strange horses came.
By then we had made our covenant with silence,
But in the first few days it was so still
We listened to our breathing and were afraid.
On the second day
The radios failed; we turned the knobs; no answer.
On the third day a warship passed us, heading north,
Dead bodies piled on the deck. On the sixth day
A plane plunged over us into the sea. Thereafter
Nothing. The radios dumb;
And still they stand in corners of our kitchens,
And stand, perhaps, turned on, in a million rooms
All over the world. But now if they should speak,
If on a sudden they should speak again,
If on the stroke of noon a voice should speak,
We would not listen, we would not let it bring
That bad old world that swallowed its children quick
At one great gulp. We would not have it again.
Sometimes we think of the nations lying asleep,
Curled blindly in impenetrable sorrow,
And then the thought confounds us with its strangeness.
The tractors lie about our fields; at evening
They look like dank sea-monsters couched and waiting.
We leave them where they are and let them rust:
'They'll moulder away and be like other loam'.
We make our oxen drag our rusty ploughs,
Long laid aside. We have gone back
Far past our fathers' land.
                              And then, that evening
Late in the summer the strange horses came.
We heard a distant tapping on the road,

A deepening drumming; it stopped, went on again,
And at the corner changed to hollow thunder.
We saw the heads
Like a wild wave charging and were afraid.
We had sold our horses in our fathers' time
To buy new tractors. Now they were strange to us
As fabulous steeds set on an ancient shield
Or illustrations in a book of knights.
We did not dare go near them. Yet they waited,
Stubborn and shy, as if they had been sent
By an old command to find our whereabouts
And that long-lost archaic companionship.
In the first moment we had never a thought
That they were creatures to be owned and used.
Among them were some half-a-dozen colts
Dropped in some wilderness of the broken world,
Yet now as if they had come from their own Eden.
Since then they have pulled our ploughs and borne our loads.
But that free servitude still can pierce our hearts.
Our life is changed; their coming our beginning.

EDWIN MUIR

# Selected Written Sources

Balfour, E. B. *The Living Soil and the Haughley Experiment*, Faber and Faber, 1975

Bonham-Carter, V. *The Survival of the English Countryside*, Hodder and Stoughton, 1971

Braudel, Fernand. *Capitalism and Material Life*, Fontana/Collins, 1974

Brown, George M. *Greenvoe*, Penguin Books, 1976

Chivers, Keith. *The Shire Horse*, J. A. Allen, London, 1976

Cregier, Sharon E. *Cruiser Courier* (Monthly). Edited and published at the Department of History, University of Prince Edward Island, Charlottetown, PEI, Canada, C1A 4P3.

Dent, A. A. *The Horse Through Fifty Centuries*, Phaidon, 1974

Galvayne, Sydney. *Horse Dentition*, Glasgow, c. 1890

Hart, Edward. *The Golden Guinea Book of the Heavy Horse*, David and Charles, 1976

Hayes, Capt. M. H. *Illustrated Horse Breaking*, London, 1896

Keegan, Terry. *The Heavy Horse: Its Harness and Harness Decoration*, Pelham, 1973

Neale, K. L. *The Colony Stud of Suffolk Horses*, The Home Office, Surbiton, 1976

Rarey, J. S., *The Art of Taming Horses*, London, 1858

Richards, Audrey and Robin, Jean. *Some Elmdon Families*, Audrey Richards, Crawley Cottage, Elmdon, Saffron Walden, Essex CB11 4LT

Rider Haggard, L. *I Walked By Night*, Boydell, Ipswich, 1974

Schumacher, E. F. *Small Is Beautiful*, Abacus, Sphere Books, 1974

Telleen, M. and J. *The Draft Horse Journal*, Rt 3, Waverley, Iowa, 50677, USA

Watmough, J. *Heavy Horse and Driving*, Watmough, Ltd, Idle, Bradford, W. Yorks.

White Lynn, Jr. *Medieval Technology and Social Change*, Oxford, Paperback, 1976

Whitlock, Ralph. *Gentle Giants: The Past Present and Future of the Heavy Horse*, London, 1976

Villiers, Guy. *The British Heavy Horse*, Barrie and Jenkins, 1976

Young, John R. *The Schooling of the Western Horse*, The University of Oklahoma, USA, 1954

# Index

217